Christopher Creighton (John Christopher Ainsworth-Davis) has been an actor, writer, director and musician, sometimes working under a family pseudonym of John Ainsworth. He is married with one son and two grandchildren. He lives in London's Hampstead with Trinidad-born Greta, his wife of forty-four years. His son, Christopher John, presently lives in Los Angeles where he is both a musician and a diplomat and father of Samantha, four, and Jack, one.

Christopher, at seventy-two, still religiously practices the piano for an hour a day, but he is happiest of all at sea yachting with his friends off the south-east coast of Kent. He has always been a sailor - from Sea Cubs to Sea Scouts to the Royal Navy, and thence to the Royal Yacht Club at Ramsgate.

Publisher's Preface

The following account is one of the most extraordinary stories to emerge from the Second World War. Simon & Schuster issues this book under the assurances by the author, Christopher Creighton, that the story is true. The Publisher has not been able to verify his account by independent research. Indeed, the documentary trail is often at odds with the author's narrative. In secret intelligence work it is very difficult to come up with absolute proof and in May 1945 Berlin was the end of the world.

According to Creighton, evidence went missing and in the fog of war, files were adjusted by those with a hidden motive. Creighton further describes how the records were compromised in order to create a legend that served a darker purpose.

In the end, readers will have to make their own judgements about what they believe. What is not in doubt is that this book is a thrilling story from a remarkable man.

London, July 1996

BRIAN

Op. JB

ALL GOOD WISHES

by

Christopher Creighton

27/05/03

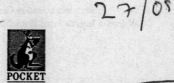

POCKET
BOOKS

LONDON · SYDNEY · NEW YORK · TOKYO · SINGAPORE · TORONTO

First published in Great Britain by Simon & Schuster Ltd, 1996
Published in paperback by Pocket Books,
an imprint of Simon & Schuster Ltd, 1997
A Viacom company

1 3 5 7 9 10 8 6 4 2

Simon & Schuster Ltd
West Garden Place
Kendal Street
London W2 2AQ

Simon & Schuster Australia
Sydney

A CIP catalogue record for this book is available from the British Library

ISBN 0-671-85565-4

Printed and bound in Great Britain by
Caledonian International Book Manufacturing, Glasgow

For my father

'A-D'

who could never know

This book is also dedicated to my former comrades-in-arms: the late Commander Ian Lancaster Fleming, of the Royal Naval Intelligence Division, and the men and women who took part in Operation James Bond: the Operational Wrens of the Women's Royal Naval Service; the Royal Naval and Royal Marine Commandos; the men and women of the German Freedom Fighters (the GFF); and one WAVE, a lady lieutenant of the United States Navy and the Office of Strategic Services (the OSS), forerunner of the CIA.

Winston Churchill to Ian Fleming about Op.JB – June 1945:

'*This must be* THE OPERATION THAT NEVER WAS.'

and

Winston Churchill to the author, October 1942.

'*Guard above all your reputation as a young man of no character; for if anyone should become proud of you – you are lost!*'

The Code Names

Christopher Creighton	*Christopher Robin*
Susan Kemp	*Miss Kanga*
Ian Fleming	*Pooh* [Winnie – the]
Winston Churchill	*Tigger*
Desmond Morton	*Owl*
Patricia Falkiner &	*Alice*
Barbara Brabenov	
Martin Bormann	*Piglet*
Ribbentrop	*Roo*
King George VI	*The Author* [A.A. Milne]
Adolf Hitler	*Rabbit*
The SS	*Rabbit's friends*
The Gestapo	*Rabbit's relations*
Note: All from 'Winnie-the-Pooh', except:	
Admiral Mountbatten	*Charlemagne*

Contents

Preface	ix
Acknowledgements	xii
Note on Sources	xiii
1 Contact	1
2 Cloak and Dagger	9
3 In Search of Gold	35
4 Patricia	45
5 Hard Training	55
6 Target Identified	67
7 Off the Rails	77
8 In the Enemy Camp	89
9 Water Power	107
10 In the Ruins of the Reich	119
11 Countdown	129
12 Our Yankee Doodle Girl	141
13 Piglet's Sty	151
14 At Close Quarters	161
15 On the River	171
16 Comrade Colonel Natasha	191
17 A Cutting-out Action	207
18 Final Twists	215
Appendix	245
Index	247

Acknowledgements

I should like to record my deep gratitude to Bridget Winter and Milton Shulman for their unstinting help, advice, expertise and support during the writing of this book. I should like to thank ex-Major Shulman, Canadian Army Intelligence authority on the Wehrmacht, for his insatiable, ferret-like devil's advocacy, and Duff Hart-Davis for his skill and patience in straightening out the text.

Note on Sources

Because Operation James Bond was so secret, very few records are available to prove its authenticity. I do, however, have letters and memoranda from Admiral of the Fleet Earl Mountbatten of Burma and Ian Fleming, which irrefutably show that the operation took place. A letter from General Lord Ismay supports the one from Sir Winston Churchill mentioned in the Preface, and encourages me to publish my story now that the time is ripe. I also have my own Royal Navy identity card, stamped in January 1945, and a few pages of my own Naval Report on the operation, dated June 1945.

With permission, I can look at some documents and supporting items held in safe custody by the M Section Security Control, and on occasion I have been allowed to show certain of these to interested parties – but only in extreme secrecy, under security escort, and with suitable undertakings of confidentiality from the people concerned. I have also had the privilege of being shown relevant sections of Martin Bormann's interrogation report, an 800-page document compiled in England between May 1945 and early 1946, in which he gives his own version of the history of the Nazi Party from the 1930s until 1945; each page is signed by Bormann and his interrogating officers. It is surely one of the most important historical documents of the century.

Preface

I am well aware that many readers will find this story incredible. All I can say is that I have done my best to write the truth about an operation which took place more than fifty years ago, and of which – by its very nature – few records survive. I should add that I have limited powers of literary invention: I could not possibly have thought the story up. Nor could I have assembled all the detailed technical information it includes. On the contrary, I have had to rely on my own memory and on official reports written by me or by my colleagues immediately after the events described.

During and after the Second World War my work as a secret intelligence officer demanded the highest degree of security; and although I obtained written permission from both Sir Winston Churchill and Lord Mountbatten to tell my story, both of them specified that I must wait until they were dead before I did so. At the same time, they enjoined me to do nothing that would endanger the lives of former colleagues. Later, Ian Fleming also wrote to say that I should tell the story one day, and revealed that our joint operation had been the secret inspiration for his colossal success with the James Bond novels.

Half a century on, the passage of time has eroded the need for secrecy, and I have decided that everyone should at last know what became of Martin Bormann. Yet the threat to survivors of the operation which brought him out of Berlin remains very real. Millions of pounds' worth of his personal fortune are still unaccounted for, and there are plenty of people motivated by greed or hatred – the KGB and the Odessa (the association of Nazi SS veterans), to name but two organisations – who believe that the money belongs to them, and would kill to get their hands on it. I have therefore used pseudonyms for all members of our team who are still alive, including myself: at the last count, the survivors numbered thirty-three.

It has not been easy to tell the story. When I first tried to publish it, in the 1970s, I was told by my superiors that the book would be suppressed, and I would be arrested, if I did not comply with their directives. These forbade me to mention the M Section or Ian Fleming; I was not to use Morton's name, but must call him 'Uncle John'; I was not to reveal that I had been a regular naval officer. These restrictions made a realistic, factual account impossible. Episodes from my war service therefore appeared in Brian Garfield's novel *The Paladin*, published in 1980. Many names and details were changed, and in any case the narrative stopped short of Operation James Bond.

Since then many more corroborative details have come to light, including contemporary reports and letters from people closely involved, among them Mountbatten and Ian Fleming. The effect of this new evidence has been to build up and authenticate the story in a way that was not possible earlier. Even now, however, I have had to withhold certain incidents, partly for the sake of people who appear in the book, partly to accommodate the wishes of senior political figures in Europe. I hope to be able to release some of these facts at a later date, particularly those which have an important bearing on the history of the Second World War.

The morality of snatching a high-ranking Nazi, and hiding him from the international judicial process taking place at Nuremberg, did not concern us. That was the politicians' business, not ours. Our job was to bring Bormann out of the ruins of Berlin, and, by a combination of luck and training, we managed it.

My main purpose in telling the story now is to pay tribute to my former brothers- and sisters-in-arms, the young men and women, many of them Germans, who made the hazardous passage down the Berlin waterways with me. In the course of the operation fourteen of them were killed, and all risked death many times. It was their bravery and determination that enabled us to pull off an outrageous coup. In particular, it was the extraordinary courage and resourcefulness of the girls – the British Wrens, the German Freedom Fighters, and one outstanding American – that brought us through.* Well into the 1990s the Ministry of Defence announced that women were to be allowed to go into operational action in the face of the enemy for the first time. Our girls did that very thing, and triumphed, fifty years ago.

I must point out that I did not cast Operation James Bond; I merely took part in it. In 1945 none of the players had an international reputation. Ian Fleming was a Royal Naval intelligence officer unknown to the public, and the fictional agent James Bond had not even taken shape in his mind. Few people in England or America had heard of Martin Bormann, and certainly no member of the public knew what he looked like. Although Fleming was already thirty-six, the rest of us were in our twenties: lively young naval officers, ratings and other ranks charged with a dangerous but routine wartime mission, which we carried out to the best of our ability.

I repeat: this is my personal story; it is not a history, and I claim nothing. Readers must accept it or not, as they will. For, like Aristotle, I am interested only in the truth, and not in what people believe.

Christopher Creighton
London, January 1996

---

* I realise that in 1996 the term 'girls' seems inappropriate for mature young women in their teens or early twenties. But 'girls' was the word we used at the time: far from wishing to be patronising, we regarded them with the utmost admiration.

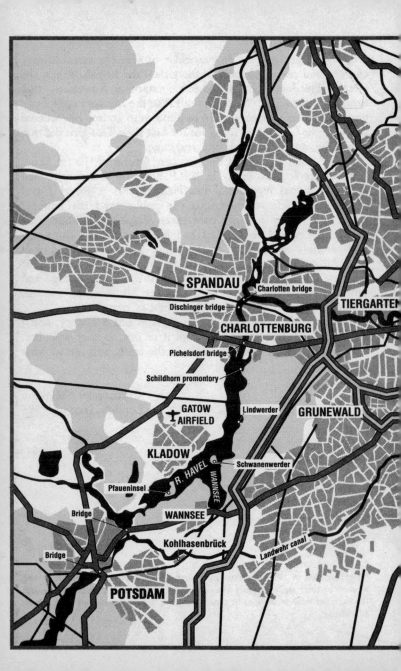

1

Contact

On Sunday, 21 January 1945, the secret feelers we had put out in Ireland at last elicited a response. A coded message received via Dublin told us that a senior officer of the newly formed Unified German Secret Service would meet me at 0700 on 23 January, at a precisely designated rendezvous near the estuary of the River Liffey, in the eastern suburbs of the Irish capital.

I was only twenty years old, but already a veteran of many covert operations. To my colleagues in the Royal Navy I was Lieutenant Christopher Creighton, and the official record described me as 'a well-built young man of some six feet two and a half inches tall, with ginger mousey hair and a nose that is far too big for his face – or anyone else's'. That was accurate enough. But to the Germans this same tall young fellow was Leading Seaman John Davis, a renegade and traitor, whose strong Fascist leanings at school had turned into active support for the Nazi cause, and who would sell any secret for cash. My dual personality had been carefully built up over a long period by my chief, Major Desmond Morton, creator and director of the ultra-secret M Section.

On the evening of 21 January I flew in a two-seater training aircraft from HMS *Daedalus*, the Fleet Air Arm station at Lee-on-Solent, to the Royal Naval base at Liverpool. Next evening I went aboard MGB *316*, a motor gunboat used to good effect by the naturalist and painter Peter Scott earlier in the war. The vessel proceeded immediately to sea for our 130-mile passage to Dublin. It was a wild night, but the wind was in the north-east, almost dead astern, so that the forty-foot boat ran easily before the storm, riding on the waves. Her two officers and crew of eight were far too professional to ask me what I was doing: to them, this was just one more operational sortie. They gave me the use of a bunk next to the wardroom, and for a couple of hours I got my head down: then it was 0300, and we were approaching the Irish coast.

At 0330 we made landfall off the mouth of Dublin harbour. By then the north-easterly had risen to Force 7 on the Beaufort scale – a near-gale. Gusts lifted the crests off the waves and hurled spray into the air. From the warmth of the cockpit-bridge we could see nothing except black sky, inky water and wraiths of swirling mist, with the red and white lights that marked the harbour entrance flashing dimly through the murk.

The MGB captain, having ordered his coxswain to hold the boat steady, submitted that I should abandon the operation. 'What do you reckon, sir?' he asked anxiously. 'Looks a bit heavy to me.'

'It does,' I agreed. 'But we're on a lee shore. The wind and sea'll carry me in. And anyway, those are the lights of Dublin. Nobody can resist them!'

At 0400 I asked the captain to turn abeam of the wind. Out on deck, the gale made it difficult to hear. 'As soon as I'm clear, you'd better withdraw,' I shouted. 'Don't hang about.'

'Aye, aye, sir.'

As the boat came broadside to the waves, I slipped over the lee side and swam quickly away before she could roll back on me. I was wearing a black Siebe Gormann shallow-water diving suit, with oiled-wool thermal submarine underwear beneath. I also wore a Davis submarine escape apparatus oxygen breathing-set, with mouthpiece and nose-clip in place, and was held buoyant by two lifebelts, one full of kapok and the other of air. On my shoulders was a haversack inside a waterproof cover, and strapped to my waist I had a variety of equipment, including a Sten sub-machine-gun, a Smith & Wesson .38 revolver, a fighting knife and a 62B grenade, all encased in elephant-size condom sheaths, specially made for us by the Durex rubber company. On my left wrist I wore an underwater writing-tablet, on my right a compass with a luminous dial. Two 36 grenades were attached to my left thigh.*

I knew from previous experience that the entrance to Dublin harbour is between two lighthouses fifty feet high and some three hundred yards apart. The North Bull Wall lighthouse was flashing a white light and sounding a bell; on the lip of the Great South Wall the Pool Beg lighthouse showed an occulting red light, on for several seconds and then briefly off, and sounded a horn. With a lee shore, and the sea crashing and sluicing into the sudden confines of the harbour entrance, the waves were forced up into over-falls some fifteen or twenty feet high, and I had to take careful aim between the two lights, making use of the waves – almost surfing on them – to avoid being smashed on to a lighthouse or wall.

The roar of wind and sea was constantly split by blasts from the horn to port and the clang of the bell to starboard. Because I was being flung up and down, left and right, under and over, it was the devil's own job to keep the red and white lights evenly balanced; but by steering with twitches of my flippers as the waves tumbled me along, I managed to pass safely through the harbour entrance, with the walls and lighthouse towers standing out in black silhouette against the street lights of Dublin, like impregnable pillars of death. Later, when I came to write my report, I described this passage ashore as 'routine' and carrying little risk. In fact it was highly hazardous and frightening, and, as usual on such occasions, I was scared stiff.

It was a relief to reach the relative calm of the harbour, and I swam on into the mouth of the Liffey, helped not only by the wind, but also by the last of the flood tide, which was surging up the channel. By 0515 I was in the river itself, hugging the Great South Wall to take advantage of the inshore eddies. Then, as the tide turned, the freshet current tumbled and bustled to meet me in miniature over-falls, and I had to swim a good deal harder to make progress.

---

* The 62B grenade, spherical and about the size of a grapefruit, was made of plastic. A relatively powerful weapon, it was capable of killing the crew of a submarine or tank with its blast. The 36 grenade, smaller and shaped like an orange, could be thrown farther: when it went off, its metal jacket exploded into lethal fragments.

Having passed under the first bridge, I swung hard to port and entered the River Dodder, a tributary of the Liffey. Again I was carried forward, this time by side-eddies from the big river, which continued to flood the tributary for some time after the tide had turned. An hour later I came gently ashore and walked along the river bank until I reached a large stand of trees, which I knew was Herbert Park. There I removed my diving gear, shed the sopping-wet thermal underwear, rubbed myself down and dressed in my nondescript civilian clothes, which had remained miraculously dry inside the biggest Durex sheath ever seen. As soon as I had buried the diving equipment with a small shovel brought for the purpose, I ate some chocolate and drank a cup of coffee laced with brandy from my thermos flask; then I set off for the rendezvous in the Cruagh Wood.

At the edge of the wood I took three bearings with my compass and jotted them down on my underwater writing-tablet. My calculations put me fifty yards south-west of the precise spot where I was due to meet the Germans. In the dim light of dawn a mass of bare twigs and branches created a hazy blur and reduced visibility to a few yards – a circumstance favouring me, the first-comer.

At 0650 I moved about fifty yards into the wood and settled myself against the trunk of a tree, well hidden from all but the most determined and professional of hunters. There, inland, the gale had eased, and in the shelter of the park the wind-noise was much reduced: even so, small sounds would be hard to hear, and I waited on full alert, with my mind running back over all the lessons I had learnt in training and on earlier operations. In particular I thought of the Iroquois Indians of Canada, from whom I had learnt the arts of tracking, hiding, soundless approach and silent killing.

Now, as always, the basic tenets were to keep quiet and remain motionless. I therefore eased my body into a position which would allow me perfect stillness and yet not bring on cramp. I silently exercised my muscles and relaxed into the disciplined, listening watch of the Iroquois.

Ten minutes later, just on 0700, I heard a branch snap, followed by muttered curses – the unsubtle noises of people entering the wood while trying to keep quiet. Listening with intense concentration, I reckoned that there were four men, and that two of them were pretty large. They were whispering in German, trying to identify the exact spot designated for the rendezvous: the third big ash in from the edge of the wood, specified by the map co-ordinates. I was ten yards from the chosen tree, silent and motionless.

Then I saw them. They were indeed four: two large, one of medium height, one quite small, all wearing civilian overcoats and hats. They stamped around, peering this way and that, waiting for me to appear. I was in a very strong position. I could have killed them all with a burst from my Sten gun, or by lobbing the 62B grenade, which was swinging from my belt, into their midst.

Yet violence was out of place here. I had no intention of killing the Germans, because I wanted them to lead me once again to Joachim von Ribbentrop, the German Foreign Minister. Equally, they would not want to kill me, because they needed my help. The best thing I could do was to impress them with the strength and skill of Leading Seaman John Davis, traitor extraordinary.

I had already deduced that the smallest man must be the diplomat and leader. His medium-sized companion was surely an intelligence officer. The two heavy fellows were merely SS thugs. Having taken one more careful look round, I silently broke cover and walked forward into the middle of the glade, my Sten gun levelled at their heads.

With no mean satisfaction I watched all four of them start as I materialised among them. They had neither heard nor seen me coming. They had not sensed my presence. But here I was, a ghost from the forest.

'*Guten Morgen, meine Herren,*' I said loudly, in more or less the only German I could muster.

'Herr Davis!' gasped the small man, whom I now recognised from earlier operations. He broke into a smile, half nerves, half relief, and genially clapped his hands a few times, applauding my silent approach. 'How quietly you have come!' he exclaimed. 'You are so good at that!'

His colleagues looked far from happy, but without further ado they escorted me to a car, blindfolded me and drove me to a country house. (Judging by our speed and the time that elapsed, I reckoned that we travelled only five miles or so.) Inside the building my blindfold was removed, and I was introduced to a tall, distinguished-looking man with grey hair. An exchange of prearranged code-words established that this was indeed Ribbentrop's emissary, and he greeted me warmly, pressing me to a large breakfast of steak and eggs, washed down by schnapps and coffee. In excellent English he addressed me on equal terms – one aristocrat to another, as he saw it; then, having sent everyone else out of the room, he proceeded to secret discussion.

In all this I rigidly maintained my role as a traitorous upper-class twit. My voice was distorted by a public schoolboy's drawl; my demeanour was oafishly nonchalant and uncaring. I was a juvenile crook, manifestly in love with money, cruelty, murder and, most of all, with myself. It was a role I knew all too well, since I had been playing it for five long years and had lived it to the full. I had committed all the basic crimes of which humans are capable, and by continuing with my role had given the impression that I revelled in it.

Ribbentrop, the emissary confided, had still not decided whether I was a genuine Nazi sympathiser, or simply a soldier of fortune working for my own benefit. The distinction, however, seemed unimportant, for always in the past I had proved reliable, provided the price was right. The emissary asked why I had proposed this new contact: what did I have in mind?

I replied that my message was for Ribbentrop's ears only. The officer, smoothly bypassing my evasion, said that, as it happened, the Reichsminister had a project of his own, from which I could expect to earn a very handsome amount in Swiss francs, to be paid into a numbered account, in my name alone. For the moment, he could say no more, except that Ribbentrop wanted me to meet him in Germany as soon as possible.

'Good!' I said. 'I'm keen to visit the Fatherland again without delay. But first I have to make some essential arrangements in England.'

'Of course,' he replied. 'I understand.' He went on to say that when I did travel to Germany, as a mark of good faith he would accompany me to Switzerland, where he would open a bank account in my name, and deposit a substantial sum. For my part, I would have to pose as a German. I would therefore be required to have photographs taken for travel documents and a German identity card. I would also have to be measured for a cover uniform.

Naturally I agreed; but I sensed that behind these arrangements there lay a hidden threat. If I failed to keep my part of the bargain, whatever it might prove to be, information about my movements would be handed over to the Allies, and might easily result in my being tried for treason. That was a risk I had to take.

Our meeting ended amicably, and two days later, on 24 January, I drove to Northern Ireland. In Londonderry I proceeded to HMS *Ferret* naval base, and thence by the same motor gunboat to Liverpool. Back in England, I reported to my chief that this first encounter had gone well: it looked as though we were in business.

2

Cloak and Dagger

My involvement in secret intelligence work derived from a concatenation of acquaintances and events which had their origins long before I was born. In 1919 my father, Jack Ainsworth-Davis, went up to Christ's College, Cambridge, to read medicine. Also at Christ's, sponsored by the Royal Navy, was the nineteen-year-old Sub-Lieutenant Lord Louis Mountbatten. Friendship with him brought my father into the circle of two other privileged undergraduates, the Duke of York (later King George VI), and his younger brother Prince Henry, later Duke of Gloucester, both cousins of Mountbatten. When my father won a gold medal as a member of the British 4 × 400 metre relay team at the Antwerp Olympics in 1920, all three were there to support and congratulate him.

Another friend of my father's who had a powerful effect on my service career was Joachim von Ribbentrop, the champagne salesman and diplomat. Before the First World War my father was sent to school at the Lyceum in Metz for a year, to learn German, and Ribbentrop was a fellow pupil there. It may be that the two boys were drawn together by their proficiency on the violin: later, in his memoirs, Ribbentrop recalled how important the violin had been to him then, and revealed that he had nursed an ambition to make music his career. My father also became an accomplished player.

In any case, their friendship continued in adult life, and during the 1930s Ribbentrop often visited our house at 69 Harley Street in London, first as Hitler's plenipotentiary in foreign affairs, then as German Ambassador to the Court of St James's. My father, a surgeon, treated him for some minor ailment, and in 1936 Ribbentrop went out of his way to entertain me, then a boy of twelve: he took me to the zoo in Regent's Park, and to several football matches, the most memorable being the rugby international at Twickenham between England and the All Blacks in January 1936, when young Prince Alexander Obolensky scored a phenomenal try, running diagonally the whole way across the field.

In due course Mountbatten also came to exert a strong influence over my life; but more far-reaching still was that of Desmond Morton, an old family friend, and one of the most effective intelligence officers ever to have served this country. Born in 1891, he was sent to Eton, and then to the Royal Military Academy at Woolwich. During the First World War he served with the Royal Horse and Field Artillery, and received a bullet in the heart, which remained *in situ* for the rest of his life. He was frequently in action, and won a Military Cross, a Croix de Guerre and a mention in despatches. After the war he was officially 'seconded to the Foreign Office': in fact he entered the Secret Intelligence Service, and in 1930 he formed the Industrial Intelligence Centre, an allegedly commercial body which was in reality a cover for his major preoccupation. This was the founding and running of the M (for Morton) Section, an ultra-secret intelligence organisation financed and protected, outside government control, by successive monarchs: George V, Edward VIII and George VI.

In the early days Morton directed the Section from an office in London and from his home on Crockham Hill, near Westerham, in Kent, with the enthusiastic support of his close friend and ally Winston Churchill, who lived just below him in the Vale of Chartwell. In 1932, when the M Section began operating, Churchill was out of office; but it was from Morton and his contacts in Europe that he obtained much of the information about German rearmament which eventually convinced the governments of Baldwin and Chamberlain that Britain and the other Western democracies were in deadly peril.

Morton was a tall, brawny, dark-haired man with huge ears, who sported a thick but tightly clipped moustache. His piercing black eyes missed nothing, but he had bad, irregular teeth (perhaps that was one reason why he so rarely smiled). Austere and patrician in manner, he cultivated an exaggeratedly upper-class English voice, although he was a Scot: he could be bombastic and overpowering, especially when proselytising for his chosen religion, Roman Catholicism. Certainly he converted my parents to Catholicism in the early 1930s, and he stood godfather at my second christening, when the name James was added to my existing John and Christopher. In 1932, when my parents divorced, he also became my guardian, and, as was the custom in those days, I knew him as 'Uncle'.

With the break-up of our family, my mother needed somewhere to live, and it was Morton who found her Chartwell Cottage, on the edge of Churchill's estate. We rented the house for only a few months, but they proved a halcyon period for me, and the friendship which I, a lad of eight, struck up with Winston Churchill lasted for the rest of his life.

No matter that he was out of a job and in the political wilderness: he entered into our games with the enthusiasm of an overgrown boy. Between our cottage and Chartwell itself, I and my two sisters built a robbers' camp – a stockade of sticks and wool tied up round the trunk of an enormous tree, with an old rope going up into the branches. One day Churchill arrived with a wheelbarrow full of new ropes and pulleys, and made us a proper hoist – only for the mechanism to jam when he himself went aloft, so that he could not get down. Our nanny, Dorothy, whom we couldn't stand, looked up and cried, 'Children, children, what on earth have you done with Mr Churchill?' while he became more and more furious that no one would rescue him.

Another time, out of sheer boisterousness, I knocked down part of a brick wall that he had been building, and he pretended to be seriously injured. Back in the kitchen at Chartwell, I watched Mrs Churchill administer a spoonful of some medicine or tonic which he was taking. 'Ah!' I said, thinking of *The House at Pooh Corner*, 'Tigger taking Roo's extract of malt.' Whereupon he immediately growled back, 'I suppose you're Christopher Robin.' Somehow the borrowed names stuck, and we used them ever after, not merely in family surroundings, but as our *noms de guerre* as well.

In those days, across the road from Chartwell's main gates, a path led up through some woods to a clearing where an old gipsy woman lived in a caravan, with only a donkey for company. We children thought of the 'Donkey Lady' as a witch, and used to bait the life out of her, occasionally using her caravan as long-stop in our games of cricket. Once Churchill asked me to take a little package up to her, and I knew that it contained money, because he adjured me not to lose it. Sixty years later his daughter Mary (by then Lady Soames) was astonished when a mutual friend mentioned my recollection. She herself had been only twelve at the time when we lived at Chartwell, but she immediately remembered the Donkey Lady, and the fact that her father had given the old woman surreptitious financial support.*

Later Morton was instrumental in having me accepted by Ampleforth, the Benedictine abbey and public school in North Yorkshire; but in 1939, with war on the horizon, his influence on me turned infinitely more sinister. For at least three years he had known of my relationship with Ribbentrop, and when, in the summer, Hitler created my other surrogate uncle Foreign Minister, Morton spotted that in the long term, because of this association, I might possibly prove valuable as an intelligence agent.

His initial move – with the direct connivance of Mountbatten and Admiral Sir Dudley Pound, the First Sea Lord – was to enter me for the Royal Navy under a name which could be used for cover purposes in future. It was under this pseudonym that I entered the Royal Naval College at Dartmouth in September 1939, aged fifteen and a half. In this book I have used a second cover-name, Christopher Creighton, a combination of my own and my father's middle names, but for security and ease of reference I have applied it to my wartime *alter ego* as well.

Cover-names were nothing new in naval intelligence. During the First World War, Admiral Sir Reginald 'Blinker' Hall, the DNI, had devised a simple but effective practice of entering on the Navy List names of officers who did not exist. These were mere phantoms, ghosts; but great care was taken to prepare, plant, prune and generally keep up-to-date the spectral entries.

* Until now this story has never appeared in print. But obviously if I had not lived on the Chartwell estate, and had not known both Churchill and the Donkey Lady well, I would never have heard of it.

From time to time they were promoted; some were even decorated, and occasonally one was gazetted as 'killed in action'. The result of this highly successful intelligence ploy was that a suitable name was always available whenever an emergency arose and someone suddenly needed a cover identity, which might be checked out on the Navy List by enemy investigators or agents.

In the Second World War, for reasons of operational security, some naval officers in the M Section used one or more *noms de guerre*. I had three. Since then cover has always been part of my life – as this story will reveal. Cover is one of the key weapons of intelligence work, especially in irregular sections such as mine; and with cover go deceit, murder, betrayal, disloyalty, brutality, amorality, and the total renunciation of God, and of anything touching on decency or friendship.

In theory I could have remained at school for the time being, and in normal circumstances I would probably have stayed at Ampleforth until I was eighteen. But if I had, I would never have been trained to an acceptable level of discipline and knowledge. For this, Dartmouth and the navy were uniquely suited. In the hectic early days of September 1939 Morton, Churchill and Mountbatten had very little time to decide on my future; but Mountbatten reckoned that if naval training had been good enough for the King, it must be good enough for me. In his usual direct and bluff manner, he told me to use the name Christopher Creighton at all times – never John Davis – and Dartmouth's captain was ordered to take it out on my backside whenever I slipped up and forgot.

In taking this drastic step of inducting me into the world of secret intelligence, Morton and Mountbatten took my mother partly into their confidence. They did not, however, tell my father, because they considered him a poor security risk. At Cambridge he had proved himself a fine scholar and a proficient musician: his Quinqua Jazz Band, with Mountbatten on drums, had attracted stars of the calibre of Noel Gay (R. W. Armitage), Claude Hulbert and his brother Jack, and Jack's wife, Cicely Courtneidge. Later he had played Grieg's Violin Concerto under the baton of Sir Adrian Boult, and he had developed into a brilliant genito-urinary surgeon. As a man, he was warm and generous. But he was also inclined to be silly, and to show little common sense. Although at heart the stoutest of patriots, he could not keep quiet or make discreet inquiries if he heard anything unusual about me: instead, he would contact all his old friends in high places, including Mountbatten, and demand to know what was going on, causing great difficulty and embarrassment.

Because of Morton's special requirements, I never completed the full course at Dartmouth. In March 1940, as an acting midshipman, I was appointed to the M Section, where, for the first time, I came face to face with the startling realities of wartime secret operational intelligence. I was still only sixteen when I undertook my first operations, and barely sixteen and a half when I guided in a Combined Operations attack on the German submarine base in Donegal, an episode in which I killed for the first time, murdering four men, three with my bare hands.*
But then in October 1940 – as a further stage in his deception plan – Morton had me enlisted into the Royal Air Force as an aircrew officer cadet pilot under training. At first I was posted to the RAF's No. 2 Initial Training Wing at Cambridge, but that was merely another form of cover. The instruction my fellow cadets and I received there was hardly designed to teach us to fly aircraft. Rather, our course included commando and paratroop training, unarmed combat, silent approach and killing, karate, jujitsu, weapons training with fighting knives and firearms of all types, use of explosives, sabotage, swimming and diving, handling two-man kayaks, and the maintenance and repair of engines, both diesel and petrol. On the intelligence front, we learnt about codes and ciphers, wireless telegraphy and electrical

---

* At that time the services were crammed with people – of both sexes – as young as fifteen, sixteen and seventeen, who had falsified their ages in order to join up (my own age was given in the books as eighteen). We had sixteen-year-old midshipmen as officers of the watch and in other responsible positions. There were many first-rate pilots under sixteen flying Spitfires and Hurricanes in the Battle of Britain. The RAF knew perfectly well what was going on, for on the attestation form for those joining up was a prominent note which read: 'Your age on attestation will be taken as your true age, whether or not at a future date it is proved to be incorrect.'

engineering. This comprehensive programme was interspersed with live training operations, particularly in German-occupied France and Belgium.

My father would have been appalled if he had known what Morton was doing behind the scenes. In a deliberate character assassination, the 'shred, doctor and forge' unit of the M Section had been falsifying the record of John Davis, blackening that name with a criminal record which showed various petty offences dating from 1940. Going still further back, they created reports from Ampleforth which revealed that, while still scarcely fifteen, I had become an ardent disciple of the Fascist leader Oswald Mosley, and an avid supporter of Germany against England. In these and other files it was made to appear that I had a spiteful character, that I had been disowned by my father, and that I would do anything for money or personal advancement. Finally, Morton had the school records rearranged to show that I had remained at Ampleforth for an extra year, until the autumn of 1940, and had then gone straight into the RAF. Some idea of the forgers' efficiency may be gained from the fact that my name appeared on the Nazis' published list of young British men who had been members of the Mosley movement – a circumstance which helped authenticate me as a traitor in German eyes.

All this clearly made it impossible that John Davis, the disaffected trainee pilot, was the Royal Navy officer with the cover-name Christopher Creighton; and should I ever be seriously challenged, and in danger, it could be shown that I had been somewhere else, and in another service, all the time. It was a brilliant ploy of Morton's to make me live, work and have my being under an artificial name and to reserve my real name as a cover.

So well did the deception go that later Mountbatten told me it had caused him some distress. My father, believing me to be the black sheep of the family, wrote and begged him to use his position to get me a commission (in my real name I was still a leading seaman). Mountbatten wrote back to say that, even with his undoubted influence, this was something he simply could not do. Later he protested to me that he had told no more and no less than the truth: in another name I was already a lieutenant, RN, so how could I become a sub-lieutenant, RNVR, as well?* At a conciliatory moment my father showed me the letter, and I was even more distressed than Lord Louis, because I still could not tell the truth, even to my own kith and kin. I was particularly moved to see that Mountbatten had signed his letter 'Dickie'. Churchill, hearing of my distress and wishing to make me feel better, said, 'Guard above all your reputation as a young man of no character; for if anyone should become proud of you, you are lost.'

With the advantage of fifty years' hindsight, I can see that I was by no means ideal material for Morton's purposes. Whether he perceived the flaws in my character, or whether he was so carried away by the possibilities of the Ribbentrop connection that he ignored them, I cannot say. Yet the fact remains that I was far too emotional and volatile a character, and too easily swayed by religious feeling, for the kind of work he wanted me to do. It is true that naval training minimised some of my deficiencies and taught me a good measure of self-control; nevertheless, I realise now that I was dangerously impulsive, temperamental and prone to emotional swings.

The worst of these were usually brought on by what I called – and call – my black angel, who first scared me when I was only fifteen. In August 1939 I went with the Ampleforth Sea Scout troop to a summer camp at Moidrey, in northern France. One evening I sat alone in the village chapel, playing the organ. When it became too dark for me to see the keyboard any longer, I walked towards one of the two exits, only to find, standing in the porch, a black figure, which called out my name. Terrified, I immediately turned and ran for the other door – but the black

* This was by no means the only occasion on which Mountbatten wrote a false cover letter. In April 1943, as part of the classic strategic deception known as Operation Mincemeat, Lieutenant-Commander Ewen Montagu persuaded him to write a personal letter which was intended to fall into the hands of the enemy and contribute to the impression that the Allies' next target for invasion was Greece or Sardinia, rather than Sicily. The tissue of lies, expertly put together in the name of expediency and victory, succeeded beyond Montagu's wildest hopes. Later he described the incident in his book *The Man Who Never Was*. Like many other deception operations, this one was sanctioned by Winston Churchill.

figure was there too. I was paralysed by fear and stood rooted to the spot.

I saw that the figure was not attempting to enter the chapel, but was waiting for me outside. Why? Instinctively I knew the answer. I was on consecrated ground, in a chapel of God, with the Host in the tabernacle. The black figure could not, dared not, enter. For the moment I had sanctuary. Crossing myself, I prayed to St Benedict and St Laurence of the great abbey and college of Ampleforth, my school and religious home. I prayed because I was a coward, and wanted God to save me from the black thing in the doorway – which then, in my mind, spoke to me.

'John!' I heard it say. 'Soon you will be mine. Not in death, but in life. You will place my mark on the world conflict that is about to start. You will be with me. You will serve me. In the name of war you will commit crimes. In the name of victory, and in my name, you will do vicious deeds. You will be one of my angels of death.'

Could I believe my inner ears? Suddenly, through the black figure, I saw another, reassuringly human and solid. 'John,' it said, 'you're late for supper. What on earth have you been doing?'

Father Jerome Lambert, the scoutmaster, looked at me closely. 'What's the matter? You're white as a sheet.'

I liked and trusted Father Jerome. I knew he would not laugh at me, so I told him what had happened. He listened quietly, looking serious, then took me by the arm and led me to the door, dipping his fingers into the font of holy water as he passed. He glared at the spot where the black figure had stood, and flicked drops in that direction. 'In nomine Patris, Filii et Spiritus Sancti,' he intoned loudly, making the sign of the cross. Then he gave the black angel a rocket. 'You just get out of here and stop annoying my boys,' he snapped, 'or I'll set the Holy Ghost on you.'

I found that reassuring, even comical, and we walked out of the chapel together.

'Too much imagination,' Father Jerome chided.

But imagination had nothing to do with it. I had seen my black angel, and knew he would return.

Sure enough, that same evening I was abruptly called home. Back at Southampton next day, I was met by Desmond Morton, who drove me to the Hampshire village of Longparish, where I

17

lived with my mother and sisters. Hardly had we arrived when he dropped a bombshell. 'John,' he said, 'you're not going back to Ampleforth next term. You're going into the Royal Navy.'

The black angel had lost no time – and that evening he visited me again. I awoke in the middle of the night, soaked in sweat, and there he was, standing at the foot of my bed. He had followed me from France and had come to claim his pawn, his knight, his paladin, just as he had promised he would. When he advanced slowly towards me, I tried to repel him by raising my fingers in the sign of the cross and commanding him, in the name of Jesus of Nazareth, to leave me. But my arms and hands seemed paralysed. I could not move. With a feeling of utter degradation and terror I realised I was powerless to stop him possessing me – as he would often do in the weeks, months and years that followed.

Looking back, I can see how completely I was in Morton's grip throughout most of the war. From 1940 to 1945 I was his puppet, manipulated by him and executing his orders. All the same, many of the actions I carried out on his behalf had such terrible consequences that guilt still overwhelms me when I think of them. The fact that they might have been for the greater good, and maybe helped a bit, will never atone for the loss of life and the suffering that I brought about.

This is not the place for a full description of all the operations in which I took part. Nevertheless I feel it is essential that I list briefly those that contributed to the image of John Davis the traitor, and so by the beginning of 1945 made me, in Nazi eyes, a credible candidate for the rescue of Ribbentrop and Bormann. In other words, I sketch here those operations whose cumulative effect was to qualify me for the operational command of Operation James Bond.

In early 1942 Morton, Churchill and the Allied Supreme Command were anxious to test the feasibility of a direct assault on one of the Channel ports held by the Germans, their aim being to decide whether such an attack should be an integral part of the major Allied invasion they were already planning for D-Day. If the exercise was to yield useful information, the port would have to be properly defended: nothing would be learnt if the Germans were taken by surprise.

Morton had for some time been trying to establish reliable contact with the German intelligence service, the Abwehr, and especially with its chief, Admiral Wilhelm Canaris, who was known to be anti-Nazi at heart. Now he ordered me to try to make contact with Canaris, through Dublin, and to betray to the Abwehr the exact date and time of the planned British raid on Dieppe. Morton's secondary aim was to establish me as a double agent.

I announced my arrival in the Irish capital by firing a message in a small canister out of a specially constructed Very flare-pistol into a first-floor window of 52 Northumberland Road, Dublin, the German Legation. The note proposed a meeting in nearby woods. My contacts kept the rendezvous, and I was taken off to a country house, where I was held close prisoner. Had my story of a criminal record in England not checked out, and had Ribbentrop not confirmed from Berlin that my father was indeed a friend of his, and that he knew me well, I would have been executed.

As it was, to my everlasting shame, I carried out Morton's orders down to the last detail. I travelled to Cork, then by U-boat to Brest, and on to Berlin. There I was taken to Tirpitzufer 22, in the centre of the city, to meet Canaris. The lift was broken, and I had to walk up a mountain of stairs. Canaris turned out to be a tiny man with a red face, deeply lined, and even on that hot summer's day he sat at his desk wearing a heavy, long black overcoat. Before he spoke, he studied me for some time with an air of contempt, and I looked back at him – this man who, Morton told me, had been the lover of Mata Hari, and had sent her to her death as a spy. As we sat there sizing each other up, several dachshunds sniffed and snapped at my ankles.

'Why?' said Canaris suddenly.

Taken aback, I could think of no reply.

'Why do you want to do it?' he asked harshly. 'Why do you want to betray your country and give us secret information?'

I told him. For money. Out of dislike of my father, and the police, and the British system. I brought out my cover-story, which by then I could have recited in my sleep.

Still he gazed at me. 'I don't believe you,' he said quietly. His tone was even, with no edge of hostility. 'But for intelligence purposes, I'll go along with what you say. Ten thousand pounds is the amount, is it not?'

I nodded. He brought out a bundle of rolled-up £5 notes from a drawer in his desk and laid them in front of him.

'When you've given me all the details, you can pick these up,' he said. 'They're yours. But if your information turns out to be false, they'll be no use to you. You'll be strung up until the scream is cut from your throat by a piano wire – a B natural, or possibly a B♭ string; but you won't notice the difference. It won't be done by us. We don't do things like that. But unfortunately the SS are in on this.'

I gave him accurate details of the forthcoming raid, picked up the money and returned to England. Now to all my crimes committed in the name of king and country I could add that of Judas Iscariot.

Late in July I went back to Germany to inform the Abwehr that the code-name for the operation had been changed from 'Rutter' to 'Jubilee', and to give the latest details of forces, beaches and commanders. Yet Hitler and his Commander-in-Chief, West, Field Marshal Gerd von Rundstedt, demanded further evidence that the forces I had named were indeed to be used, and were ready and waiting in the places I had mentioned. Back in England, I went so far as to take a German agent with me round some of the bases along the south coast.

On 14 August I crossed to Cherbourg, and on the night of the 18th–19th, with the assault due to begin in the early hours, I was taken, handcuffed, to the cliff-top known to the Allies as the Rommel Battery, but to the Germans as the Bismarck. Around 0300, Canaris appeared and told me that if the main attack had not started by 0600, I would be dead. The SS put a loop of piano wire round my neck and attached the other end to a block set in the ground near the cliff-top. One kick would have sent me over the edge.

From that eminence I was forced to watch every phase of the massacre that followed. I saw the destruction of practically every Canadian tank on the beaches. Almost sub-consciously, I counted three hundred men killed just below me. Of those, I made a specific count of thirty-seven human beings disembowelled.

At 1500 Canaris gave me a bag containing another £10,000 in

big white £5 notes, and told me what a fine job I had done in destroying my countrymen and their allies. The contempt in his voice was icy. Hating myself, I walked along the beaches, past the dead and wounded. Many men were terribly injured, but they received no attention. My instinct was to help them, but my SS escorts would not let me. I tried to pray for them, but could not. I knew that God would not listen to a hypocritical traitor who had helped engineer one of the worst betrayals in history. Instead, I prayed with all my heart that someone would shoot me. Later, close to the harbour, I dropped the notes into the water as a kind of penance – all but one, which I kept for Morton. He had no sympathy at all. The money had been expertly forged.

In October 1942, on another mission of deception, I first kept a rendezvous with Abwehr agents in Lisbon. Then I was flown to Paris and handed over to General Ernst Kaltenbrunner, head of the SS in France, who had orders to transport me to a secret rendezvous. Nobody told me what our destination was, or whom I was going to see; and by the time we had travelled by car and train for two days and two nights, I was thoroughly confused. At one stage somebody told me we were going to Vinnitsa, in the Ukraine: then I heard that we were heading for Hitler's headquarters known as the Wolfsschanze (the Wolf's Lair), in East Prussia.

When we eventually arrived, I found Ribbentrop waiting for me. He was friendly, but seemed preoccupied. Two SS guards chained my wrists together and escorted me along a corridor to a room whose walls were entirely covered by maps. The only occupant was the Führer himself, wearing his normal uniform of brown jacket and black trousers.

When Ribbentrop gave the Nazi salute, I said quite loudly, in English, that I was sorry I could not do the same. Being handcuffed, I could not salute my Führer, and the leader of all British Fascists and Mosleyites. As soon as this was translated, Hitler gave an order: the SS guards removed my chains and left the room.

'After your considerable services to the Third Reich at Dieppe,' said Ribbentrop in an oily voice, 'the Führer is confident that you will not try to harm him.'

How wrong he was! Even before the chains were off, my mind was spinning as I tried to assess my chance of killing both Nazi leaders, and maybe even escaping as well. Hitler was pacing up and down about six feet from me. If I moved at the instant he turned away, I could reach him in one second, get him in the death-clasp in two seconds, and break his neck in three. In a maximum of five seconds the leader of the Third Reich would be finished. I reckoned that Ribbentrop would be so shocked that in that time he would be unable to move, and I would get him too. In twenty seconds both men would be dead, without a whisper – for a man caught in a death-clasp cannot make a sound.

Wild, ridiculous thoughts chased each other through my brain. In some extraordinary way Hitler resembled my father: take away the forelock and some of the moustache, and there was a definite likeness. Then I wondered if Ribbentrop would be very angry if I *did* kill him. Through my head ran the old naval maxim that a captain can do little wrong if he heads towards the sound of the guns, and, without orders, engages the enemy. There were a hundred examples – Nelson, Collingwood and Earl St Vincent, to name but three. But Hitler was not firing any guns; I was not the captain of any ship; I had no authority from my superiors to attack and kill. On the contrary, I was in Germany to convince the Abwehr, Ribbentrop and now the Führer that the Allies were about to attack Norway rather than North Africa. With an effort I fought the idea down.

Hitler said something in German, smiled, came right up to me and put his hand against the side of my cheek. Even before Ribbentrop translated, I knew that he too was congratulating me on my performance at Dieppe. Then he was off again on his little walk, out and back, out and back. I could not help noticing that he looked bouncy and well.

When I came down to business, and spoke of Allied intentions in Norway, he exclaimed to Ribbentrop, 'There! I told you. That was exactly what I said.' His good humour lasted until the end of our interview, and at the close he made many protestations of friendship, talking of the jobs I could have in Germany when the war was over and my country was a province of the Third Reich.

What I did not realise until much later was that our meeting had been closely monitored by Martin Bormann, Hitler's private secretary, and head of the Nazi Party Chancellery, who, by making himself indispensable to the Führer, had manoeuvred himself into a position of immense power. At the time I did not know who Bormann was, and certainly did not notice him. But he noticed me.* He also saw that Ribbentrop was trying to build himself up in Hitler's eyes by falsely representing that it was he, Ribbentrop, and not Canaris, who had handled the Dieppe deception from the German end. Further, Bormann heard Ribbentrop claim that it was he who had found me in England in 1936, through his friendship with my father, and had nurtured my latent treachery by persuading me to join the junior section of Mosley's British Fascist Party while I was still at school.

Bormann saw how impressed Hitler was, not only by the information I had given the Nazis, but also by my father's gold medal in the 1920 Olympics, his friendship with Mountbatten, and his connections with the royal family. Bormann realised that I was someone who might well be useful to him in the future; but for the moment, with his usual patience and cunning, he gave no sign of his interest. At that time, in 1942, one of his main aims was to bring down the strutting Ribbentrop, with his cheap champagne and phoney use of the prefix 'von'. Bormann loathed and despised the Foreign Minister, whom he regarded as an upstart; but still he would give him a sickly smile, as, having farted quietly in his trousers, he moved off across the room and blamed the resultant stink on him.

At the beginning of 1943 Mountbatten had me drafted into a secret unit called COPP (Combined Operations Pilotage Party), irreverently known as 'Mountbatten's private navy'. It comprised only thirty-five officers and men, charged with the task of pre-invasion beach reconnaissance. What the members of COPP didn't know about silent approach from water was not worth knowing.

My months at COPP were the happiest of my war, and Morton was pleased that I had joined the unit, as service with such a secret and centrally placed formation could only enhance my reputation among the Nazis as a source of top-level information. Already he

---

* The details that follow are taken from the 800-page transcript of the debriefing carried out at Birdham, the M Section's training base near Portsmouth, after Bormann had been brought to England in May 1945. It is referred to hereafter as the Birdham transcript.

had another job for me; and this one turned out still more traumatic than Dieppe.

At the beginning of 1944 we put out hints to my Nazi contacts in Ireland that I would soon be in a position to supply precise details about what we called the Second Front – in other words, Operation Overlord, the Allied invasion of Europe planned for D-Day. On Morton's instructions, I let it be known that my price for these paramount secrets would be £100,000.

Various preliminary meetings convinced the Germans that I knew what I was talking about. Then on 5 May 1944, in his secure office, Morton told me that the Allied landings would begin at dawn on Monday, 5 June, in the Pas de Calais. He pointed out every detail of the beaches we would attack, code-named Sword, Juno and Gold for the British, Omaha and Utah for the Americans. Again and again he hammered 'Pas de Calais' into my brain. One wall was dominated by a large-scale chart of the same region. I came away in no doubt at all that the Pas de Calais was our target. I had no means of knowing that Morton was double-crossing me for his own ends, and that in fact the invasion was planned for the Bay of the Seine, in Normandy, a hundred miles to the south-west.

Back in Ireland again, I was paid £10,000 as a deposit, and the money was placed in a Dublin bank. But before I could carry out my next great betrayal, a fresh crisis blew up.

On 11 May 1944, on the orders of General Dwight D. Eisenhower, Supreme Commander of the Allied Expeditionary Force, a large-scale landing exercise took place off Slapton Sands in Dorset. Code-named Exercise Tiger, it was designed to be a final rehearsal for D-Day, but it turned into a tragedy: proper intelligence and escort security precautions had not been taken, and as the force approached the beach it was attacked by three German E-boats.

By chance I was among a group of COPP officers and other observers aboard a landing-craft. Like most of the participants, we saw practically nothing, and took the E-boat activity as a dummy diversionary assault, part of the exercise. But the attack was all too real. The E-boats struck almost unopposed, as the transports had practically no naval escort, and 420 US servicemen were killed.

A decision was immediately taken at the highest level to shroud the disaster in secrecy. If any mention of it leaked out, the confidence of the American GI in the feasibility of the D-Day landings would be severely shaken. Eisenhower delegated responsibility for the cover-up to Morton, who immediately launched Operation Tiger Hunt. In this, all the men and women who had witnessed the fiasco were rounded up: most were arrested and taken into protective custody, but about thirty were ordered to report to HMS *Tormentor*, a Combined Operations base on the Hamble River, near Southampton. The cover-story put about was that they were being taken back to Slapton Sands to see if a second visit would shake up their memories and produce some explanation of how the tragedy had occurred. They boarded the landing-craft alongside the Bugle Inn, and proceeded west, down the Solent and towards Dorset. But at the Needles, off the Isle of Wight, they struck a mine, and the boat sank with all hands. At least, that was what the official report concluded.

As for myself, ordered back to Ireland on 20 May, I told the Standartenführer with whom I had been negotiating that I would go no further, and give no further information about D-Day, until the balance owed to me – £90,000 – had been paid. Within twenty-four hours the cash was deposited in the same Irish bank, for transfer to a Swiss account. At once we left for Cork, and travelled by E-boat to Cherbourg.

By the evening of Monday, 22 May, I was in the castle of the Duke of Rochefoucauld, which had been appropriated by Field Marshal Erwin Rommel, Commander-in-Chief of Army Group B, as his headquarters. In the castle library I stood facing Rommel and his senior staff officers.

The field marshal was short but athletic-looking: like all senior Wehrmacht officers, he wore no tie, but had his white shirt buttoned high up to the neck, and the only colour about him was the scarlet of his field marshal's tabs on his lapels. In manner he was courteous and not openly aggressive: but as he stood in front of a map, holding a baton, his eyes bored into me, and a half-smile played round his lips. His personality was so powerful that I remember nothing of my surroundings, save that the walls of the library were hung with magnificent tapestries. Like Canaris, Rommel had seen right through me, to the truth in my soul; but for the time being he continued with the masquerade.

'So,' said Rommel in strongly accented English, 'what have you to tell us?'

'It's the Bay of the Seine, in Normandy,' I said, parroting Morton's instructions. 'A fortnight today, early in the morning of 5 June.'

The field marshal's English was evidently limited, for he went on in German, with his ADC interpreting. He demanded more specific information: the code-names of the beaches, the precise strength of the Allied groups in each area. As I spoke, he never took his eyes from mine, and when I had finished, he said, in English, 'Judas boy!' Then, in German, 'What is your price for this betrayal of your country, your family, your friends?'

'A hundred thousand pounds.'

Rommel shook his head and asked the SS officer alongside him why I should be believed. Out came the usual spiel: the record of John Davis the turncoat, the arch-hater of Britain. Rommel's response was that I hardly sounded the sort of person on whom he should rely. The SS man respectfully pointed out that my information about Dieppe had proved 100 per cent accurate, and had led to a heavy Allied defeat. Moreover, he added, I was a friend of Reichsminister von Ribbentrop.

At that Rommel walked up to me, looked straight into my eyes, and said, 'Soon you will have to face yourself. Deep in your soul you will pay the extreme penalty, from which there is no reprieve.'

His eyes continued to bore into me, until I felt they were drilling at my heart.

'Tell me, Judas boy, why should I believe you? All our information, logistics – everything points to the Pas de Calais.'

'Why should I give false information?'

He paused for a long moment, then echoed, 'Yes . . . why?'

Suddenly footsteps came clattering down the passage outside. The door opened to admit an SS Obergruppenführer, a full general, who came rigidly to attention before Rommel. A loud 'Heil Hitler!' rent the air.

Rommel appeared far from happy. He returned the greeting not with a Nazi '*Heil*!' but with a normal soldier's salute.

'We come from the Führer,' said the general.

At once I knew something was wrong. I hastily flung out a Nazi salute, but it availed me nothing, and, with Rommel's permission, the SS officer questioned me all over again. I gave the same answers, but I could see that the man did not believe me. Soon his demeanour became almost triumphant. Rommel picked up the tension and watched me closely, with undisguised fascination.

'And have you been paid for your information?' the general asked.

'A portion, yes.' I concentrated all-out on maintaining my role as a traitorous upper-class twit.

'Might I see your identity card?'

Striving to appear nonchalant, I took out my Royal Navy seaman's paybook and handed it over.

The general studied the book carefully, then glanced up with a look that terrified me.

'I don't mean this document, Herr Leading Seaman John Davis. I was referring to your real one, which shows you to be Lieutenant Christopher John James Creighton, an officer of British Secret Operational Intelligence.'

My heart turned to ice. I knew I could no longer maintain my role as a traitor.

'Herr Lieutenant Creighton, Royal Navy,' the general continued, 'I do not accept your information about the Allied invasion. We have irrefutable proof that you have been sent to mislead us. You are under arrest.'

Two other SS officers grabbed hold of me, none too gently, but Rommel stepped forward and took command. 'Stop!' he called. 'Step back from him!'

The men let go as Rommel came close to me. 'You are Lieutenant Creighton? British Royal Navy?'

I knew I had been caught. There was no point in denying it. Unconsciously my demeanour changed. The languid, traitorous twit vanished, to be replaced by a regular naval officer with quietly controlled discipline. I came softly to attention in front of the field marshal and said, 'Yes, sir, I am.'

Rommel nodded. 'Ja, Kapitänleutnant. It was a good try. Now you are a prisoner of war. You will go to an Oflag, a camp for officers.'

The SS general intervened sharply. 'General Feldmarschall! This man is an enemy agent. I have written authority to take charge of him, in the name of the Führer.'

The officer held up a sheet of paper. Rommel read it. The electric tension in the air revealed everything. Rommel seemed glad, almost relieved, that I was not a traitor after all. To the obvious annoyance of the SS men, he clicked his heels and bowed his head curtly – from the field marshal, a salute. He put out a hand. I took it gratefully. It was firm and warm.

The SS prison at Cherbourg Castle was a ghastly place, and the fortnight I spent there was the most ghastly of my life. I was flung into a stinking stone cell, with verminous straw covering part of the floor, and I had not been there long when four men in cvilian clothes crashed open the door and walked in. One, speaking passable English, said, 'Good evening, Mr Creighton, Royal Navy. We are from the Gestapo. We always like to be polite and gentle – at first, anyway – to give you a chance to answer our questions as a friend.' He paused as they circled me, then went on, 'Please, Mr Creighton, just tell us the *real* place and time of the invasion of France . . .'

Their patience did not last long. Suddenly they rushed me, ripped off my trousers and underclothes and bent me right over. A revolver barrel was stuffed up my rectum, twisted round and jerked out. Flesh ripped, and blood spattered down on to the filthy floor.

That was how it began, and that was how it continued. For as long as I could, I clung to my cover-story, until I feared I would never be able to walk properly or play the piano again. After a week my face was battered, my mouth torn, my nose split, my ears lacerated. Some of my fingernails and toenails had been ripped out. Blood seeped from my fingers, my toes and the soles of my feet. I had nothing to eat, and only sips of dirty water to drink. In my cell there was no basin, not even a bucket. The straw became fouled with urine and diarrhoea.

For day after day the monotonous voices of the interrogators droned on. 'You know it's not the Bay of the Seine. Don't you? You know it's the Pas de Calais. Just tell us.'

Plenty of real patriots, many incredibly brave men and women, have suffered far worse than I did, and never given in. I did not come within light years of their achievement. My courage and my pain threshold were of a far lower order.

One morning, when once again they had hitched up their electrical gear to my testicles, the moment came when I could not go on. My mind had become so exhausted and muddled that a sort of temporary insanity took over. What difference was there between the Bay of the Seine and the Pas de Calais, in any case? Weren't they one and the same? If that was so, it would make no difference if I *did* say 'Pas de Calais' to my torturers. This agony would stop.

But there was another way to stop it: concealed in one of my lower left molars was my L-pill, a capsule of potassium cyanide, which would pass harmlessly through the system if swallowed by mistake, but killed in ten seconds if bitten through. As I struggled to decide, there rose before my eyes visions of all the people I had killed, or whose deaths I had caused. I saw again all the vicious acts I had committed. Suddenly everything was crystal-clear. This was my punishment. God intended that I should die here and now, in retribution for my manifold sins.

I hardly had the strength to suck the L-pill out of its cavity. But at last I managed to put it between my teeth. Visions of all the people I loved swam in and out of focus before my eyes: my mother, my sisters, my beloved Patricia. Yes, Patricia most of all. Then, with the discipline bred into me by the Royal Navy, I bit through the capsule.

Drops fell on my parched tongue and throat. I waited, tense in expectation of searing pain, terrible cramps, a smell of almonds. Nothing whatever happened.

For a few moments I lay there stunned in the filthy straw. I could not imagine what had gone wrong. Morton himself had given me the capsule . . . The issue of the pills was rigorously controlled . . . He could not have made a mistake. Then I realised: he had given me a dummy, full of water. He did not intend me to die, even if my suffering became impossible to bear. For him to have done that, there must be some reason. But what was it? Did he mean me to break, to tell the Gestapo what they wanted to know? Through the fog in my brain I remembered how he had kept repeating the words 'Pas de Calais, Pas de Calais, Pas de Calais'. Was *that* what he meant me to say?

In any event, my resistance came to an end. After the umpteenth twisting and electrifying of my vital organs, the hundredth smashing of my head and neck and body, I could hold out no longer. My will to fight on had gone. Through the clotted blood in my mouth I whispered, 'Yes, it's the Pas de Calais.'

Suddenly everything stopped. The beatings ceased. I only had to repeat the words a couple of times, and I was left alone. A great flood of relief surged over me, only to merge into feelings of abject guilt and shame. I had failed utterly. I had let down each and every one of my friends. I had betrayed my country. If ever I returned to England, I hoped they would hang me as a traitor. Still better that someone should come and shoot me: get it over and done with. Put an end to the physical and – worst of all – the mental anguish. 'Roll on, death,' I prayed. 'Dear God, come and get me.'

For a short spell, doctors took over. They injected Pentothal, filled me with drugs. But I was left locked in my cell, still without food or water, wallowing in shame and degradation, close to death.

Then one morning an SS officer with an escort came to the door. It was 0815 on the morning of 5 June, he told me. I had promised that the Allied invasion would start at 0530 that morning in the Pas de Calais. Nothing had happened. Nobody had landed. There was no sign of an invasion fleet. Clearly my information had been false. I was to be shot in the main square.

I was half dragged, half marched to the main gate, where the commander of the castle challenged the SS party. The officer produced an order for my execution, signed by Walter Schellenberg of SS intelligence, and this apparently sufficed. I was flung into the back of a truck: inside, there were more SS men and some women, who jeered and kicked at me as I lay on the floor.

As we set off, I lapsed into semi-consciousness; but after a few minutes I registered that the truck slowed down and turned left. Judging by the bad surface, this was a smaller road. Suddenly, in the back, everything changed. I felt myself being lifted off the metal floor. A coat was slipped gently under my head and shoulders. A woman knelt down to take my pulse. When my eyes cleared enough to see, I was astonished to find that I was looking at Dr Jenny Wright, a surgeon-lieutenant in the Royal Naval Volunteer Reserve, and, beyond her, at some of my colleagues from the M Section.

The next thing I remember is that we arrived at a large farmhouse overlooking the sea, and drove into one of the outlying barns. I was helped out of the truck and taken down into an underground bunker occupied by British and French sub-units of the M Section. Cleaned up, given first aid, and sustained by some liquid warm food down a tube, I gathered all my remaining strength to give a brief report. Then I lay down on a bunk and fell into the deepest sleep of my life. A few minutes later, a cipher signal bearing my report crossed the seventy-five miles to Southwick Castle, high above Portsmouth, the Supreme Headquarters of the Allied Expeditionary Force.

I did not know until later that Operation Overlord had been postponed for twenty-four hours because of bad weather. Before dawn next day – 6 June 1944 – our forces had begun landing in the Bay of the Seine. By evening they had secured the beach-head and pressed slowly inland, and the greatest combined operation in the history of warfare had been successfully launched.

A week later Morton came to see me in the Royal Naval hospital at Haslar. He was bluff as ever, and gave no sign of feeling sorry for me. On the contrary, he freely admitted that he had authorised my L-pill to be filled with water. It had been essential that I genuinely try to kill myself, he said, so that the Germans would believe that the first name I had given them was false. Only by such extreme methods could they be led to believe that the name they exacted under torture was the real one. He also admitted – without remorse or apology – that he had secretly informed the German Unified Secret Service that I was a lieutenant in Royal Naval Intelligence. This master-stroke, he said, finally convinced the Germans that I had accurate data, and that the invasion really would come in the Pas de Calais.

Later, with some sarcasm, I asked him if he had sprung me from SS custody as a special favour, to save my life.

'Of course not!' he exclaimed, obviously shocked. 'You were sprung in the hope that the Germans would believe you to be an officer of some importance, and that they'd think we wanted to rescue you before you could be forced to reveal other top-level secrets.'

This, he said, had made them all the more inclined to believe me. But before he left, Morton warned me against becoming big-headed. He agreed that I had made a positive contribution to the great deception which preceded D-Day; but he pointed out that my terrible adventure had been only one small pin-prick in a multitude of secret operations carried out to deceive the Hun.

'Aren't you even going to say "Sorry"?' I challenged him as he started through the door.

He seemed genuinely surprised.

'Good gracious, my dear boy,' he replied. 'One never says sorry in war!'

As the door closed on Morton, I started to feel that I would never recover. The physical damage I had suffered was the least part of it; my grief and shame were overwhelmingly greater. But my despair did not last long.

A shadow fell across the doorway, and a Wren officer peeped into the room. Patricia!

Second Officer Patricia Falkiner looked stunning anywhere. But there to me in hospital she looked astonishingly beautiful: of medium height, slim-waisted, with dark hair, she had huge green eyes, and a face almost too perfectly formed to be real.

'Christopher!' she whispered.

At the sight of her, suddenly so close to me, I burst into tears. All through the war this girl had been my life: she had supported me and loved me through the terrible years of deception, murder and betrayal.

She walked over, perched on the side of the bed and cradled me in her arms. Tears began pouring down her face as well.

She pulled away to look at me. I knew that my appearance was ghastly: bandages everywhere. I looked like the Invisible Man rigged up with drips. She touched a bare part of my cheek.

'It's not as bad as it looks,' I lied. 'In a month or two it'll be OK.'

She stared at me, her face working, then gently kissed my face and broken lips. But it was the sight of my heavily bandaged hands that shocked her most.

'Not your fingers, Christopher! Will you still be able to play the piano?' She picked up one hand and looked at the thick white layers of dressings.

I didn't yet know the answer to her question, but I nodded optimistically. For a few moments we held each other close and gently kissed, borne up on a sudden wave of hope and happiness. One thing I knew for sure: but for Patricia, I would be dead. Bang on cue, the radio, tuned to the BBC Home and Forces programme, launched into the hit-song of the moment by Julie Styne, 'I don't want to walk without you, Baby'. It was our favourite song, too.

Once again my potential value as an agent was brought home to Martin Bormann. As he later described at his debriefing in England, immediately after D-Day Hitler flew into one of his tantrums, venting his spleen on the SS officers who had refused to accept what I told them in the first place.* 'If they'd listened to that boy,' the Führer screamed, 'we would have smashed the Churchillian-Jewish vulgarians off the face of the planet!' Why had his officers not consulted him? If they had, he would have backed the loyal and faithful Hannes (myself). The English boy had been right all along. Hitler told Bormann he wanted to see me again, to thank me for my faithful service to the Nazi cause, and to find out what other precious information I might have for him.

* Details from the Birdham transcript.

—————

3

In Search of Gold

In London the morning of 4 January 1945 was wild and bitterly cold. Drifts of snow from a recent blizzard were still piled on the capital's pavements, but now a blistering wind brought an onslaught of ice-cold rain. Through it, a tall, lean naval officer fought his way across Whitehall, from his flat in Berkeley Square, down St James's and along Pall Mall to the Admiralty. There he flashed his identity card at the Royal Marine sergeant at the entrance and went along the corridor to Room 39, headquarters of the Royal Naval Intelligence Division.

Commander Ian Lancaster Fleming had worked from that room for the past three years, as personal assistant to the Director of Naval Intelligence, Rear-Admiral John Godfrey. But on that foul January morning his career was turning sharply in a new direction. He had just returned from the Far East, where he had been liaising with the naval intelligence divisions of India and Australia; and he had come home on 'secret recall', which meant that although he was back in the United Kingdom, his records would show that he was still on appointment far east of Suez – to be precise, on leave with his brother Peter in Ceylon. He had come home by FEASTS, the Far East Security Transport Service, a secret shuttle which flew from New Zealand via Australia, Ceylon, Aden, Alexandria, Malta, Marseilles, Cherbourg and across the English Channel to HMS *Culdrose*, the Fleet Air Arm base in south Cornwall. Since the service used relays of the most modern aircraft of the Royal Air

Force and the Royal Australian Air Force, the journey took only seventy-two hours, a record in those days. Never having travelled by this means before, Fleming was delighted to find how much time it saved.

As he later told me, for a few minutes he sat at his desk in Room 39 'nonchalantly simmering with excitement', and wondering what his abrupt return might portend. He soon found out: a signals Wren brought him a message, for which he signed. The outer envelope was marked simply 'Commander Fleming, RNVR', but inside it was a second, bearing the legend 'COMMANDER I. L. FLEMING, RNVR. PRIORITY A 1 IMMEDIATE. MOST SECRET. EYES ADDRESSEE ONLY.'* The message inside told him that he had been appointed a deputy director of a special organisation designated by a naval code-number, and ordered him to report to the section's director, Major D. Morton, at 1415 hours that day.

Having often heard whispers of the esoteric M Section, Fleming was intensely curious as well as excited, and when he walked back to St James's to have lunch at his club, White's, he found that for almost the first time in his life he had no appetite. As he told me later, he reckoned that to be appointed to the M Section was 'the very best secret intelligence job', and to become a deputy director of it was the fulfilment of a private dream.

Soon after 2 pm he was outside the Ministry of Works, and by 2.15 he was sitting opposite Major Desmond Morton, in Room 60, the poky little den on the ground floor which the director of the M Section chose to occupy. The walls were drab yellow, and devoid of decoration. There was nothing, not even a calendar, to divert the eye, except for a single shelf of books.

Needless to say, Morton had done his homework on his new recruit, and had memorised every detail of his background. Fleming, he knew, was a Scot by blood, despite a middle name that marked his direct descent from John of Gaunt, the great Duke of Lancaster – a contradictory combination that reflected the contrariness of his nature. Many people liked and admired

---

* Some historians claim that by this stage of the war the phrase 'Most Secret' had entirely superseded the earlier 'Top Secret'. In fact, the M Section continued to use both.

him, but others considered him a playboy naval officer and called him 'the Chocolate Sailor'.

If they were envious, they had good reason, for he came from a wealthy family, and his connections undoubtedly helped him. His father, Valentine Fleming, had been an MP and a close friend of Winston Churchill: both served as officers in the Oxfordshire Yeomanry, and when Valentine died a gallant death in the trenches during the First World War – a week before Ian's ninth birthday – Churchill wrote a moving tribute in *The Times*. But it was Commander Fleming's genuine talents, rather than his background, that appealed to the people who employed him.

At the beginning of 1945 he was thirty-six, but he seemed younger: tall, with receding dark hair, and extremely good-looking, he had a patrician air, almost that of a Roman nobleman. The one irregular feature of his face was a broken nose – the legacy of a football collision at school – which many young ladies found added to his attraction. When they heard that at Eton he had been victor ludorum (champion athlete) for two years in succession, their fate was usually sealed.

Before the war he had never quite found his *métier*. He had dropped out of the Royal Military College at Sandhurst, gone to learn German in Austria, tried his hand at journalism and then become a moderately successful stockbroker. Throughout the second half of the 1930s he had been overshadowed by the brilliance of his elder brother Peter, who had established a reputation as the author of such outstanding travel books as *Brazilian Adventure* and *News from Tartary*. Yet once Ian had been recruited into naval intelligence on the recommendation of Montagu Norman, Governor of the Bank of England, his talents found a proper outlet.

As personal assistant to Admiral Godfrey, he proved once again the truth of the adage that most sailors, however competent, do not possess the flair needed to make good intelligence officers: more important were originality, imagination, slight eccentricity and wit. Fleming had these in abundance: he also had courage, efficiency, a fine sense of discipline, charm, and an enviable ability to talk people into doing what he wanted. All this made him a formidable recruit to the world of naval intelligence, and he had flung himself into his new life with a zest that alarmed many of his colleagues.

Some of the schemes he dreamt up were distinctly hare-brained, but in June 1940 he came within inches of a spectacular success. Just before the defeat of France he all but convinced Admiral Darlan, Commander-in-Chief of the French Navy, to bring his powerful fleet over to England. Fleming had been thwarted only by being ordered home prematurely. Had he succeeded, the massacres at Oran, Casablanca and Toulon might well have been avoided, and, in addition, the Allies would have had the immense advantage of the French warships joining them from the outset.

Godfrey's praise for Fleming's work had soon become unstinting. On 10 December 1942 the admiral wrote: 'His zeal, ability and judgement are altogether exceptional, and have contributed very largely to the development and organisation of the Naval Intelligence Division during the war.' What Godfrey could not write, for security reasons, was that Fleming had taken part in five top-secret operations, vital to Allied intelligence, and had distinguished himself in all of them.

Now, in Room 60, Morton filled in a little of his own background, explaining that, on the instructions of the Prime Minister, the M Section had launched a major undercover operation, and that he, Morton, had appointed Fleming to direct it. In a few minutes the PM would summon them for a briefing on the state of play.

As they waited, Morton emphasised and re-emphasised the need for total security. However cleverly they might plan, however resourceful they might be, all would come to naught unless they observed secrecy on a level beyond anything Fleming had experienced before. It was not just a question of paying lip-service to the rules, or of classifying the operation 'Most Secret – A 1 Immediate'. It was also a matter of Fleming and his subordinates being totally discreet. Even at the highest level, only a handful of people outside the M Section should know of the project's existence. It had never been mentioned in any document, except under its naval party assignation, or code-number. It never would be mentioned. It had simply never existed, and never would.

It was the same with Fleming. In the context of his new appointment and the coming operation, he simply would not exist. Everything that he and the men and women of the M Section did would be obliterated from the records. His official files would show that he had been in Jamaica when in fact he had been in Portsmouth, in Scotland when he'd been in Rome, and in New Zealand when he'd been in Berlin. At that very moment it would appear that he had continued on his Far Eastern tour. With luck, it would be impossible for anyone to prove that he had led this operation – or indeed that there had been such an operation at all. It would be The Operation that Never Was.

The red, internal secure telephone on Morton's desk buzzed twice. The Prime Minister was free to see them. Out of the door they turned left, then right down a spiral staircase, heading for the government war rooms flippantly known as 'the Hole in the Ground'. Four flights down, well below the level of the Thames, they came to a watertight door. Across the passageway lay the Cabinet War Room. A Marine pensioner opened the first of the double doors, which were about eight feet apart, and both fitted with small glass panels. A second Marine, armed with a revolver, stood sentry between the doors, unable to hear proceedings in the War Room, but with a full view of everything that went on in there.

Churchill welcomed Fleming warmly, as the son of an old friend, and, in his usual fashion, brought up some fond reminiscence of Val. Then he was quickly into the business of the day. As the Allied armies closed in on the remnants of the Third Reich, his thoughts had turned more and more to the vast fortune the Nazis had plundered from the defeated countries of Europe. In particular, he had been considering how the Allies might recover the cash, gold, jewellery, works of art and property deeds the Nazi leaders had hidden away. He believed, he said, that Hitler's henchmen intended to use these assets to finance their safe and comfortable retirement, once Germany had finally collapsed. The Prime Minister's orders were simple and clear. Fleming was to thwart any such plans by locating and retrieving as many of the stolen assets as possible.

Back upstairs in Room 60, Morton clarified some essential points. First, the M Section was to seek out only those Nazi assets outside Germany and the occupied territories. Those inside came under the jurisdiction of the Supreme Commander in Europe, General Eisenhower, and since D-Day, six months earlier, a special unit under his command had been working with some success in that field.

During the past two years, Morton went on, M Section agents had been actively pursuing leads in Europe, and their reports indicated that billions of pounds' worth of Nazi loot were held within the Swiss banking system, not only in numbered accounts, but also in safe-deposit boxes in various banks, and in large vaults in other buildings owned and operated by the banks throughout the Swiss Confederation. In recent weeks agents had been able to pinpoint two banks, one in Zurich, one in Basle. All they needed now was account numbers, and the names of the account-holders and signatories. As soon as these were in Morton's hands, the Section would have *carte blanche* to launch almost any operation that might be deemed necessary.

Latest reports from Vienna indicated that at least some of the vital missing information had been uncovered by agents working in Austria, and strenuous efforts were being made to relay the numbers and names back to M Section control, either by courier or by wireless; but so secret was the whole operation that no risks could be taken. If the slightest leak occurred, and information were intercepted by the Nazi authorities, it was obvious that numbers and signatories would be changed immediately, and the M Section would have to start all over again.

Morton's briefing lasted for most of the afternoon, and made it clear that, although the task ahead was simple in concept, its execution would be complicated and dangerous. Towards the end, Morton brought up the question of who would be the operational commander, working under Fleming's executive authority, and he put forward my name. When Fleming asked what my qualifications were, Morton told him that in the morning he must read my file; then he must meet me and make up his own mind about whether I would fit the bill.

In conclusion, Morton referred again to the question of breaches of security, and warned Fleming that the M Section took the dimmest possible view of any failing in this direction. Penalties were harsh: on some occasions the extreme punishment of execution had been invoked. Such ruthlessness had always been the Section's policy, and many lives had been saved by it.

Fleming (as he told me later) had always considered himself nonchalant, not easily impressed, and well able to conceal his emotions. Morton's exposition, however, startled him so badly that his face 'expressed everything'.

Throughout the meeting, one simple question kept bothering him. Where *was* the M Section? It could hardly be here, in Morton's dingy little office. The set-up seemed altogether too modest to control an organisation with the capabilities about which he had been learning.

In fact he had misunderstood Morton's style. Morton was *always* frugal and modest, and secretive to boot. He was without doubt the most secretive man in the kingdom. He was secretive about almost everything – not just about vital intelligence, but about his private life, his friendships, his hobbies, his hopes, his dreams (if ever he had any) and himself. He was the most private of men.

He positively enjoyed the plainness of his office and its air of complete unimportance. What need had he of ostentation? At the end of any one of his security telephones was a subordinate ready to answer a query or initiate action, upon the instant. It was in the Ministry of Economic Warfare – a cover organisation, under whose umbrella secret bodies flourished – that the Political Warfare Executive, Special Operations Executive and the M Section had their being.

In that first interview with Fleming, Morton naturally revealed almost nothing of his organisation's background. In fact he had created it in 1932, and from then until September 1939 it had been financed and protected by the reigning monarch. Then, when Churchill became First Lord of the Admiralty, it passed on to the books of the Royal Navy, and from 1941, when Mountbatten became chief of Combined Operations, it was financed through Combined Ops. Its civilian arm was housed at Northways, a huge block of flats overlooking Swiss Cottage, in north London, where it operated under cover of the Flag Officer, Submarines, and the wartime headquarters of the British Submarine Service. Close by, various specialist departments were deployed in commandeered houses in Eton Avenue and Belsize Park. The operational service arm – mostly Royal Navy personnel, but including Royal Marines and operational Wrens – was located at Birdham, a large country house in Hampshire, and in other mansions far from centres of civilisation.

Officially, Morton merely advised the Prime Minister on intelligence matters, as his personal assistant. Nowhere was it recorded that he had become the supreme chief of special, secret intelligence operations. His role was pitched far above the Prime Minister's 'secret circle', and was never revealed to even the most senior of his Civil Service staff. Private secretaries and other intimate members of his circle, even though fully trusted, had never been included. At that supreme level of security the maxim was: those who do not absolutely have to know – however important they may be or think they are – should not be burdened with such knowledge. Once, in a private meeting with Fleming, Churchill put the matter in sharp perspective. 'My secret circle think that they know everything,' he said. 'Pray do not spread disillusion by telling them something they do not know.'

One of the M Section's greatest strengths was that it reported only to the Prime Minister, on the authority of the King. Its operations were not controlled or limited by any outside body; nor was its security placed at risk by having information about its activities passed unnecessarily to civil servants. Other organisations were less fortunate. MI 6, the Secret Intelligence Service, answered to the civil servants of the Foreign Office, and MI 5 (responsible for home security) had the disabling millstone of the Home Office round its neck. The M Section, in contrast, kept well clear of everyone else. Like its director, it was frugal, modest, independent and totally secret: as far as anyone outside it was concerned, it did not exist.

Next morning, 5 January, Fleming returned to the Ministry of Works and was escorted by two of the M Section's security officers to a safe room. There Morton met him, and handed over a small strong-box, together with its key. Fleming signed for both, but before Morton left, he told his new recruit, 'I warn you. The file you are about to read does not exist.' That remark appealed tremendously to Fleming, who later told me how delighted he was to read, for the first time, documents which were not there.

The security officers searched the room, checked that the window was fast, and took up their post outside the door. Two more officers stood guard on the pavement below the window, in Storey's Gate. Left alone, Fleming read my record with astonishment. If he himself had not been on the periphery of some of the events described, he would have doubted the accounts' veracity; but because he had often been involved, usually putting effective cover in place, he knew that the narratives were genuine. Furthermore, he saw that it would have taken a story-teller of incredible skill and invention to dream up some of the events that had occurred. Overall, what touched him most was my innocence in allowing myself to be inducted into the M Section, and the naive way in which I had submitted to the Svengali-like influence and control that Morton had exercised over me since my early childhood.

Having read to the end, he put the files back into the strong-box, locked it, and knocked on the door for the security officers to come and take it away. He then lit a Morland special – his favourite brand of cigarette, encircled by red and gold bands – and stood looking out of the window over St James's Park.

'Well, there it is,' he said, a remark he often made when he was moved.

Later that afternoon he saw Morton again, and said he would interview me at Ramsgate, where I was then serving, as soon as possible, but that he had serious reservations about taking me on as his operational commander. He had immediately discerned that my record embodied many contradictions. On the one hand, I seemed to be a straightforward naval officer with much greater practical experience than his own, even though I was sixteen years his junior; on the other hand, I had several times acted as a hired assassin, or carried out missions of deception which broke all normal rules of morality. Was I really the kind of character with whom he could work?

'Fear not, dear boy,' Morton told him blandly. 'You'll get on.'

It was evident that moves had to be made fast. Morton handed Fleming a signal reporting that some of the essential information they needed had been passed the day before to a young radio operator working for the M Section in Vienna. Things were so dangerous in the city, however, that transmission might have to be made from somewhere outside. Vienna and its environs were teeming with SS, Gestapo and German troops, as well as with the vicious local brand of Austrian police. It would be safer for the message to be sent from a secret location out in the country.

When Fleming asked about the operator – who he was, and how

reliable – he got a surprise. Morton revealed that the agent was a young woman, an operational Wren, one of their best. Being a member of the M Section, and assigned to the operation now beginning, she was effectively under Fleming's command. This gave him a jolt: so far in his naval career he had never had to deal with operational Wrens, and although he had read about them in his briefing, he had not really come to terms with their existence.

Until then his attitude to women had been distinctly old-fashioned. He believed in the mastery of the male sex, and considered women inferior: they were there to be chased, brought down, taken to bed and then discarded. The fact that he had enjoyed no mean success merely encouraged him in his belief – but his superiors had noticed it, and it had gone down in his record as a failing.

Now, suddenly faced with the need to suppress his prejudices, he rose to the occasion and told Morton that he felt sure this operator in Austria must be a splendid girl. He wished her every success, and looked forward to getting her report.

4

Patricia

That same afternoon in the Austrian Tyrol the River Salzach was in spate, draining away the vast volume of water which had fallen in recent storms. So heavy had been the rain that most of it had run straight off the steep slopes of the Kitzbühel Alps without first turning to ice, and every stream that fed the Salzach had become a hurtling torrent.* The river flowed from east to west through the centre of Austria, which was still full of Hitler's mechanised armies.

Technically, it had been incorrect to describe the country as 'occupied', since Dr Arthur Seyss-Inquardt, nominated Chancellor by President Wilhelm Miklas under Nazi duress, had called the Nazis in and the following day enacted the 'Auschluss' bill incorporating the once-great Austrian Empire into the Third Reich. The result, however, was the same as in other European countries: the place was alive with all the arms of a repressive dictatorship.

On the evening of that terrible day, 5 January 1945, a young woman dived headlong from the north bank into the raging waters

---

* My account of that day's events is based on the testimony of Hans Gerhardt, who, although a Nazi sympathiser at the time, turned against the Germans and informed on them. Later in 1945 he gave himself up to Austrian resistance fighters, and a detailed report of the incident described here found its way to England.

of the Salzach. To any casual observer, it would have seemed an act of terminal folly. Over the past seven years many young people had committed suicide, and maybe this was just one more: perhaps the girl had decided to finish things once and for all.

Yet her manner in the water soon showed that she did not have self-destruction in mind. She swam strongly across the current, her strokes slow and professional. To Hans Gerhardt, a student who had picked her up in his powerful binoculars, it was clear that she had reckoned on the speed of the river, and was not allowing herself to be panicked by the ferocious rate at which the water swept her downstream.

As he watched, Gerhardt felt a prickle of excitement. Something odd was going on here, and he had better report it to the authorities. Ever since being forced into the Hitler Youth at the age of twelve, he had been brainwashed into embracing the cause of National Socialism: like thousands of fellow students, he had been led to accept Nazi racist theories, and to believe that Jews, Russians and even some Austrians were degenerate, and so should be isolated or obliterated.

He saw that the girl in the river was making good progress. In fact, during rigorous training with the Special Boat Section of the Royal Marine Commando, she had learnt that the rate of a current makes no difference to the time taken to cross a river. Of course it needed courage and determination to take full practical advantage of that law of mechanics, but she knew what she was doing, and kept her head.

Some way downstream she came safely ashore and crawled up the bank to the cover of some bushes. There she took a towel and dry clothes from the waterproof bag strapped to her shoulders. Having rubbed herself down, she dressed in dry kit, with winter coveralls. Then with a miniature compass she took several bearings, and noted them on a map. She also made three all-round lookout sweeps, but did not pick up young Gerhardt, who was still watching her.

Patricia Falkiner would have been a recognised beauty in any country. With her huge green eyes, dark hair and trim figure, she had always been outstanding. At school at St Mary's Convent in South Ascot, she had benefited from the inspired leadership of the headmistress, Mother Ignatius, and then, early in 1940, on her eighteenth birthday, she had joined the Royal Navy. After rugged basic training at Westwood College, the Wrens' intake base in Hampstead, she passed out as a Wren proper, and then applied for a place in the Code and Cypher Branch. Once she had taken the necessary specialisation exams and sat the Admiralty Selection Board, the Director, Wrens, Commandant Dame Vera Laughton Mathews, hustled her off to the Officers' Training Course. Three months later she emerged as Wren Third Officer Falkiner, with one blue braid stripe on each cuff.

In the years that followed her life became extremely stimulating, for she was appointed to the government Code and Cypher School at Bletchley Park, Buckinghamshire, the establishment which kept constant watch on enemy signals and played a leading part in breaking vital German and Japanese codes, including the top-secret Enigma-Ultra.

On her twenty-second birthday Patricia was promoted second officer; but soon after that, in the autumn of 1944, she accidentally stumbled on information of the utmost secrecy and sensitivity, at a level for which she did not have security clearance. This made things difficult both for her and for the authorities. The normal fate of someone in her position was to be locked up on the Isle of Man for as long as hostilities lasted; but to incarcerate a girl of her ability and training would obviously have been a dire waste of talent.

An intelligence officer came to see her, and she was spirited away to No. 1 Dorset Square in London, the headquarters of SOE, the Special Operations Executive. There her fluency in German, her high proficiency in wireless telegraphy, codes and cyphers, and her black belt in judo, all made a strong impression. Her accomplishments, reinforced by the fact that she had acquired secret knowledge, suggested that she would be ideal for operations SOE was planning in France and Germany. Such work was strictly voluntary, and Patricia could easily have declined to do it; but then she met a senior officer from the M Section who appealed to her sense of duty and told her it was vital that she should serve with this particular branch of operational secret intelligence.

So it was that at the start of 1945 she came to be standing on the north bank of the River Salzach as dusk settled among the mountains. Up in the foothills behind her was a safe house, a log cabin used by the Austrian resistance, who worked closely with British intelligence in London. Between her and the hut lay four miles of treacherous tracks, and she could not move before dark; but she knew from her briefing that the cabin contained a transceiver on which she could pass her all-important information to the M Section's control station at Bletchley.

Her climb to the hut took four hours, including, at the end, a fifteen-minute wait for surveillance, during which she watched – as best she could in the dark – every possible line of approach, and listened intently for the smallest sound that might betray a Gestapo or SS trap. When all seemed well, she went on to explore the hut, which stood on a crag jutting out over a steep ravine. The site seemed ideal, and indeed it had been chosen both to give maximum security and to ensure the best possible radio communication.

After a careful look round the windows, to make sure that none had been forced, she produced two keys for the outer door. The inner door had a combination lock, for which she had memorised the code. Once inside, she again checked the security of the windows and the back door, making an inch-by-inch search of the entire cabin. Everything was just as the Austrians had told her it would be.

Having drawn the curtains, she lit a small oil lamp and went to work. She was frightened, tired, cold and ravenous. She knew that there was tinned food and brandy in the back room, but nothing so mundane as hunger could distract her from her task.

Going to an unobtrusive cut in the floorboards, she prised up a plank and eased out the radio transceiver. From the false back of a cupboard she brought out two accumulators and connected them up. The specially adapted B Mark II transceiver was live. Then she plugged in the aerial – seventy-five feet of it wound round the cabin in loops and ingeniously hidden behind the wallboards – which the set needed to communicate across 125 miles of Alpine peaks with the receiving station in Liechtenstein.

Next she slit a pouch in the pocket of her shirt, carefully brought out a tiny crystal – one of three she carried sewn into her clothes – and fitted it into the transceiver which operated on frequencies between 3.5 and 16 megacycles per second. Then for a minute or two she massaged the cold fingers of her right hand. It was good basic training that the transmitting fingers be relaxed and warm:

otherwise, her mode of transmission, her key-signature, might differ from her usual style and rhythm. Her correspondent might then suspect that an impostor, an enemy agent, was posing as her, and submit her signal as suspect. The whole operation might end in failure and disgrace – for her, anyway.

At last she took the morse key between thumb and first and second fingers, and began to transmit. First she sent the code-letters for TOP SECRET, PRIORITY ONE. That would clear all other Allied traffic off the waveband. Then followed the coded call-sign of her correspondent, and her own code-name, 'Alice'. In a similar site high in a mountain station a few miles east of Vaduz, the Liechtenstein capital, officers of the M sub-section (Switzerland) picked up her transmission. Within seconds they responded. Secret code-words and -numbers were exchanged, and the correspondents accepted each other's bona fides. Then, at her maximum efficient operational speed of a hundred letters a minute, Patricia sent her signal.

The M Section's secret wireless-telegraphy control station was housed in commandeered farm buildings in Buckinghamshire, a couple of miles from the government's decoding and deciphering establishment at Bletchley Park, where Patricia had worked until recently. The complex, which housed not only the M Section's operators and equipment, but also other highly secret units, was guarded day and night by Commandos disguised – and working – as farm labourers, with a herd of cows to milk, flocks of chickens to look after, and crops to sow and harvest. Every precaution had been taken to make sure that the buildings betrayed no sign of non-agricultural activity: the film designer and model-maker Zoltan Korda had gone over the place to confirm that no alien equipment remained uncamouflaged. Hundreds of feet of aerial wire, for instance, were wound invisibly round the branches of nearby trees.

Within minutes of Patricia sending it, the duty operator safely received her signal, relayed from Vaduz, in five-letter groups of code. Seeing that the message was marked for the director of the M Section, and headed EYES ADDRESSEE ONLY, the duty Wren officer picked up a red telephone marked simply 'M', and passed the signal straight to London.

There, Morton and Fleming had come back from dinner to continue their discussion in Room 60. Having taken down the message, Morton asked his companion to hand him the code-book, which stood at the far end of a shelf. Reaching for it, Fleming was amazed to find that it was a copy of A. A. Milne's classic children's story *The House at Pooh Corner*.

'Don't look so surprised,' Morton told him. 'This is our bible.' He explained that not only did the book provide the basis for the M Section's code signalling system, made up from a combination of page, line and word numbers: its chararacters had also been borrowed to provide names for key personnel. 'Who's Winnie the Pooh, then?' said Fleming incredulously, and then immediately answered his own question: 'The Prime Minister, I suppose.'

'Wrong! Somebody said he should be Winnie, but he wouldn't have it. He was already Tigger. And I'm Owl.'

At that Fleming burst out laughing. For a moment he was afraid he had overstepped the mark, and that Morton might take offence. But then he too softened and gave one of his rare laughs.

'Winnie the Pooh's free,' Morton said. 'You can be Pooh. From now on, you *are* Pooh.'

Churchill, as usual, was working late in the Cabinet War Room, and when Morton took him the decoded signal, his face lit up. 'Splendid! Spendid!' he exclaimed, as he read the name of the Swiss bank that held most of the Nazi assets in trust, and the key numbers of the accounts in which the funds were lodged. All that remained to be discovered was the names of the signatories; and Fleming reckoned that with some skilful diplomacy in Basle, and a modicum of luck, it should be possible to unearth these as well.

For all his enthusiasm, Churchill was worried about 'this girl of yours, this Alice'. Morton assured him that Patricia Falkiner was extremely competent, and could look after herself. The Prime Minister, warming to his theme, remarked on how the Royal Navy, of all the services, constantly excelled itself. Now, by exhibiting such skill and courage, Miss Falkiner had gallantly maintained the traditions of her service. Should they not get her out of danger right away?

Morton promised that he was on the point of doing that very thing: he was about to send a signal ordering her to return to base by one of the well-tried routes kept open by MI 8 or MI 9.

'Pray add a word or two from me,' Churchill said. 'Say she's done a magnificent job, and we are all very proud of her.'

The Prime Minister was evidently in a mood to talk, but Morton slipped away on the excuse that he must initiate the signal, leaving Fleming alone. For a minute of two Churchill sat in silence, sucking hopefully at a moribund cigar; then, after two or three futile attempts to revive it, he suddenly hurled it over his head with such unerring accuracy that it landed in the fire bucket strategically placed behind his chair.

With the signal from Austria still on the desk in front of him, he began to unburden himself on the subject of women being employed on operations. He had always been fiercely against it, and his opposition extended even to the use of girls on the anti-aircraft batteries in Hyde Park, where his daughter Mary had served as a subaltern in the Women's Royal Army Corps. He complained that his desire to keep women out of action had been thwarted again and again by SOE, by the M Section and by other intelligence units. Morton, in particular, had disregarded his wishes entirely – and now Miss Falkiner was at peril in an operation which he, Churchill, himself had originated.

As he listened, Fleming felt some sympathy, for he recognised that Churchill's obsession derived from the ultra-conventional upbringing his mother, the American Jennie Jerome, had given him. Fleming himself had had difficulties on that front: after his father's premature death, he and his three brothers had been left in the hands of their formidably eccentric mother, Eve.

In the cabin deep in the Kitzbühel Alps, a coded message, including the Prime Minister's congratulations, beeped out in Morse from the transceiver on the table. But Patricia no longer sat in the chair. Her place had been taken by a man in SS uniform, wearing the insignia of a Standartenführer. The only other sound in the room was a rhythmic creaking, and a shadow passed to and fro across the man's face with the regularity of a pendulum.

The girl, nearly naked, swung by her wrists on a rope tied round a beam in the roof. She was only semi-conscious. Three other SS officers stood near her, each holding a leather belt armoured with a metal buckle. Blood dripped from the girl's shoulders and ran down her legs, but her head and hands had been carefully avoided.

Young Hans Gerhardt stood watching, numb with horror. In the last few minutes his enthusiasm for the Nazi cause had evaporated. Never had he imagined bestial brutality of this order. In a few moments of shattering disillusion he realised that what he should have been fighting for, these past seven years, was the freedom of Austria, not a foreign regime crazed by hatred. Now he desperately wanted to help – to save – the girl strung up before him. But what could he do, unarmed as he was, and one against four? If he tried to intervene, his life would be over. Better to find out and commit to memory the names of the men involved in this butchery, and pass them to Austrian resistance fighters. He struggled to control himself, and to remember every detail of what took place.

The girl stirred towards consciousness. Again the Standartenführer told her that it would be easy to escape further punishment. All she need do was tell them the contents of the signal she had just sent. It surely must have been very important, for her to have come so far, and to have taken such elaborate precautions.

They took her down from the beam and sat her on a chair. The sudden change of attitude made her sick, and she vomited violently over her tormentors. When one of them threw a bucket of cold water over her, she shuddered and moaned. Gerhardt could see that she was in terrible pain, and exhausted. Then suddenly he thought he saw a spark light up her eyes, as if she had thought of something.

Once more the senior SS officer promised that if she revealed what she had sent to London, her ordeal would be over. She muttered that she would tell him nothing. Nor would she send another message, cancelling her first.

The SS man seized Patricia by the hair and dragged her to her feet. Seconds later her remaining clothes had been ripped off. Once more she was hung from the roof, this time by her ankles, upside-down, and higher, her face level with that of the SS commander. When he gave her one last chance to change his mind, she spat in his face.

The German pulled out his razor-sharp dagger, with the SS motto, *Meine Ehre heißt Treue* (My Honour is My Loyalty), engraved on the hilt. With one violent sweep he slashed downwards at an angle across the girl's breasts. Blood spurted, but the victim made no sound. Hans Gerhardt, staring in horror, suddenly felt that she knew that this was *her moment* – a flash of intuition granted to very few.

The SS officer approached her again. Her jaw muscles suddenly tightened as she bit hard and swallowed. Inside her mouth potassium cyanide trickled from the capsule she had carried hidden in a specially hollowed-out molar. Within seconds her head jerked back and her body writhed convulsively. Her torturers jumped away from her, instinctively afraid of the strong odour of almonds, as if merely smelling it might kill them too.

In the final second before she died, Gerhardt heard the girl whisper one word. It was 'Christopher'. My name.

5

Hard Training

For the time being I knew nothing of this tragedy. After my own ordeal at the hands of the Gestapo, I had spent several months recuperating, and only recently had I been pronounced fit for duty. I had then been appointed to HMS *Fervent*, the Coastal Forces' shore base at Ramsgate, in Kent, where I took command of a flotilla of obsolescent motor torpedo-boats, with mostly Norwegian crews. Clearly, the authorities realised that, although I was once again physically fit, the stress of previous operations had left indelible scars, and the powers-that-were meant me to serve out the remainder of the war in relative quiet.

The afternoon watch of 6 January 1945 was anything but that. A violent storm was raging, and we spent half the day searching for forty American servicemen whose troop transport had foundered in the gale. Before it went down, our three little MTBs, helped by other rescue vessels, had managed to take off most of the passengers and crew; but several men were still missing, and although we returned again and again to look for survivors, searching the perilous waters around the Goodwin Sands, in the end we retreated into Ramsgate Harbour, tails between our legs, defeated.

As we came alongside, there on the quay was a Royal Naval commander, watching us, so I brought the ship's company to attention and saluted.

'Mr Creighton?' he called down.

'Sir.'

'I'll see you in the wardroom as soon as you're secure.'

'Aye, aye, sir.'

What did *he* want? I hardly cared. A few minutes later, exhausted, soaked to the skin, frozen and still in shock, I staggered up to the wardroom mess, which had been established in the ancient and distinguished Royal Temple Yacht Club, above the port. In the bar I sat down alone with a schooner of brandy, still shaking uncontrollably, and unable to dismiss from my mind the thought of the men whose lives had been lost. My self-esteem had sunk to its lowest ebb. I told myself that the men could have been saved if I had bothered to learn a little more about my job. At twenty, I was far too young to lead a flotilla; I had not had anything like enough training; I was both incompetent and arrogant. As usual, guilt threatened to overwhelm me.

Then suddenly everything changed. Into the bar walked the commander I had seen on the quay. He came over and said, 'My name's Fleming.'

We shook hands, but I hardly knew what to answer.

'That was a grand show you put up,' he began warmly.

'No, sir. We should have got them all.'

'My dear chap! I hear it was a great effort. But I must say, you handle your flotilla a little recklessly.'

His praise and enthusiasm were welcome – yet I could not shake off my depression. Then he asked, 'Is this place secure?'

'Well . . .' I was taken by surprise. 'We can go out on to the quarterdeck.'

Beyond the French windows of the bar was an extensive flat roof which commanded tremendous views of the sea. Out there in the wind, with huge over-falls bursting white above the Goodwins in the distance, the visitor looked round and said, 'Mr Creighton – or rather, Christopher Robin – I've come from Owl and Tigger.'

I could not believe my ears. I had only just been pronounced fit for duty again, and the pyschological scars left by my experience at the hands of the Gestapo were far from healed. Fleming saw what I was thinking and sent me off for a hot shower, a visit to the sickbay and a change of clothes, saying that we would meet for dinner.

Later, in a secluded corner of the dining-room, he went straight to business. By order of Major Desmond Morton, with the full backing of the Prime Minister, he was to carry out a secret operation, and he wanted me to join him.

My immediate reaction was one of furious resentment. They could not be coming for me *again*! Surely there was someone else who could fill the breach. Why bloody *me*? There was no part of my body or my morality that had not been twisted and perverted in the course of some ghastly covert operation for the M Section. The idea of diving into those murky waters again revolted me. I struggled to control my emotions.

Fleming watched me closely. I realised that he could see what I was thinking. He had read my record, and knew what I had been through.

'Do they insist it must be me?' I asked.

'No. Your name was put forward, of course. But the decision's entirely mine. And I made it a few moments ago.'

My appointment at *Fervent* would be cancelled immediately, he said. I would be reappointed to the M Section in command of the new C sub-section, which would carry out the operation. As a deputy director of the M Section itself, Fleming would be in overall charge, with myself under him. The set-up would be a traditional naval one, like that aboard a ship: Fleming would be the commodore in overall flag command, and I, like a captain, would have operational command. He told me not to worry, and promised he would make things as easy for me as he could.

In the middle of his explication he stopped and said, 'Are you going to take me at face value? Or would you rather check me out with Morton?'

'Don't worry,' I reassured him. 'I've done it already, when I went to the heads just now. You're from Room 39, the NID.'

That delighted Fleming. He grinned broadly and launched into an enthusiastic exposition of the need for attention to detail. Both of us, he said, must take infinite trouble over every little facet of the operation. Our discipline and security must be rock-like. We must leave nothing whatever to chance.

As to what the operation was, he did not yet choose to enlighten me. But he sprang another surprise. To ensure that I would not be junior to any other officer in the command, he said, I had been promoted acting lieutenant-commander.

I was astonished. Although only 'acting', I would probably be the youngest lieutenant-commander in the navy. The promotion was totally unexpected, and left me unnerved. Fleming was glad to see that at last I showed some signs of animation, but he pointed out that, although I was still not twenty-one, the age assigned to Christopher Creighton on the Navy List was a few years more than that.*

In conclusion, Fleming issued some specific orders. I was to sew in my new half-stripe, bring all my special gear, and report to Birdham in two days' time. I had been given a direct order. According to Admiralty Instructions there was only one reply. 'Aye, aye, sir,' I acknowledged.

Birdham! The name brought back a flood of memories, some wonderful, some terrible. I had spent months there before and after operations earlier in the war: I knew every inch of the place, and had many close friends there. But immediately I decided that under no circumstances would I make a conventional return as commander, with salutes and bosun's pipes. On the contrary, my re-entry would be outrageous.

Ostensibly, Birdham – a cover-name, of course – had always been part of Combined Operations, first under Vice-Admiral Lord Louis Mountbatten, more recently under Major-General Robert Laycock. A Commando training establishment for both the Royal Navy and the Royal Marines, it was also the principal operational headquarters of the M Section. It was based in and around an ancient manor house, which was tucked away in thirty acres of undulating park and woodland near Portsmouth. Parts of the house were very old – sixteenth-century, at least – with fine oak beams and panelling; but it had been extended by later additions, and, most recently, by the construction of modern huts

---

* The promotion was entered on my identity card and in my record, and published in M Section signals and bases, where it mattered and remained secret. But it never appeared in the *London Gazette* or the Navy List, where it would have aroused unwelcome interest. (All regular officers scan the list constantly, to assess their own promotion chances.) This unusual procedure was covertly approved and activated by both the Sea Lords concerned, Admirals Sir Dudley Pound and Sir Andrew Cunningham, and of course by Admiral of the Fleet His Majesty King George VI.

and annexes in the grounds. Although the normal complement was about twenty-five Commandos and operational Wrens, the place could accommodate at least two hundred.

The house, well screened by trees, stood a mile back from the nearest main road, at the end of a gravel drive, and security was tight: the main gates were guarded round the clock, and the grounds were encircled by a barbed-wire fence which carried an electric current, so that if anyone touched it the point of disturbance showed up in the control-room. Yet the most effective security equipment was the system of R/G (red/green) lights. One of the greatest scientific successes of the war, it used infra-red to enable operators to see signals on their receivers in the dark, without showing any light to the enemy. The equipment had been used on D-Day to great effect by my old unit, COPP, to help the Allied Expeditionary Force land at precisely the correct spots. At Birdham the monitors picked up anyone moving around the park at night and showed them in a green haze – provided they were in the open, for the infra-red beams detected heat, and could not pick out people in cover.

On the evening of Monday, 8 January 1945, the duty officer at Birdham was Second Officer Susan Kemp, an operational Wren of striking looks and physique. To anyone who did not know her, her auburn hair, blue-grey eyes and well-endowed figure might have been dangerously misleading. Like all the operational Wrens at Birdham, she wore khaki battledress, with the red and navy-blue anchor, tommy-gun and wings of Combined Operations on each shoulder, and above these insignia the words RN COMMANDO. These gave rise to mirth among some uninitiated naval officers, who failed to realise that they had been earned the hard way.

Like her comrades, Susan was trained to a very high standard. She had completed the strenuous Commando and unarmed combat courses on the Duke of Argyll's Highland estate at Inveraray and at HMS *Armadillo*, the shore base a few miles north-east of Holy Loch. Competing not only against all ranks and ratings of the Royal Navy, but against the Royal Marine Commandos as well, she had passed out first in her class. She had gone on to do a course that few men ever attended, and this had taught her the highest standards in jujitsu, attack and defence with fighting knives, silent approach and killing, the use of firearms (including German and Italian weapons), and endurance at sea and in the mountains. Altogether, she epitomised the exceptional standards achieved by the operational Wrens at Birdham.

Towards the end of the second dog watch, that Monday afternoon, one of the cypher girls handed her a message from 'M' which read: WITH IMMEDIATE EFFECT ACTING LIEUTENANT-COMMANDER C. J. J. CREIGHTON RN APPOINTED (C) SUB-SECTION – IN COMMAND.

As Susan told me later, she and most of her signal Wrens 'let out a howl of approbation'. Everyone in the Section had known me for so long that I was an old friend, almost a fixture, and the news that I was returning gave rise to a surge of chatter.

Susan had met me first in 1940, soon after she had arrived at Birdham as a newly spawned Wren officer, aged twenty. I was barely seventeen, and had just returned from the secret assault on the German U-boat refuelling base in Donegal. Those, my first kills, had left their mark on me. Susan had seen it in the lean, gaunt look of my face and the horror in my eyes – 'visions', she later said, 'that she would never forget'. I tried to laugh off the experience, as I had been schooled to do at Dartmouth; but, to her distress, she had often seen the look return.

Memories flooded back as she walked down the winding stairs from the signals office and across the minstrels' gallery to look down on the medieval hall below. She felt mildly annoyed with herself for indulging in such nostalgic day-dreams. She was officer of the day, and, in the absence of her captain, she was in command. Moreover, she was determined that her C sub-section should be fully efficient, operational and in good, seamanlike order when I arrived to take over.

Her brief reverie was broken by a red lamp flashing at the foot of the main stairs. Picking up a telephone, she learnt from the duty communications officer that three of the ten R/G lights which stood guard over the perimeter wire had been neutralised, apparently by outside interference.

Immediately she ordered action stations. Every light in the building snapped out, leaving only the dim red glow of the night-vision circuit. From all parts of the base armed Marine Commandos and operational Wrens sped to pre-arranged positions. Within seconds Susan had been joined by three duty colleagues, Penny Wirrell,

Joan Prewitt and Caroline Saunders. Already they had blacked their faces with boot polish; now they strapped on their .38 Smith & Wesson revolvers and made sure that the sheaths of their two-edged fighting knives were round at the back of their webbing belts, so that they would not stab themselves if they had to belly-crawl.

At the last moment Susan handed over officer of the day command to John Morgan, a tall, fair-haired captain in the Royal Marine Commandos, and led her girls out of the library window. Since her call to action stations, one minute and forty-two seconds had elapsed.

The night was crow-black, the wind bitter. Susan led off at a fast jog towards the R/G surveillance light that had been put out of action last, with the other three spread out in line abreast, about ten yards apart. They did not see the intruders standing on high ground above them – but the tallest of the four men could see them. He, too, had an R/G receiver: as he scanned down through it, the manor house appeared lit up green, and when he swung ninety degrees to his left, he could see the line of Wrens moving up towards him.

Susan was still advancing when Penny nipped across and whispered a message picked up on her portable transceiver: the control monitors in the house had detected active intruder R/G beams focused in their direction. All four girls immediately went to ground and lay flat in the bracken, which they knew would shield them from the beams.

As she stared into the darkness, Susan found she was breathing short and sharp. She was cold but also sweating, the result of fear. A moment later Penny crawled up to her, relaying control's message that the intruders were only forty yards to their north-west, and still approaching. Control also reported that the Commando section was seventy yards to the west, pinned down by the enemy R/G surveillance. They could not cross the open ground without being seen; but if an engagement started, they would immediately speed to the Wrens' aid.

Out came the order, 'Intercept, disarm, detain.' Susan loosened her Smith & Wesson in its holster and eased her fighting knife in its sheath. Close to her she could hear small movements as her companions did the same. Then, almost in unison, all four of

61

them went up on one knee and shuffled into two pairs, ready to spring.

The intruders became audible; then they began to take human form. At fifteen yards, four men loomed out of the blackness. At ten yards their outlines were very clear. Could they be Germans? Surely not, at this late stage of the war. No matter: they had no business to be where they were. 'How many times have I exercised for this very situation?' thought Susan. 'How many nights have I lain awake, sleepless with the fear of having to make a kill?'

Five metres. The sweat running down her backbone seemed to freeze instantly. Four men, four girls: on paper the odds would have looked impossible. But all four girls held Special Service black belts in the martial arts, and they had the supreme advantage of surprise.

A large boot crunched down into the bracken four feet from Susan's head. Another pair of boots went past a little further away. She waited until all four men were between the two waiting pairs, then touched Penny on the shoulder. The two girls sprang together. Susan struck her man square in the back and cut downwards with a wrist-and-arm double blow across his gun arm. His revolver flew harmlessly away into the dark, but, as her momentum carried them both forwards and sideways, the man managed to pull away. As she faced him, she heard the Commandos running down the hill towards them.

The intruder lunged at her head. She dived under his arm. Using her thigh as a fulcrum on the back of his knee, she jerked sharply and threw him hard, face first on to the ground. Instantly she pounced on his back, snaking her left arm round his throat and pulling it back tight. She felt the man struggling violently against her, but the fulcrum balance, the vital pivot of jujitsu, was in her favour. With her left hand she grasped her own right elbow, and forced her right hand and wrist down hard behind his head. The man was held in the classic Japanese stranglehold, the death-clasp.

'Move another inch and I'll break your bloody neck,' she shouted, in a voice whose menace surprised her.

Her victim, knowing he was beaten, ceased to struggle. Penny and Joan had also disarmed and held their adversaries: Caroline was having some trouble, and her man was threatening to break loose when the Commandos arrived with a rush to take charge of the prisoners.

Susan felt flushed with pride, as tall and strong as any man in the section. She reached out to each of the other girls, hugging and congratulating them. Caroline had a gash on her right cheek, but a few stitches would close it, and with proper attention it would leave hardly a mark.

Five minutes later in the galley, still dimly illuminated by the red night-vision lights, Susan confronted her black-faced captives; and when John Morgan wiped some of the boot-polish off the face of the tall man with whom she had fought, a slow but traumatic realisation came over her – for the chief intruder, I am afraid, was me.

Morgan called the room to attention and saluted, asking me, as the sub-section's new commanding officer, if Birdham's defences had been proved adequate by the mock-attack exercise.

'Absolutely,' I assured him. 'First class. Everyone did brilliantly, especially the Wrens.'

I could see that Susan was seething with rage; but it was not until a few minutes later, when we came together alone in the library, which served as captain's office and conference room, that I realised just how infuriated she was. When she threw her beret down on the table, I did the same, denoting that ranks were temporarily suspended, and that, within reason, she was free to say anything.

'You bloody fool!' she led off. 'That was an incredibly dangerous and stupid thing to do. I might easily have killed you.'

I pointed out that this was unlikely, as the Wrens had been ordered to take the intruders prisoner, not to kill them. She agreed, but said that if she or any of the girls had got into serious difficulties, they would have shot to kill. Those were her standing orders.

With what, in her later report, she described as 'provoking calmness', I asked exactly how she would have killed me.

'By pointing my gun at you and pulling the effing trigger,' she said very loudly.

'Show me what you would have done,' I said, shamelessly continuing the provocation. 'Have a go at that.' I pointed at one of the thick wooden beams in the ceiling. Normally she would have had the sense not to react to such a taunt; but now she was so fired up that she whipped out her revolver, took aim and pulled the trigger. All she obtained were sharp, metallic clicks. The bullets in all six chambers were dummies, switched for live ones by Morgan, who had made this and all the other safety arrangements for the exercise, on my orders.

The discovery made Susan even angrier. She accused me of employing dirty tricks to poke fun at her and the other girls, by allowing them to go out in defence of the base with dud ammunition. I came back at her aggressively, pointing out that neither she nor any other of the Wrens had bothered to check their ammunition before loading it. If the raid had been a real one, some of the Section might easily have been killed because of her negligence. I went on to explain that the exercise, which had been sanctioned by Morton, had been designed primarily for her benefit, and that of her operational Wrens. Its lesson was this: that everything, absolutely everything, must be checked two hundred and fifty times, and then checked again.

Susan became contrite, and apologised for her oversight. But I had not finished. There was another point. Officers of the day did not, in the absence of their captains, lead out parties of Wrens to intercept potentially hostile intruders. They assumed command of the base from control.

She could not get out of that one, either. She studied the deck at length, and again apologised. Still I was not done.

'If you have one flaw,' I said, 'it's that you're too anxious to prove yourself. Just be a bit more patient. Things are about to start up in a big way, and your chance will come sooner than you think – provided you don't kill yourself and all the girls first!'

I paused and added, 'Your trouble is that you never went to Dartmouth and had your backside beaten for cock-ups like this.'

'I'd rather be beaten than have you tell me off,' she answered quietly. And with that, thank goodness, our antagonism evaporated.

Action stations were stood down. The lights came on again. In the giant mirror above the fireplace we both looked like chimney-sweeps, our faces streaked with boot-polish and sweat. It was time for showers and dinner.

Susan went out, only to pop back a second later. 'I really might have killed you, you know,' she said.

'Well ...' It was some time before I could add, 'As long as you didn't.'

Left alone, I looked at myself again in the mirror, and did not much like what I saw. Susan was right. The exercise had been a stupid idea. It was only by the grace of God that nobody had been killed. My first training session as an operational commander had been a fiasco. Worst of all, I had given a sanctimonious lecture to the dearest, kindest friend I had ever known. Had promotion gone to my head? Was I qualified to command C sub-section? Once again my black angel threatened to overwhelm me.

Susan, however, knew me far better than I knew myself. Suddenly reappearing, face still black, wearing a dressing-gown built for a giant and with an enormous towel wound round her head, she looked like a Japanese circus clown, and made me burst out laughing. She formally announced that her Wren officer's steward was allowing no black faces in to dinner, not even those of acting lieutenant-commanders. She had therefore brought me a sponge bag and towel – and the water was piping hot.

She also confessed that what had really annoyed her about the exercise was that it had enabled me to sneak back into Birdham unannounced, and she had been unable to welcome me as her new commanding officer in accordance with King's Regulations and Admiralty Instructions, with a Marine and Wren guard of honour, bosun's pipes and all. A formal ceremony would have given her the chance of saluting me for the first time.

'Don't be bloody ridiculous, Susan,' I said.

'Then just welcome back to Birdham, dear old buddy,' she replied. We hugged and kissed as we always had, back on our old fraternal footing.

6

Target Identified

For me, it was if time had stood still. Suddenly I was back in the familiar routine of rigorous Commando training. At 0600 next morning a bugle sounded reveille, and by 0630 the entire ship's company, women as well as men, was out on the quarterdeck – in this case the lawn in front of the big house – wearing skimpy vests, shorts and gym shoes, for a ferocious session of physical training, taken by a Marine sergeant instructor. With everyone well warmed up – indeed, nearly on their knees – we went for a run round the track inside the perimeter fence.

That was merely the start of the day's exertions, for the main concentration of physical effort was on hand-to-hand combat. Clearly, this had to be very closely supervised and controlled, and the instructors, Royal Marine sergeants, were marvellously disciplined. I can still hear one of them barking out the basics of fighting with knives:

> If someone has a knife and I haven't, am I sorry? No! I'm very happy. Because if I have a knife, he knows it, and he's going to fight me level. But if I haven't got one, and appear to be a little bit scared, I'll get him to come close to me.

That was the whole basis of our training: to make an opponent come close to you. Rule One, when tackling an assailant with a knife, was never to worry about getting your hand or arm cut: as the attacker came for you, the key move was to sweep his knife-arm aside, regardless. We also constantly practised ways of killing with our hands. The death-clasp, in which Susan had got me, was the most effective, but we also learnt to kill by leading with a hand to the attacker's face, routing your palm up over his chin and driving your first two fingers into his eye-sockets. A still simpler trick was to get a finger into an opponent's mouth and rip out his cheek, a move against which there was no defence. By dint of non-stop practice we learnt to move extremely fast. Such was the speed of our reactions, in fact, that our vitality alone was enough to disconcert an opponent.

In all this, men and women trained together, all ranks and ratings, one sex often fighting the other. But every bout was closely supervised by an instructor, and if he saw anyone getting into real trouble, he would immediately bellow '*STILL*', the naval command that brought activity to a halt. Men and women also ate together, and in general relations were extremely close. I do not mean that we slept with each other, although inevitably a certain amount of cohabitation did occur. Rather, we lived as one big family, and shared one another's emotions, which were heightened by the physical strain of our existence and by the fact that the operation ahead was certain to be dangerous. The result was a great deal of emotional display – much hugging and kissing – which outsiders may well have found childish, but which to us seemed perfectly natural.

Potential officers and petty officers for the M Section were usually selected while still at school. Morton took it upon himself to get to know, if not to make friends with, the headmasters and headmistresses of leading Catholic establishments. Mother Ignatius of St Mary's, Ascot, and 'Posh' Paul Neville, OSB, of Ampleforth, were only two of his contacts. Among Protestant schools, he firmly avoided his own *alma mater*, Eton, as he did Harrow, Westminster and Rugby; but he had a strong penchant for Marlborough, Radley and Winchester. As for girls, he preferred those from Roedean, Highfield and Frances Holland. A few of our people – Dr Jenny Wright, Penny Wirrell, John Morgan – had been recruited from universities, but most had entered the services at eighteen, and therefore had had no chance to go on to higher education.

The fact that we had so many girls was due largely to the advocacy of Dame Vera Laughton Mathews, the Director, Wrens. A woman of medium height but immensely strong character, Dame Vera was round and jolly and slightly deaf, so that she often leant forward with a hand to her ear to catch what was being said. In the First World War she had herself been a Wren – and incidentally a close friend of my mother, who joined the Women's Royal Flying Corps. Now, in the Second World War, she was eager that any of her girls who volunteered should be allowed to go operational (that is, into action) and fight level with the men, as the young women of Special Operations Executive had done with such success in France and elsewhere. Her only regret, she said, was that she herself was no longer young enough to go into the front line.

In his recruiting, Morton looked for good qualities, bad faults, even criminal tendencies that he might be able to exploit. He sought pure intelligence – English, foreign languages, mathematics and science were the credits he wanted at School Certificate – but also the ability to lead and command. He wanted physical toughness and good co-ordination, which, with training, would produce a high level of skill in jujitsu, unarmed combat, silent killing and the use of weapons. He also demanded loyalty of the first order, which would endure, if necessary, through torture to death. All candidates for the M Section went through prolonged psychiatric examination. The final endurance test for both boys and girls was twelve strokes of the cane administered by a Marine Commando sergeant across their bare buttocks in front of their class. They were not strapped down, but had to stay down and not cry out: then, immediately afterwards, they had to lead a section on exercises in the countryside, without faltering. Such were the indoctrination and training that out of each course of twenty-five, only about five failed at this ordeal, and usually only one of these was a girl.

While we prepared for possible action, Morton and Churchill had been busy, and on 11 January Ian Fleming flew to Switzerland bearing a personal letter from the Prime Minister. Ostensibly a Foreign Office courier, he travelled in civilian clothes and on a diplomatic passport. Arriving in Basle, he made his way to a pre-arranged rendezvous at a bank, where he met the Swiss Finance Minister, Ernest Nobs, and two senior colleagues in a closely guarded conference room. The letter from Churchill asked that positive action be taken against the murderers, thieves and swindlers of the Nazi hierarchy; but when the minister read it, he claimed to be unable to help. He did not even know – he said – whether the Nazis held any accounts in his country.

Playing his cards with some skill, Fleming revealed that he already knew not only which banks were involved, but also the numbers of the suspect accounts. All he needed was the names of the signatories. Apparently unimpressed, the minister replied that, even should such accounts exist, he would commit a grave criminal offence under Swiss law if he revealed any names. Countering, Fleming pointed out that the Nazis were international criminals: Swiss law surely demanded that the accounts of such people should at least be frozen and investigated. The minister agreed that this would be true if the accounts were held by individuals, or even by companies, partnerships or associations; but he claimed that accounts held by an independent sovereign state such as Germany were no less immune than the German Legation and its diplomats.

The discussion appeared to have reached stalemate. But before the minister left, he asked one searching question. If the British government *did* somehow gain control of the assets in question, what would be done with them? Fleming was prepared for this one. In the first instance, he replied, Britain would ask the Swiss government to act as trustee of the funds until an international committee of experts could be appointed to deal with them. The objective, then, would be to determine where the funds and valuables had come from, and to restore them to their rightful owners. As for any residue left unclaimed, this could be distributed among the countries and people most severely in need of reparations after the war.

'So funds would be available to help German and Italian citizens as well?' the minister asked.

'Unequivocally yes,' Fleming replied. 'Mr Churchill is adamant on that point.'

Soon after that the minister took his leave. But before he departed he became strangely insistent that his visitor should stay on for a few minutes and have some sandwiches and coffee. Left alone in the vast room, Fleming wondered what was going on; and when the coffee arrived he was surprised to see that it was brought in by a young army officer. When the man had gone, Fleming took his cup across to the window and looked out; then, hearing the door open again, he glanced back, to find he had been joined by an attractive, blonde woman in her thirties, wearing a smart two-piece suit, and carrying a briefcase and raincoat. She introduced herself as Madame Claudine Fouchet of the Swiss Intelligence Service, and suggested that he might like to accompany her, to see something of interest.

Barely an hour later they arrived at what a casual visitor might have taken for a normal hamlet, tucked away in a high valley of the Alps. Fleming's trained eye, however, noticed the small gun-batteries and machine-gun emplacements discreetly deployed to guard the approaches. Innocent-looking chalets flanked a pair of heavy steel doors let into the side of a mountain.

Inside, Fleming's guide explained that this was a secure vault of the National Bank of Basle, carved out of living rock, and in a quick tour of part of it she showed him treasure that would have made King Midas sick with envy. Crates stacked to the roof held ingots of gold and silver. There were diamonds, sapphires, emeralds and other precious stones beyond counting. Crown jewels from the German royal family, the Hohenzollerns, were stored alongside items that had belonged to Marie-Antoinette. Huge wooden racks held oil paintings by every great master – from the Czech House of Luxembourg and Premysl, from France, Belgium and Holland, from Denmark and Norway, from the Grand Duchy of Luxembourg, from Italy and Yugoslavia, from Leningrad and the Ukraine.

Fleming was astonished by the sheer volume of what he saw, and when he posed a simple question he was equally amazed by the answer.

'And what part of all this belongs to our German friends?' he asked.

'All of it, Mr Fleming,' replied Mme Fouchet. 'The whole lot.'

Back on a military airstrip outside Basle, as they parted, she handed him a white envelope, which she said the Finance Minister had asked her to give him. Inside was a single sheet of white paper, which bore one typed line only: *Nationalsozialistische Deutsche Arbeiterpartei 60508.*

*　　*　　*

At Birdham Fleming lost no time in discovering that membership number 60508 of the German National Socialist Workers' Party had been allocated to a man called Martin Bormann. At first the name meant nothing to us. Familiar as we were with Hitler's other henchmen – Goering, Goebbels, Himmler, Ribbentrop and Hess (still languishing in British captivity) – we had never heard of Bormann, who was then 44 years old.

Research soon put us right. Bormann, it turned out, was head of the Nazi Party Chancellery. His position was unostentatious, but one of enormous power. He had started his political career as a humble assistant to Hess, the deputy Führer, but since Hess's flight to Britain in 1941, he had made himself more and more indispensable to Hitler, and in 1943 had become his private secretary. Quiet, unassuming, mole-like, but also bad-tempered and vindictive towards enemies, he was described as a short, squat man with a hook nose, always there, always at the Führer's elbow, closer to him than anyone else on earth. Moreover, as head of the Chancellery he was the man who controlled the colossal Nazi assets abroad.

In Fleming's view, this simplified our task enormously. All we had to do now, he announced, was to find out where Bormann was, kidnap him, bring him secretly back to Britain with his chequebooks, and invite him to start signing some rather large cheques. As he often did when faced with an almost impossible proposition, Fleming casually remarked, 'It's a piece of cake.'

The obvious way to start was to reactivate my own Nazi contacts, so we obtained Morton's permission to set up the reconnaissance trip to Ireland described in Chapter One. The moment I returned from it, with news that Ribbentrop had specifically asked to see me, Morton came down to Birdham for a meeting with Fleming, Susan Kemp and myself. We began by speculating on whether the Foreign Minister's invitation might be the preamble to a German peace feeler, but we soon dismissed the possibility. Everyone felt sure that Stockholm or Lisbon would prove to be the channel for surrender negotiations, and that any initiative would probably come through Count Folke Bernadotte, the Swedish head of the International Red Cross.

Nevertheless, all four of us felt excited, and hopeful that we were on to something important. Otherwise, why the offer of large sums of money, and the show of good faith? Why else should Ribbentrop want to contact me on his own initiative? We all felt that a meeting with him would smartly advance our quest for Bormann.

What we did not know was that by then Bormann's relationship with Hitler had undergone a fundamental change. From worshipping his great Nazi leader, the toadying, ever-efficient, self-effacing secretary had swung round to a position from which he loathed and despised him.* By March 1945 Bormann saw that the war was well and truly lost: the only man who would not face the truth was the 'schizophrenic megalomaniac' in charge. Cool and calculating as ever, Bormann decided that he would manipulate Hitler right to the end, whenever that might come. When Ribbentrop mentioned that he had again been in contact with me, Bormann saw more clearly than ever that I might be extremely useful in helping him to escape: he reckoned that 'the dirty English boy' could be trusted in any criminal activity, and would do anything for money.

Without knowing that fate was already pushing Bormann in our direction, we decided to follow up Ribbentrop's overture; but I immediately voiced my doubts about my ability to carry the initiative through on my own. On previous solo operations in Germany, France, Algiers, the Dutch East Indies and elsewhere I had done reasonably well, but always I had been carrying out carefully prepared plans and orders. Only on a minor scale had I become involved in negotiations, diplomacy or intrigue. Although I could handle operational command, for which I

---

* The pages of the Birdham transcript covering this point are full of wild, intemperate language, suggesting that Bormann had had several drinks before that session of interrogation. Describing how he abhorred the sight of Hitler, he called him 'contemptible, revolting and inhuman'. At the end of the war it would be he, Martin Bormann, who won out. He would be the tops. He would win the gold medals and become the richest man in the world: chief banker, cashier-in-chief, boss man, head of everything. Having escaped from the idiocy of the Third Reich, he would set himself up in a realm where, as king and emperor, he would rule all before and under him. He, who had been so loyal and quiet and humble, would burst out into the universe, cut down the muck and piggery, and rule omnipotent.

had been trained as a professional sailor, I was a novice in diplomatic manoeuvring, and I felt that on this new mission I might well be out of my depth. I therefore submitted that Fleming should accompany me on the next trip. He agreed at once, as did Morton, and our little committee promptly endorsed the idea. It would be no problem to invent a cover-story which showed why it was essential for me to travel with a companion.

Our system of using code-names from A. A. Milne had already been extended to include the principal Nazi players: Ribbentrop had become 'Small' and Hitler 'Rabbit'. Of the characters remaining unassigned, there was one who stood head and shoulders above the rest as being ideal for Bormann, and this was Piglet.

Fleming, as I have said, was 'Pooh'. But for our forthcoming journey it was decided that he should use the cover-name he himself had devised for the operation as a whole: James Bond. He had lifted it, without permission, from the real man of that name, author of a classic ornithological work, *Field Guide to Birds of the West Indies*, which Fleming had picked up during his first trip to the Caribbean in November 1944. After the war, when he called his fictional hero James Bond, he claimed it was the most boring and nondescript name he could think of; but early in 1945 it was merely the one at the front of his mind.

Among ourselves, the name was quickly abbreviated to 'JB'; from that moment we spoke among ourselves about 'Op. JB', and the official stamp, used on documents relating to the operation, bore only those cryptic letters. Fleming reiterated the need for absolute security laid down by Morton: the name James Bond was not for operational use, even within C sub-section, he said, and he added two important riders. The first was that only the officers directly involved in the operation need know anything about it – and this firmly excluded MI 5 and MI 6. His second point was there was no case for co-operating with inter-Allied intelligence. We did not want word of what we were doing to reach the ears of any of our allies, least of all the Russians, who, with their intense suspicion of Western motives, would naturally assume we were trying to seize the Nazi assets for ourselves.

We composed a message for my contacts at the German Legations in Dublin and Geneva, explaining that when I next came over I would be accompanied by my colleague Mr James Bond. There was some doubt as to whether we should send the signal in English or in German; and while we wavered, Fleming, typically, said, 'Send it in Irish!'

It was hardly surprising that at first Fleming found life at Birdham strange and distasteful. By nature rather fastidious and aloof, he was appalled by the idea of having to train with women and even fight them; but Susan was not prepared to treat him differently from anyone else. 'Look,' she said, as she saw him hesitating on his first morning, 'you're going to get hurt, so you might as well start with me.' When he did move in to attack her, she threw him all over the place, for he was out of practice and unfit, and she was far too quick for him.

At first he took a lot of punishment; but, to his credit, he did not mind. On the contrary, he warmed to the job with every day that went past, and trained with ever greater skill and enthusiasm, often with blood pouring down his face.

Then, one morning, our lives were revolutionised by the arrival of nearly a hundred German Freedom Fighters (GFFs), young men and women, mainly Jews, who had escaped from the Nazi regime, found asylum with the British, and now were determined to take an active part in the liberation of their homeland. A little convoy of three-ton trucks pulled up outside the manor house, and out tumbled a motley collection of boys and girls. At first glance they resembled any other British Commando unit, for they wore smart khaki battledress with Combined Operations Commando flashes; but a closer look revealed that many of them were swarthy and strong-featured – and under their veneer of confidence, they seemed uncertain of themselves, even homesick.

From all round the base nearly a hundred British personnel of Op. JB converged on the main driveway to scrutinise the new arrivals on the lawn opposite. The granite-hard Royal Marine sergeants were already outraged by the mere idea of having to train German Jews, and the sight of this lot milling about set their eyeballs rolling. Then the Germans' leader stepped forward. A tiny man in his thirties, only about five feet three inches tall, he was immediately remarkable for his intense blue eyes and mop of curly black hair prematurely turning grey. Marching smartly forward, he announced himself to Susan as Major Israel Bloem. Her reaction was typically outgoing and direct. She asked him if she might go over and welcome the new arrivals. After a moment's hesitation, Bloem agreed, so she walked across, spoke a few words in German, and ended with 'Shalom!' The effect was instantaneous. One of the new girls embraced her, and suddenly everyone was hugging in the best Birdham manner. Not even the hoary old sergeants could escape. To them the idea of being embraced in public was well-nigh high treason – but somehow they too succumbed.

Fleming, watching from the front door of the house, muttered, 'What the hell's going on? This is disgraceful! No discipline whatever!'

'You poor old thing!' cried Susan. 'Nobody's hugged you.' So she gave him a kiss on the cheek, brought him out and made him take his cap off. Soon he too was surrounded by a throng of young Germans.

It was Morton's idea to draft the Freedom Fighters into our sub-section. Now that we had identified Bormann as our target, it was clear that our theatre was likely to be Germany, and to have natives of the country in our ranks would obviously give us an enormous advantage. Further, there seemed every chance that, if we found Bormann at all, we would find him in Berlin, the ultimate focus of the Allied encirclement, which was already closing round the remains of Hitler's Third Reich and tightening towards his capital.

7

Off the Rails

As Sub-Section Commander I had quite a lot paperwork to deal with, and on the afternoon of Friday, 12 January 1945, with operational training out of the way, Susan Kemp and I were in our office, sorting through requestmen, defaulters, and various odds and ends. Then at 5 pm the signals officer, Penny Wirrell, came in with copies of the evening's communications, the first of which read:

> Most Secret. Immediate. From Department P 5 to 'M'. Repeated M Sub-Section Commanders. Regret Second Officer Patricia Falkiner WRNS (Code Name 'Alice') killed in recent Austrian operations.

Neither Susan nor I raised an eyebrow at the news. To have displayed emotion would not have been in the Royal Naval tradition. Complete indifference was the name of the game – nonchalance on the grand scale. I looked up at Penny, who was plainly shaken, and handed the message back to her. 'File it, please,' I said quietly. Then I glanced at my watch and added, 'It's after four-thirty, Miss Wirrell. Where's the tea?'

I knew Susan must be shocked, for she and Patricia had been very close friends. Besides, this was the first reported casualty of Operation JB. As for myself, I felt as if a knife had been driven into my heart. I had been in love with Patricia since 1941. Admittedly we had not been able to see each other for months, but that had not lessened our devotion. The shock of suddenly hearing that she was dead hit me all the harder because I was not even aware that she had joined the M Section. The last I had known of her employment, she had been serving at Bletchley Park. Because I had spent months recuperating, and then gone to HMS *Fervent*, I had not been authorised to know what she was doing. Quite properly, Morton had not revealed the nature of her work: he told me only that she was on special secret communications duty.

Patricia dead! I could not take it in. The person closest to me in the world had gone: the loyal, intensely loving girl who had held me together through the four ghastly years of betrayal and horror into which I had been forced. Even though I had abandoned every tenet of decency and honour, she had supported me with understanding, sympathy and love. Now I would never see her again.

Dimly I heard Susan telling me that it was Patricia who had sent the vital signal from Austria, that it was she who had put Op. JB on the road. No one yet knew exactly what had happened: something terrible had gone wrong. But it was Patricia's courage that had got the message through.

Before I could absorb the full impact of the disaster, I felt myself being seized by rage that sent me blind with sudden hatred. Why had she been drafted into the M Section so late in the war? I wondered furiously. Why had nobody told me what she was doing? Why had lies been told to prevent me finding out?

Only Morton could have organised all this, I decided. Nothing of the kind could have happened without his directive. From Patricia's induction into the Section, right through her training, into her operation, and to her death: every step must have been engineered by him.

Apparently I sat for some time without speaking, as Susan tried to explain that, because I had been away for nine months, I could not possibly have known. Her own shock was compounded by the heartless way I had been left to find out what had happened, and she went through several minutes of what she later called 'silent agony'. Then suddenly I left the room, announcing that I was going to London.

For a while she stayed in the office, trying to pull herself together and bitterly wishing that she could have done something for me at a moment when I needed help so badly. Several times in the past she had seen my emotions get the better of me; she knew me better than I knew myself, and now she realised that my discipline and self-control were probably at breaking-point.

She therefore went quickly to my cabin to check what I was doing, and noticed that my webbing belt carrying a .38 Smith & Wesson revolver was not in its usual stowage. This in itself was nothing unusual, for during the war it had been normal and proper for officers – and Commando officers in particular – to carry side-arms wherever they went. But now the war was nearly over: the Germans were on their knees, and the chances of Nazi paratroopers dropping from the skies were negligible. Besides, she knew that I never carried side-arms outside the base except on exercises or operations. Being an extremely level-headed young lady, she went straight back to the office, picked up the red security telephone and asked to be connected with Commander Fleming at the Admiralty.

I, meanwhile, had taken my 350cc Ariel motorcycle and ridden into Portsmouth, where I put the bike into the luggage van of a train for London. By 7 pm I was feeling my way through Whitehall in a dense yellow fog; so thick was the pall that I almost rode into the sandbags piled up outside the Ministry of Works to protect the building from V2 rockets. I didn't care. I had walked or ridden or driven this route many times when my heart was light, my spirit alive and dedicated. That day I moved slowly, not because of the fog, but because my heart and spirit were overwhelmed, my dedication subverted and shattered.

A Grenadier Guards sergeant squinted through the gloom at my two passes, one my naval identity card, the other a special pass for entry to the Cabinet War Room. Together the documents gave me access to the chiefs of staff, the Cabinet secretariat, the Prime Minister, Desmond Morton, and indeed the whole spectrum of the wartime High Command.

As I entered that huge, gloomy building, memories suddenly began to assail me; like the apparitions conjured up for Macbeth by the witches, ghosts of all the people I had killed rose up to haunt me. Most of them had been perfectly loyal and innocent people, allies who had become innocently caught up in our operations: all were now dead as a result of my own treacherous activities.

It was down in the labyrinthine bowels of this building that I had been briefed for all my most amoral operations. It was here that Morton had ordered me, in the summer of 1942, to hand the Abwehr our plans for the raid on Dieppe: a betrayal that had led to four thousand Allied casualties. Later, I had tried to exorcise my guilt by confessing to Vice-Admiral Lord Louis Mountbatten, who had been commander-in-chief of the operation, in the hope that I would be reviled and condemned to a court martial. The result was quite the opposite: Mountbatten listened patiently, said he had known all about my involvement, and congratulated me for having done 'jolly well'. My guilt had remained inviolate.

Now I ran up a few steps and on to the landing. This time a Royal Marine checked my papers more thoroughly. I asked where Major Morton was, and the corporal directed me to the Cabinet War Room. High up on one wall was a slit like a letterbox, set in a green baize surround. As I turned left, I glanced up at it, remembering how I had once challenged Morton about the security of the building on this very spot. As we went in, I had said to him, 'You know, the security in this place is bloody awful.'

'Oh, is it?' he replied. 'I see, I see. Let's have a little experiment, then. You move fast and try to get through that door over there.'

As I did so, invisible partitions on either side of the letterbox flew open, and there were two Royal Marine Commandos covering me with sub-machine-guns.

Now, I knew, two men were watching invisibly as I went in. I descended two flights of the spiral staircase that so delighted Churchill, who liked to pretend that he was in a submarine whenever he went up and down, even though he knew perfectly well that submarines did not have spiral staircases. At the bottom was a watertight door. Again I showed my pass, and I was through to the Hole.

Hardly knowing what I was doing, I carried on down to the lowest level, thirty or forty feet beneath the level of the Thames, a cavernous, partly finished floor fitted with bunks for emergency accommodation. Its farthest reaches were alive with rats, whose eyes glowed red in the light of the odd electric bulb burning dimly among the girders in the ceiling. Churchill sometimes opened up on these wretched beasts with his revolver, for target practice: he had never been known to hit one, but once a bullet ricocheted off the concrete floor and wall and knocked a file out of General Ismay's hand, to the intense disapproval of General Montgomery.

I did not smile at that memory, for other ghosts were crowding thick around me. My conscience was back in the Pacific aboard the Dutch submarine K-XVII, commanded by Lieutenant-Commander Besançon. In December 1941 I alone had wiped out the entire ship's company with two tiny cylinders of cyanide inserted into their oxygen supply, and a box of high explosive, disguised as whisky, both timed to release their venomous contents when I was safely away. Those Dutch submariners' only sin was that they had seen, and reported, the Japanese fleet sailing towards Pearl Harbour: news of it had been suppressed, to ensure that the attack went home and America came into the war, and it was deemed essential that the Dutchmen and their secret must die.*

Undoubtedly the war had turned me into a fiend and mass-murderer: on the Day of Judgement I would stand alongside the SS and the Gestapo in the dock, and to say that I had only done as I was told would be no excuse. And what would Patricia think, now that the whole of my dirty career was open to her view? Maybe it was better that she was dead, so that she could never face me with my crimes in human form.

Eventually I realised that in wandering the lower deck I was trying to keep grief at bay. Rage took over once more and drew me back up to the main floor. Yet there again memories overwhelmed me. I looked in on the small mess-room near Churchill's sleeping quarters. The year before, when I had partially recovered from the injuries inflicted by the Gestapo, Churchill had sent for me, and told me to report to this very room. As a surprise, he had arranged for Patricia to meet me there. We had talked and held hands on the very spot where I now stood.

Until then I had always been disciplined. Discipline ground into me at Ampleforth and Dartmouth had seeped into my very soul. In training and operations I had almost always been able to rely on my self-control. Now, though, I felt under such stress that I hardly knew what I was doing: I felt as if some alien power had taken me over and digging his spurs into my flanks, goading me along.

I showed my pass again, this time to the Royal Marine pensioner

* A fuller account of this incident is given in Chapter Nine and Appendix.

stationed at the double doors that led to the Cabinet War Room. Inside, I found Morton sitting alone at the huge table which took up most of the floor space, absorbed in some papers: as always, he was immaculately dressed in a dark suit. He was side-on to me, so that I could see the left half of his face as he read, but he looked up when I came in.

In the past our relationship had always been friendly, even affectionate. But that evening I felt only icy hatred.

At once I pitched in, challenging him to tell me about Patriçia. Surely he, the great intelligence supremo, had heard of her? In case he hadn't, he might like to be reminded. Without being invited, I took him rapidly through her service at Bletchley and in the M Section. I accused him of forcing her into the Section, and, before she had had a chance to be properly trained, launching her into the most dangerous theatre, in Austria. This made him no less guilty of her death than the people who had murdered her.

When Morton tried to reply, I cut across him as if he had not uttered. I accused him of taking elaborate precautions to ensure that I would never find out Patricia's fate. I knew, I said, that he had ordered her to write to me saying she was in Washington, when in fact she had been at Birdham. As for her death, it was disgraceful that I had been left to discover the truth by accident.

Morton did at least apologise for that. The plan had been that I should hear she had been killed in an accident in Washington. The leakage of true information had been 'an unfortunate mistake'.

'Mistake?' I retorted bitterly. 'How could it have been a mistake, when you yourself planned it down to the last detail? You always do, with your murders – or, if you prefer it, with your assassinations.'

'Look!' Morton began to speak forcefully, with a mixture of sarcasm and exasperation. 'In case you haven't noticed, the Prime Minister and I are trying our best to finish off the most ghastly and bloody conflict ever to affront the face of this earth. People are getting killed all the time. Merely because someone close to *you* has been lost, and security dictated that you couldn't be told about it, you come in here and start being both insurbordinate and threatening. By what God-given right d'you think you're behaving like this?'

'Because,' I said viciously, 'for me Patricia Falkiner was the dearest creature on earth. That's something you apparently don't understand or care about. You're so bloody ruthless, you trample everything in your path. Why don't you put your own head on the chopping-block and risk yourself, for once?'

However much I question myself after the event, I have never been able to say how my webbing belt came to be round my waist with the .38 Smith & Wesson in its holster. I had no recollection of taking it with me. Still less could I account for the fact that at the critical moment my hand was on the butt of the revolver.

I saw Morton draw in his breath. He was often bland, contemptuous and arrogant, but he could be brave and cynical as well.

'If you fire that thing from where you are,' he said evenly, 'you're bound to score a bull's eye. But since I've already got one bullet in my heart, I can't see that another'll make much difference.'

His cynicism failed to deflect me. Morton was the uncle I had known so well, and loved, long ago. But the man before me now was someone else: I did not recognise him at all. I realised that I was slipping out of control. Tears welled into my eyes, and I felt that the situation was becoming unstable.

Unknown to me, the Marine between the double doors at the entrance had been relieved by Commander Ian Fleming, who held a Colt .45 levelled through the crack. As he told me later, he reckoned that the amazing scene unfolding before his eyes had become locked in stalemate, and that one side or the other was going to have give ground quickly. Before he could take action, though, salvation came from another direction.

'Christopher Robin!' The familiar deep voice boomed out from the back of the room. Turning in astonishment, I saw Winston Churchill heave himself out of a chair and walk slowly towards me.

'Don't you see?' he said as he advanced. 'You were the last person in the world who could have been told the truth about what Miss Falkiner was doing. It would have been fatal to the operation. You knew her far too well.'

By then he had come close up to me, and my Smith & Wesson was pointing directly at him. Without pausing, he deftly took the gun from my hand and stuffed the barrel down inside the waistband of his siren suit, before waddling off round the table like a fat cowboy to sit down in his own armchair.

There was another factor, he went on, of which I knew nothing, but which had caused deep distress to people close to him. It was something that the need for security, which we had been discussing, had prevented Morton from revealing to anyone, even to Churchill himself. He had learnt of it only that day. He looked at his security chief, as if expecting him to take up the story.

At first Morton seemed reluctant to say anything more; but when Churchill pressed him, he began to talk – in a far softer tone of voice than I had heard him use for years. He said that just after Patricia and I had got to know each other, in 1941, I had left her one day in the upper reception room. Morton had found her there and taken her into his office for a talk. 'What I impressed on her most,' he said, 'was that she must never tell you about our relationship.'

That word startled me. *Their* relationship? What the hell was he talking about? Seeing me stare open-mouthed, Morton said, 'You know what my names are.'

Still I was baffled.

'Go on,' he urged.

'Morton,' I began. 'Desmond, John, Falkiner . . .'

I broke off dumbfounded.

'She was an only child,' I heard him saying. 'Her parents were Canadian, but both were killed in a car accident in the thirties. Because they'd been good friends of mine, I arranged for the girl to be brought to England. She lived with other friends, who became her guardians.'

Not having a wife (Morton went on), he could not adopt her; so he had her name changed to Falkiner and became a surrogate uncle, converting her to Catholicism and establishing himself as her godfather, exactly as he had with me. In due course he arranged for her to go to St Mary's Convent at Ascot, where he had also placed my two sisters. Yet throughout all this his obsession with secrecy had prevented him from telling anyone what he was doing.

His revelations snuffed out the last spark of my anger. He asked me to believe that he had done his utmost to keep Patricia out of operations. It was only when she had stumbled on the most vital of secrets at Bletchley that he had been forced to deploy her in the field.

Churchill reminded me that it was her valiant work which had got Operation James Bond off the ground. He then gave me a lecture on the morality of secret operations, emphasising that all of us – he, Morton and myself – were equally guilty of foul play, by normal standards, but that in desperate circumstances desperate methods were justified. 'If God in His wisdom destroyed Sodom and Gomorrah, together with the lives of thousands of His people, then surely in this great conflict, fought in His name, we have some such rights too.'

By then reaction was setting in. I had started to feel sick, and thought I was going to faint. On impulse Morton put out a hand. My reserve collapsed, and I hugged him, as I so often had in the past. Churchill, watching, blew his nose loudly and muttered that nobody ever hugged *him* like that. Then he took my revolver from his waistband and handed it back to me saying, 'You might need this to shoot Herr Schickelgrüber. Besides, if I keep it in my trousers any longer, I'll probably shoot my cock off.'

Minutes later I was gone – but not before I had received the most severe of reprimands from both my mentors. This sort of wild behaviour must never occur again, they told me. Had I been anyone else, I would by now be under close arrest and awaiting court martial, with only one verdict and sentence possible. Much as Churchill sympathised with me in the loss of Patricia, Christopher Robin could expect no further favours from either Tigger or Owl. On the contrary, I must pull myself together and approach my new task rock-like, as had the naval captains of old. I was in command of an operation crucial to the reconstruction of post-war Europe. I must realise the importance of the position I held, and steadfastly honour the commission that I held from the Sovereign.

Just before I left, Churchill closed his soft, podgy hand on my wrist and said again how sorry he was about it all. There were tears in his eyes.

Between the double doors, Fleming handed his watch back to the Royal Marine pensioner and retired to the small bar across the hall, trusting that a double Scotch would help him regain his senses. Never in his life had he witnessed such a scene, and he felt physically and mentally numb. So did I.*

Out in St James's Park the fog had lifted, but my heart remained heavy as lead, and for half an hour I sat hunched in an unobtrusive heap at the bottom of Clive Steps, sobbing my heart out. I felt so low that I thought of going to see my sisters, or even my mother; but my predicament was far beyond their sphere of activity or understanding. Eventually I decided to head for the Prospect of Whitby, an East End pub which was one of my favourite London haunts, in the hope that its happy memories might restore my spirits.

When I mounted my motor bike and headed for Wapping, I did not notice the jeep that followed me at a distance; but I found the Prospect doing its usual brisk trade, and took my pint of Black and Tan out on to the wooden jetty at the back, above the Thames. For a while I watched the river surging downstream on the ebb tide. I was looking straight down into the water: if the surface had been calm, I could have seen myself reflected in it and observed what a useless piece of rubbish I was. In fact the spring tide was boiling down from Teddington and above, and I knew that if a man fell in his body would not be recovered much short of the Medway or even Margate Sands. Unconsciously I shuffled forward until my toes, even half my feet, were over the rushing water.

Suddenly in the eddies I saw Patricia's face. I heard her voice call

* In 1978 I took the author Brian Garfield round the Hole in the Ground. At the time he was working on *The Paladin*, his excellent novel based on the first part of my war service, and I wanted him to see the old War Cabinet Room, which was still in more or less its original state and had not yet been opened to tourists.

I reminded Brian that there had been a direct telephone line from this room to Desmond Morton, and that I had heard Churchill speaking to him on it. The curator, who was escorting us, denied it. The only direct connections, he said, had been to the chiefs of staff and other VIPs. I was appalled: if my memory had played me false on this vital fact, how much else might I have got wrong?

I followed my two companions disconsolately into the map and telephone room. Then Brian suddenly said, 'Is this what you meant?' He held up a dusty wire he had found lying on the floor behind the main console. One end led into the box of direct Cabinet Room connections, and on it was a tag of dirty white tape bearing in faded print the name MORTON.

clearly from the water, 'Come on, Christopher! Here I am. Come and join me. We can be together again. Come on, darling . . .'

In the cold night I poured with sweat, as vertigo seemed to seize my very soul. Then from behind me another familiar woman's voice called my name. Someone pulled me back from the brink, and as I shook off the hallucination I found Susan Kemp holding my hand.

Back in the bar we sat face to face, looking at each other in silence. She read the questions in my eyes, and answered them before I asked. Yes, she had reckoned I needed help, so she had followed me to London. No, she had not been summoned by Morton or Churchill or Fleming, or even by person or persons unknown. Nobody had called her.

At last I did get one question out. 'Did you tell Fleming I'd gone to London and taken my gun-belt with me?'

'Of course I did!' she exclaimed with a sudden grin. 'I'm supposed to be your friend, aren't I? Not some gormless bloody idiot!'

My inner torment started to abate. An hour later, when we left the pub hand in hand, I loaded the Ariel into the back of the jeep, and we drove south over London Bridge towards Portsmouth. I did not exactly thank Susan for her efforts on my behalf; instead, I asked her, rather brusquely, if she would like to become my second-in-command – or number one, as the navy prefers to call it – on Op. JB. Morton and Fleming had already approved my nomination, I said. 'It's up to you.'

After some thought she accepted, but only out of a sense of duty. As she said, barely in jest, she didn't think anyone else would take the job.

8

In the Enemy Camp

The outburst cleared my mind and to some extent eased my heart. Fleming returned to the Far East for a short spell, again by the FEASTS relay. His aim was partly to wind up a half-completed project for naval intelligence, partly to create cover for Op. JB. But, as he confided to me later, his overriding personal aim was to have a final fling with a gorgeous Wren he had met in Australia.

Back at Birdham, I settled down to serious training and concentrated on the operation ahead. Life was physically demanding, for we were out at our PT and runs in every dark winter dawn, come snow, rain, ice or fog, and unarmed combat work continued apace. But now our exercises were sandwiched between periods spent exhaustively studying conditions in the remains of the Third Reich.

Here our German Freedom Fighters became invaluable – none more so than their leader, Major Israel Bloem. A remarkable man in many ways, he was then thirty-three, well-built and agile despite his lack of height. He had one physical peculiarity, in that he had lost the second finger on either hand. Bloem himself never mentioned this deficiency: indeed, he refused to talk about it, and it was only through his record that we discovered what had happened.

In 1936 a group of SA troopers (Brownshirts) had chased his fifteen-year-old sister up a street in Munich and threatened to molest her. Fortunately he had managed to scare them off. A few days later they tried again, and once more Bloem, together with some friends, saved the girl. But a week or so after that the same gang of Brownshirts cornered him on his own, told him he was a 'short-arsed Jew-boy' who had twice deprived them of some fun, and chopped off two of his fingers.

In spite of that, he was a well-balanced man. Sensitive and emotional, but none the less very disciplined, he was just the sort of leader his people needed. Rank apart, his endurance, strength and vitality, together with a strong sense of humour, made him one of the most popular men in the group. He was tough, and a strict disciplinarian; but because he was always completely fair, people respected and liked him: indeed, they almost loved him. They saw him for what he was: an outstanding anti-Nazi patriot.

His great value to us was that he could swiftly interpret the intelligence that came in from Germany, and also produce a huge amount of useful information from his own resources. If we needed any special detail, he would smile in an engaging manner and wave a finger knowingly before disappearing in search of what we wanted. A day or two later – or sometimes after only a few hours – strangers would arrive at Birdham carrying crumpled paper packets, and presently Bloem would knock on the door of the Section, ready with the answers. His informants were secret, and he would never say anything about them, except that he would protect them to the death. We respected his position, and never pressed him further.

When Fleming returned early in February, he took to Bloem immediately, and the two of them often went ashore together, chatting for hours in the local pub, and playing game after game of chess. So far as I know, Fleming never won.

I myself found Bloem easy to deal with, even though I was more than twelve years his junior. Far from resenting the fact that I was in command, he went out of his way to support me, without ever being patronising. He always addressed me as 'sir', and saluted, and whenever one of his unit failed to show me proper obedience or compliments, he would whack the offender across the backside with his swagger cane, regardless of sex – a disciplinary method that was effective and readily accepted by his people: in fact they preferred it to loss of pay and leave.

The presence of the Freedom Fighters in England was of course completely secret. Some of them were blond and Aryan-looking, but most were dark and obviously Jewish. Their ages ranged from late teens to early twenties. Many had risked their lives to escape the Nazi regime, and some had had a tough time even when they reached Britain. People whose parents had come here before the war found things relatively simple: by 1945 most spoke reasonable English, had been to English schools, and had achieved a satisfactory standard of education. Several of these became officers. Yet the majority, who had escaped while the war was in progress, had faced a very different regime, being put through brutal interrogations designed to weed out planted spies, and then sent off to the Isle of Man to join Oswald Mosley and real traitors in detention camps, under Rule 18b. Only when cleared by a German officer, such as Israel Bloem, could they be sent for military training under cover of the Pioneer Corps. Then they underwent further covert training with No. 10 Commando – the Allied Commando – so that by the time they reached us they were proficient with firearms and at unarmed combat. The hundred-odd who came to Birdham were hand-picked by Bloem, John Morgan and others.

By volunteering to fight with British Commandos in Europe, they were immediately putting their lives on the line again. And of course, if their names or families had become known, they would have been in great danger, not only during the war, but after it as well. Unlike so many of their compatriots in occupied Europe, who had knuckled under to persecution, they had stalked the thugs of the SS, ambushed them and slit their throats before departing. They were magnificent young people, who had inherited their survival instincts from Charlemagne, Attila the Hun and the Israel of Abraham. They saw themselves as God's freedom fighters, crusaders who loved their native Germany and were determined to evict the Nazis. They made it their business to risk their own lives by returning to save their people, well knowing that if they were caught they were liable to be tortured, maimed or hacked to death.

For all their heroism, they were emotional, unhappy, uncertain, and nervous of their surroundings in the United Kingdom. They were in a foreign land, far from home, and many no longer had homes at all. It was thus all-important that they should be fully integrated into life at Birdham, and here no one was more effective than Susan, now second-in-command of the base and of the operation. A 24-year-old with her looks, charm and ability naturally won over the men in short order; but her patent sincerity soon endeared her to the women as well – and when they witnessed her professional skill as a fighting Commando, they gave her their whole-hearted support. When they found that she and her Wrens were preparing to go into Germany with them and face the same risks, all races, religions and creeds at Birdham became one.

If we trained hard, we also played hard, and when off duty the ship's company gave vent to their high spirits in wild games and practical jokes. Some people gave the impression of being totally irresponsible, but that was just their way of facing up to the dangers that lay ahead.

Fleming by no means approved of such hilarity. At heart he was a serious man, and to begin with he was shocked by some of the goings-on; but although he was my superior both in his appointment as commodore and in his rank as commander, he followed naval tradition and did not interfere with the running of my ship. In private he might say, 'This is bloody ridiculous!' but in public he made no comment. Soon, however, he overcame his inhibitions and joined in the fun, becoming the most outrageous practical joker of the lot.

We had sports competitions, plays, poetry readings and marvellous evenings of Jewish entertainment. On special occasions we lit a fire in the great hall of the manor house, and feasted on spit-roasts and mulled wine – for the German girls were the most brilliant foragers and, in spite of nationwide shortages of food and drink, never returned from a foray without substantial edible or drinkable booty. Needless to say, people had affairs, but Susan kept things under control by telling everyone to be discreet and to use condoms, which were issued free, so that there was no excuse for errors.

At first, strangely enough, we had little music: a couple of guitars, a mouth organ, a penny whistle, a pile of scratched 78rpm records, and of course the radio. But there was a dearth of dancing and singing and the usual navy music-hall turns.

Then, in a cellar, we discovered an old and dilapidated grand piano. The Freedom Fighters immediately commandeered it, dragged it up to ground level and set about repairing it. With one expert directing, and two or three semi-skilled hands helping, and with the importation of some spare parts from Chappell, the London specialists (acquired under the pretext of 'operational necessities'), we soon had a top-quality reconditioned Bechstein.

A few people could tinkle, one or two quite proficiently. But, as Susan knew well, music and the piano were the other half of my life.

I had played since I was four, and at Ampleforth I managed to scramble through the LRAM examination before scurrying away to the Royal Naval College at Dartmouth. There, by general demand and captain's order, my classical bent merged into the popular music of the era. Afterwards, with the help of my father's patient Carroll Gibbons, the leading dance pianist of the day, I started to adapt properly. As often as I could manage it, I was up in his apartment at the Savoy, practising under his direction, sometimes for two sessions a week.

My debt to Carroll was, and is, immense. It was not that he taught me to play specific notes or even harmonies: rather, he opened my mind to matters of interpretation, attitude, and the harmonic progression of the music of the 1940s.

At the start of every lesson he would say, 'Touch, attack, tempo and harmonic perfection. Never thump: the piano's a sensitive instrument.' It was this apparent contradiction in his orders – to 'attack sensitively' – that formed the basis of his own perfection. Listening to him and learning to play like him were pure joy. His instruction was electrifying, and gave me a standard of knowledge, appreciation and performance of which I had never before dreamt.

Later, whenever I passed through London on a Sunday, on leave or duty, I would look in at St James's, Spanish Place, and usually I would find Carroll there. He never said 'Hullo', but in his low Canadian drawl would whisper remarks like 'I have said three Hail Marys that you will remove your foot from the sustaining pedal and allow the melody to emerge untrammelled.'

During the war I often played with a Royal Navy or Combined Services band, and I was frequently at the piano in Wrenneries (Wrens' quarters) for dances. I also used to play at the Jokers' Club in Portsmouth, mostly for my own relaxation, and sometimes, strictly against naval regulations, I topped up my meagre pay by taking small fees.

Music had become an integral part of my life and well-being. Patricia and Susan, and later Fleming, all told me that when I played the piano I became warm and relaxed: a glow came into my eyes, they said, and colour to my face. For me it was an art and a profession which almost equalled that of being a sailor – but the Royal Navy always just came first.

Early in 1941, I made an accidental discovery which later turned into one of the best-guarded secrets in the communications war. One evening I was in the Jokers' Club with Patricia, and as I sat playing she went across to the bar to get new drinks. Then she found she had forgotten what I wanted, and, when she called a question across to me, I replied on impulse in Morse code concealed within the rhythm of the tune I was playing. I was amazed when, without further communication, she returned carrying exactly the drink I had had in mind. Suddenly we realised that we had invented a secret communication system of our own: we could say what we liked to each other, and no one else knew that a signal was being sent, still less understood the message.

For some time we did not appreciate the potential of what we had stumbled on. We tried out the system to send love messages, or other frivolities, using not only the piano but other instruments too, and even our singing voices. But our games came to an abrupt end one evening when we gave a demonstration for Morton. Instantly he classified the Creighton-Falkiner musical act as Top Secret: he forbade us ever to use it or even to talk about it again in public, and when Patricia made a light-hearted remark about getting royalties on the patent, he did not find it amusing.

The idea was so simple that we found it hard to believe that no one had used it already, especially as the World Service of the BBC was daily heading its broadcasts to occupied Europe with the opening bars of Beethoven's Fifth Symphony: da-da-da-*dah*, da-da-da-*dah*, the Morse for V for Victory. Our system was officially named Secret Musical Telegraphy Transmissions, or SMTT for short, and a few of us used it in France, with considerable success.

The easiest instrument to use was the piano, though some

people managed with flutes and other instruments. A musician in England could send a simple message to a brother-in-arms – a French resistance fighter in a café or bar, or anyone who was listening and knew the secret – without fear of arousing suspicion. Naturally, both parties had to be good musicians and telegraphists, and the sender had to play popular pieces that seemed natural for broadcasts. Within the music Morse rhythms were played on a particular note or group of notes, or on their octaves within particular harmonies. Later, the system became more refined and developed into complex harmonic progressions.

In the tightest of security our idea was enthusiastically taken up by the BBC and used for its secret transmissions. Many vital messages for our agents in Europe, which could not have been sent in code or in poems, went out on the air both instrumentally and vocally. Incredibly, few of the people involved knew what a service they were rendering to the Allies' secret war: even that great star Vera Lynn, the Forces' Sweetheart, sang on without realising what the pulse of her delivery contained.

One of my most moving experiences at Birdham took place with the reconditioning of the Bechstein. We had set it up in the huge ballroom, which doubled as mess-deck and wardroom combined, and one evening I chose a moment when the place was deserted to try out the instrument and see whether I could still play; for I had not touched a piano for nine months, since my hands had been damaged by the Gestapo, and, even more important, since Patricia's death.

For a moment, as I sat at the keyboard, my hands shook and my musical spark became dull with grief for the girl I had lost. Then I touched a note, and another, and another. I found that the piano was now in superb condition: Bechsteins had always been my favourites, and this one was as good as any I had known.

I took full advantage of being on my own. A light touch of Bach's 'Amen' and the *adagio cantabile* from Beethoven's 'Pathétique' sonata led on to Gershwin and 'Summertime', thence to *Showboat* and 'Can't Help Lovin' that Man of Mine'. All my grief, my devotion and my hopes poured out through my fingers. It was the best I had ever played. The music flowed as if someone else was at the keyboard and I was just a listener.

So absorbed was I that I never once paused to look behind me, and I did not realise that the room was filling up with the off-duty men and women of Op JB. The music drew them from across the grounds, from the outlying Nissen huts and other buildings, and they flooded in like rats to the Pied Piper. When at last I stopped and turned to see them there, they did not speak or applaud, but stood gaping at me, moved to silence by the music, and by the discovery that their operational commander could play.

For a second or two I was bewildered, almost overwhelmed by the high charge of emotion in the air. There was only one way out; and, as usual, Susan provided it. 'How about "Pardon Me, Boy"?' she asked. I sat back on the stool and let fly with Glen Miller's 'Chattanooga Choo Choo'.

The place went berserk. A few people began to dance, then others joined in, and soon the floor was packed with whirling couples. Inhibitions vanished, and the evening did a tremendous amount to consolidate a close-knit family atmosphere at Birdham. Music suddenly brought everyone together. Bonds of deep affection were forged, and the festivities established me as one of the gang – which, piano or no piano, I truly was.

From that moment the Bechstein contributed handsomely to the Section's dances, concerts and musical comedy performances. Yet my own performances were soon outshone by those of Israel Bloem, who really fired people's imagination.

From his record we discovered that before the war he had been a trained classical violinist. Fleming managed to borrow a suitable instrument in London and brought it down, but it took hours of persuasion by us, and private practice by Bloem, before he would consent to play in public. Then came the poignant moment when the ship's company assembled after dinner one evening to hear him.

With one of his GFF girls as a partner, and making no concessions to his missing fingers, he launched into Brahms's Violin and Piano Sonata in A Major. For a while his bowing was messy: he missed notes and played some passages incorrectly. But then technical problems seemed to fall away, and he allowed his heart to rule. The result was magic: as his artistry blazed forth, we were overwhelmed by admiration for his talent and courage.

* * *

With the Allied armies tightening their grip on Germany, the atmosphere at Birdham became ever more tense, and inevitably a few men and women in the operational group did not measure up to the high standards required in ability, suitability or discipline. Because of the strict security, it was very rare for anyone who lapsed to be offered a second chance, and several times, with great reluctance, I had to order somebody's removal.

What happened to the people who failed, or where they went, I never knew. The difficulty was that they had had access to vital secrets, which must at all costs be preserved for the foreseeable future. Some of the defaulters, I assumed, went to the Section 18b detention centre on the Isle of Man: about others I really did not care to think, for I knew that on one or two previous occasions the extreme penalty had been invoked. This made my responsibilities weigh heavily indeed.

From 1 February all leave was cancelled, in case we had to go into action suddenly, and officers were allowed ashore – that is, off the base – only with special permission. Then on the fifth the feelers we had put out in Dublin, seeking to renew contact with Ribbentrop, at last brought a satisfactory reply.

On 8 February Fleming and I flew from Croydon to Lisbon in an aircraft with Portuguese markings. During this first leg of the journey we were ostensibly diplomats, Foreign Office couriers travelling in civilian clothes, on diplomatic passports, and nobody interfered with our baggage, which contained a small radio set, batteries and personal weapons, all of which we had negotiated in advance with the Germans. As usual on such outings, Fleming looked extremely smart and wore an Old Etonian tie (black with a diagonal light-blue stripe). But during a one-night stop-over at the luxurious Hotel Aviz a German contact ushered us into the downstairs gentlemen's lavatory, where he took our photographs and measurements with scrupulous care, explaining that if he had come to the bedroom we were sharing, alien eyes might have spotted him and reported something suspicious.

We were relieved to find that of the various odd bodies passing frequently along the hotel corridor, and casting sideways glances at our bedroom door, three were from the M sub-section (Portugal). One was Caroline Hurst, a junior operational Wren officer much admired by Fleming. But on this type of mission the rule was strictly 'hands off', and we slept soundly.

Next morning at 0530 hours we were airborne for Basle aboard a Swiss aircraft, again travelling as diplomats. At Basle we changed planes and went on in a local aircraft to Zurich. There we were greeted openly by Ribbentrop's emissary – the man I had met outside Dublin – now dressed in the uniform of an Obergruppenführer of the SS. Having met us with two of his men, he took us off in an open Mercedes flying Nazi flags from the front mudguards, and we drove north-east, nearly forty miles, to a castle overlooking Lake Constance, hard by the point where the Swiss, Austrian and German borders meet. At that stage of the trip Fleming was quite nervous, and kept asking me how I thought we were doing.

Evidently Ribbentrop had ordered the best for us. The castle was a very substantial building on several floors, and its huge rooms were sumptuously decorated, with fine, heavy furniture and large oil paintings. We wondered who had owned the place, and it occurred to both of us simultaneously that this was probably one of the very properties we were hoping to repossess. Late in the evening offers of sex, both straightforward and homosexual, were laid before us with charm and abandon.

'I always wanted to do it at Eton,' whispered Fleming mischievously as a fair-haired youth made advances. 'Let's try it now!' But since there was no knowing what an entanglement might lead to, we politely declined.

Next morning, leaving Fleming at the castle I drove back into Zurich with the emissary, who took me to a bank, and, in the manager's office, opened an account in my name with an initial credit of £100,000, in those days a phenomenal sum, perhaps equal to £3 million today. Having done some specimen signatures, I was handed a note of the confidential account numbers. (Alas, I never drew a single franc.) Fleming, meanwhile, was being politely but closely questioned about his association with me, and he brought out our well-researched story about how we had often worked together, he as the backroom brain, and I as the boy in the field.

We passed a sybaritic weekend, eating, drinking, walking and talking. The war seemed far away. Then on Tuesday, 13 February, we drove down the hill and round the edge of the lake, to cross

Christopher Robin...
(Left)

My father, nearest,
and Harold
Abrahams, centre.
Two Olympic
champions
(Right)

The winning relay
team. Olympics,
Antwerp 1920. My
father, front right
(Left)

My father's old friend Dickie
Mountbatten with his wife,
Edwina, 1941 (above)

A rare picture of Morton (M) with
Churchill; " Tigger" and "Owl"
(below)

My "Uncle", better known as
Joachim von Ribbentrop, with
Oheim Ciano (above)

10, Downing Street,
Whitehall.

October, 1954

Dear John,

Lord Ismay has told me of your wishes but
I am afraid that it is still impossible for
anything to be done and you must not now speak
of these matters. When I die, then, if your
conscience so allows, tell your story for you
have given and suffered much for England.
If you do speak, then speak nothing but the
truth, omitting of course those matters which
you know can never be revealed. Do not seek
to protect me for I am content to be judged by
history. But do, I pray you, seek to protect
those who did their duty honestly in the hope of
a future world with freedom and justice for all.

Yours y sincerely,

Winston Churchill

John Ainsworth-Davis.

Letter from Churchill
(Left)

Berlin in ruins
(Below)

Bormann
(Far left)

Broderick Hartley
(Left)

Bormann and Hitler
(Bottom left)

Broderick Hartley
(Far bottom left)

Bormann
(Right)

Hanne Nelson and
Broderick Hartley
(Below right)

Dr. Friedrich Bergold, Bormann's counsel at Nuremberg
(Above)

Taking a break with Peggy Adams, star of *The Blue Lamp*, during the filming of *Murder at 3am,* written and produced by the author in 1952
(Left)

16 Victoria Square
London S.W.1.

14th October, 1963.

To: <u>Commander "James Bond" R.N.</u>

He has always been my very dear friend and wartime
comrade-in-arms, John Ainsworth-Davis.

The enclosed contribution comes with my grateful
thanks and vivid remembrance of our operation "James Bond",
in which "Piglet", Martin Bormann, was clandestinely
transported from wartime Berlin to England via the German
waterways in April/May 1945. This eventually resulted in
the recovery of some 90% of the Nazi assets plundered from
occupied Europe, which had been deposited in neutral countries,
mainly Switzerland.

Without any doubt, you and our operation were my
secret inspiration for all that followed; a secret that I
have never revealed to anyone else. It gives me great
pleasure to tell you now.

I have missed you, and your bloody piano.

As ever,

Your most secret friend,

Ian F Fleming

If you do go ahead with a book on the subject,
you may use this note any way you will. Publish it,
if it helps you.

Time off with the
beloved piano while
directing at Warner
Bros., Hollywood
(Above)

Letter from Ian
Fleming
(Left)

Whilst acting with Noîl Coward and Eva Gabor in *Nude with Violin* and *Present Laughter* on Broadway, 1957
(Left)

Directing the film Judgement in Prague in Czechoslavakia in 1967 with, amongst others, Charles Aznavour, Shirley Ann Field and Martine Carol. Otherwise cover for further intelligence ops, this time for NATO
(Below)

into Germany. A few kilometres up the road towards Stuttgart we stopped at a small villa, where, in the garage, we tried on our newly made Waffen-SS uniforms. It was Ribbentrop's idea – and a good one – that we should pose as members of the Waffen-SS, the military arm of the Schutz-Staffeln, rather than the police, Blackshirt, side of the organisation. Ribbentrop knew Bormann was surrounded by numerous members of the Blackshirt SS, who acted as bodyguards (among other roles, such as that of exterminators in concentration camps), and if we arrived wearing their uniform they would be immediately supicious, because they had never seen us before. If, on the other hand, we appeared to be Waffen-SS, people were much less likely to ask questions.

One feature which did attract attention was my beard, neatly trimmed though it was. Beards were generally frowned on in the SS, but we quickly turned this fact to our advantage. When in public I wore a bandage over my mouth, and carried an expertly forged medical certificate explaining why the dressing was there. The bandage, making it impossible for me to utter, effectively concealed the fact that I spoke no German.

The grey-green material of the uniforms was rather heavy, but they fitted well, and in the privacy of the garage we practised a few Nazi salutes on each other, crying, 'Heil Hitler!' and raising our right arms, palms down, as we tried to keep straight faces. Emerging, we received German identity cards, with authentic stamps and photographs. A few minutes later we were away again on the 200-kilometre drive to Heidelberg. Burnt-out vehicles littered the roadside, the victims of Allied air attacks; and because of the air threat, principally from British and American Beaufighters, we had to stay off the main routes, winding laboriously through the suburbs of Stuttgart and keeping to minor roads in the country.

On the way we must have been stopped thirty times. At every road-block our identity cards were examined, but they were never challenged. Whenever someone addressed a question to Fleming or myself, the emissary replied on our behalf, and his word was never questioned.

Late in the evening we reached Heidelberg and branched left to the hamlet of Weinheim. Overlooking the village on a small hill stood an elegant, two-storey villa, which became our home for a week.

Again, we were in the lap of luxury; but the opulence of our surroundings could not make us feel comfortable. Irked by the delay, and itching to make progress, we had to be careful not to talk shop indoors: instead, we saved vital matters for our long walks, during which we were followed at a discreet distance by two SS officers.

Our hosts and escorts frequently apologised for the lack of action: the Reichsminister was extremely busy, they said, but he would be with us as soon as possible. Meanwhile, to communicate with Morton and let him know how we were doing, I fell back on my old friend the piano. Finding that the villa contained an old grand, in pristine condition, Fleming and I proclaimed our enthusiasm for music, and I made a point of playing in the evenings, with him standing alongside and turning the sheets when I indicated (he himself not having a clue how to read the notes). Then, under the pretence of tuning the piano, we wired it, running a transmitter wire down the inside of one of its legs, out of a window, up the wall and into our bedroom. There, beneath a cupboard floor, we set up our small transceiver radio; we wound its seventy-foot aerial round the outside of the roof by slinging a padded hook over the ridge at night.

On this occasion, in a variant of my normal method of SMTT, I wired up three particular notes and used them as Morse signal keys: E♭ and A♭ above middle C became live for Morse transmission, as did D♭ below. Whenever I pressed one of these, a pulse went out through the radio upstairs.

One evening, at a transmission time arranged in advance, I entertained our hosts with a medley while Fleming, in the bedroom, made contact with the M Section control station at the farmhouse near Bletchley Park. The call went out through our own mobile relay unit, which was moving eastwards through France behind the Allied advance, and then was near Châlons-sur-Marne. The fact that I began hitting the live notes went unnoticed by the Germans, but to Jane Lawson, our leading expert in codes and ciphers, it was the music she wanted to hear. In six minutes she had received my message; ten minutes later it had been decoded, and eight minutes after that it was in Morton's hands.

At last, on the morning of Tuesday, 20 February, I was escorted to the library, and there, waiting to receive me, was my father's old schoolfriend and patient, the German Foreign Minister, Joachim von Ribbentrop. As soon as the SS guards had left the room, he gave me the warmest possible greeting, taking my right hand in his and putting his left arm round my shoulders.

'My dear John!' he beamed. 'How good to see you!'

'*Oheim*!' I replied, involuntarily bringing out the German family word for 'uncle', by which I had known him as a boy.

'What a big fellow you are now!' he exclaimed.

Ribbentrop himself was a large man, and by then he had become a little paunchy. When I had last seen him, over two years earlier, we had been about the same height. But since then, between eighteen and almost twenty-one, I had gone on growing, and now, at six feet two and a half inches, I was a couple of inches taller than he.

With his hand still on my shoulder, he led me to an armchair.

'How is your dear father?'

'Fine, thank you. If he knew I was here, I'm sure he'd want me to give you his best wishes.'

'Good! Where is he now?'

'Working in the hospital at Cosford, the same as ever.' Ribbentrop knew my father had joined the RAF as a surgeon – one of the few displaying pilot's wings – but I wasn't going to let on that he was working with the foremost plastic surgeon of the day, Archibald McIndoe, at East Grinstead, and at other hospitals where badly burnt casualties were treated.

'At least it is safer in London now,' said Ribbentrop sanctimoniously.

'I don't know,' I replied. 'These damned V–2s of yours are pretty dangerous.'

'Yes, I suppose so. I'm sorry.' The Reichsminister rang for coffee, and, until it came, continued to make small talk. Listening to him, I found myself torn between feelings of genuine affection for the man who had been so kind to me when I was young, and contempt for the pompous, common, posturing ass I was now mature enough to recognise. I saw that he was carried away by the fluency of his own English, and was talking a lot of nonsense.

But then, when a servant had brought coffee and left, he suddenly became serious.

'*Lieber* John,' he began confidentially, 'what I am going to say now is for your ears only.'

'Of course.'

Germany had lost the war, or was about to, he announced, pacing up and down in agitation. Defeat was inevitable: it could be only a matter of time before the Third Reich collapsed. And when that happened, he wished to disappear. In the final chaos of disintegration, he would simply vanish.

He paused, looking at me, and suddenly asked, 'Can you help?'

I was so surprised that I gave a bit of a start. 'How?'

'By arranging my escape from Germany.'

I spread my hands as if in doubt. 'Well . . . Surely you don't need help? If you went now, before it's too late, you could easily slip out through one of your legations?'

'Maybe – but there is something else.' He went on to declare his major ambition: to seize for himself the vast assets the Nazis had accumulated abroad, so that he could live out the rest of his life in comfort and anonymity.

'Where would you go?' I asked.

'South America, perhaps. But there is one man I need to suborn. Somehow I have to bring him under my control. You know who I mean?'

Adrenalin started to race round my bloodstream, but I took care to give no sign of excitement. I shook my head.

'Bormann! Martin Bormann, the Führer's secretary. He is also head of the Party Chancellery, and personally controls all the assets outside the Reich. You have heard of him?'

Again I shook my head. 'I'm sorry. We don't know about Bormann in England.'

'It doesn't matter. My idea is this. Through you, I propose to offer Bormann a means of escape. For bringing him out of the ruins of the Reich, I shall demand a payment of twenty-five million marks. But then, as soon as we are out, I shall hand him over to you British, or liquidate him – whatever you suggest.'

I held my excitement carefully in check and tried to look worried.

'I'll make it very well worth your while,' said Ribbentrop quickly. '*Extremely* well worth your while . . .'

'I need to ask my colleague whether it's possible.'

To give myself time to think, I began to describe James Bond's character and achievements. In particular I gave him credit for building up the small unit of renegades and criminals he commanded, a formation which would be indispensable in any operation to lift senior Nazi officers out of Germany. In mentioning this unit I was embroidering rather than inventing. When he worked in naval intelligence, Fleming had indeed commanded – and still did – a group consisting largely of tough, adventurous young Royal Navy and Royal Marine Commandos, whom he called his 'Red Indians'. When they achieved no mean success not only on operations against the enemy, but also among the local female population round their base, he characteristically changed their name from the 30th Assault Unit, or 30th AU, to the 30th IAU, or Indecent Assault Unit, a move which caused uproar at the Admiralty.*

At first Ribbentrop did not seem convinced about my friend Herr Bond. The fewer people who knew our plans, the better, he said.

'You can rely on him absolutely,' I said. 'Apart from anything else, he went to Eton.'

This information had a ridiculous effect – as I knew it would on someone as snobbish as Ribbentrop. When I had Fleming brought in and introduced, his charm and natural flair as an actor worked wonders.

I gave a brief outline of what Ribbentrop had proposed, and then Fleming expatiated on his private army. In a relaxed, self-deprecating and almost supercilious manner, with plenty of pauses, he presented his secret unit as a gang of unscrupulous deserters from the regular forces, who had joined up with us and were prepared to carry out any dubious mission for satisfactory rewards. When Ribbentrop asked how the group would be infiltrated into Germany, and how we could contrive an escape plan,

---

* Early in 1945 Fleming had been called before Admiral of the Fleet Sir Andrew 'Cuts' Cunningham, then First Sea Lord, who told him that people had been complaining about the activities of his 'bloody Red Indians'. Fleming was ordered to disband the unit without further ado, or to make it part of the M Section. Whatever he did, he managed to keep it in being for the remainder of the war.

Fleming stalled him by saying that he would not divulge any plan or methods, for security reasons; but he reassured our host by reminding him that in every past operation involving the Foreign Minister, I had served him most loyally and efficiently. On the next occasion, Fleming insisted, I would prove no less reliable.

Ribbentrop seemed to accept this – and then he began an extraordinary confession. For the next ten minutes we listened in amazement as he gave an emotional account of his problems. He did not get on with many of the Nazi leaders, he confided, and his relationship with Bormann was particularly difficult. Bormann was such a low fellow! So common! He claimed that he, Ribbentrop, alone of the Nazi hierarchy had any breeding or manners: the rest were without social standing or education. They deserved nothing. He, in contrast, was a gentleman and a man of the world. Had it not been foretold in Valhalla that he would inherit Nazi gold? Now he intended to make the prophecy come true. (What he meant by this I was never quite certain.)

Feigning ignorance, we asked where Bormann was likely to be over the next few weeks.

'In Berlin,' was the answer. '*Ganz bestimmt* – absolutely for sure. He is with Hitler in the Chancellery almost all the time. He still sometimes travels to Berchtesgaden, but less and less. At the end, as your armies close in, Berlin is where he will be. He will go to ground in one of the bunkers there.'

Firmly believing that all three of us were gentlemen, Ribbentrop proposed what he called a gentlemen's agreement. We professed ourselves happy to go along with it, and said we would make urgent inquiries into the possibility of setting up a rescue party. Once we had everything in order, we would let him know, and then wait for him to summon us. As we said goodbye, he took both my hands in his, stared into my eyes, and again repeated that he had every confidence in me.

That evening, after Ribbentrop had left for Berlin, Fleming and I had to bottle up our excitement until we could take another walk in the hills. Then, safely in the open, we let off exclamations of amazement at the way Ribbentrop had conceived almost exactly the same idea as we had, and had come up with it before we had any need to reveal cards of our own. Little did we realise that Bormann had been working on the Foreign Minister for his own ends. Of course, neither of us had the slightest intention of keeping our agreement with Ribbentrop. At almost the same moment during the discussion we had decided that a double double-cross was in order. Ribbentrop would pull the first one over Bormann; then we and the M Section would pull the second over Ribbentrop and Bormann together, taking both them and the Nazi assets. Such action clearly lay within the terms of reference given us by Morton and the Prime Minister.

As we walked, Fleming demonstrated the clarity of his mind by running through possible sequences of events in fast and forceful exposition. Bormann, he pointed out, must be a crafty customer to have achieved the position he had: he might well plan to double-cross Ribbentrop – and us. 'If we get hold of him at all,' said Fleming, 'we'll need to keep him chained to us.' He had been impressed by the evident closeness of my relationship with Ribbentrop, and he reckoned that our prospects looked good. The danger was that, if anything, events were moving too quickly. The Allies had not yet crossed the Rhine, and the full pressure of encirclement was not yet upon the Germans. Our potential victims still had a lot of time and space in which to manoeuvre. 'Play hard to get,' Fleming advised. 'If Bormann does call for us, we mustn't seem too keen.'

That evening I again entertained the company at the piano in the main living-room, while Fleming made radio contact with England. Then, in a long and nerve-racking Morse transmission, I sent Morton a situation report. To receive an answer, our arrangement was that we would make contact again an hour later. This we managed, to be told that we were to return to base immediately.

We had already arranged with Ribbentrop's emissary that, within reason, we would be free to leave at any time of our choosing, to set arrangements in train at our end. So we set off next morning, and were back at Birdham three days later, on 24 February. The groundbait had been put out, and we settled down to wait for a bite.

9

Water Power

Five of our Freedom Fighters came from Berlin, and with their help we began intensive study of the city. What excited us most was the profusion of waterways: not only the rivers Spree and Havel, but also the lakes such as the Grosser Müggelsee and the Wannsee, and the network of canals which linked the natural channels in an intricate web. For people such as ourselves, familiar with every kind of waterborne activity, the whole area looked immensely attractive. This was kayak country.

All information was grist to our mill. Even old tourist brochures from pre-war Berlin, describing the Grosser Müggelsee as *ein Wasserparadies* (a water paradise) had their uses, for they showed us that the lake was surrounded by wooded hills. Expensive houses were tucked away in the hills, of course, but clearly there were plenty of places to hide kayaks and other stores. From somewhere I discovered that the rowing events of the 1936 Olympics had been held on this very lake, and that in the double sculls a British pair, Beresford and Southwood, had won the gold medal, a feat which made me think of my father at Antwerp in 1920.

We saw that the Grosser Müggelsee, in the south-eastern suburbs of the city, was over two miles long, from east to west, and nearly a mile and a half wide: quite big enough for the landing and take-off of a sea-plane such as a Catalina. The Spree flowed into it at the south-east corner and out again at the north-west, then right through the centre of Berlin and out to the River Havel in the west. Thereafter the Havel ran southwards out of Berlin, through the big and little Wannsee and round many islands – other water paradises – and on past Potsdam and Brandenburg to the Elbe.

Because the whole system seemed ideal for kayaks or war-canoes, at an early stage we conceived the idea that our operation should be water-based: a snatch party could slip away westwards (downstream) along the Spree and Havel, and then continue on the mighty Elbe, towards the north-west, until it met the advancing Allied armies. We had the personnel, the equipment and the experience for just such an undertaking. Not only were there highly trained Commandos from both the Navy and the Marines and the remnants of my own old unit COPP; but M Section Royal Marines had trained with the Royal Marine Special Boat Section, the 'Cockleshell Heroes'. What those people did not know about silent approach from the water wasn't worth discovering.

For pilotage, we had all the latest Army Ordinance maps delivered to us hot off the presses before any other unit had sight of them. The back of each sheet carried precise information about the positions of civilian and service control points, as well as those of hospitals, arms dumps, bomb shelters, lavatories and other vital installations. Besides the maps, we had Admiralty charts embellished with extra detail provided by our scouts on the ground, and German navy charts not just petty-pilfered by the GFFs, but – even more important – corrected and brought up to date by them after a down-river reconnaissance all the way to the Elbe. Because we would be travelling at night, we would need special information: on the lakes, for instance, we would not be able to take bearings, because there would be no natural features in sight. Instead, we would have to rely on forward scouts, waiting in set places, to guide us on.

As information came in, we built an enormous relief model of the Berlin waterways, ten feet across, with every lake, river, stream, bridge, canal and lock as accurate as we could make it. Then we set to memorise every detail, so that we would know, for instance, which each bridge was as we came to it, without having to refer to a map. Apart from Fleming, myself and Susan, nobody knew the precise purpose of our operation: clearly, we were hoping to snatch someone from Berlin, and bring him out by water, but the identity of our target remained absolutely secret.

Much of our attention was focused on kayaks, which were delivered to us at Birdham in kit form. In one package came the main canvas sheath, folded up together with its inboard stowage pockets and buoyancy bags on either beam; the other bundle contained the wooden struts, spars, deckboards, head-ropes and so on. There were also floats, to be strapped on to the packages so that they did not sink if they were parachuted into water. All operational hands went through drills to assemble and disassemble a kayak until they had done it five times, three times at night and twice in the sea. Unlike the much more robust kayaks used by the Special Boat Section, these fragile craft – ten feet long, with a beam of two feet six inches – would not have survived a minute in the open sea with any swell or wind; but they were ideal for calm rivers and sheltered inland waters, and they were so light that, if necessary, the crew of two could easily lift one out of the water and carry it overland round an obstacle.

The more we trained, the better integrated the whole sub-section became, not least because of the lead given by Fleming. By his own admission he had grown physically soft during his time in Room 39, but now he made amends by once more hurling himself into our tough and dangerous work-outs with rare enthusiasm, so that, although often hurt, he rapidly gained fitness and proficiency. In our personal contests of unarmed combat, I was able to defeat him easily at first, but by the end we were fighting level. Ironically enough, he found himself in greater difficulties when he was set to tackle the Wrens: his natural inhibitions made him reluctant to attack the girls all-out, with the result that they inflicted heavy punishment on him.

No one had him more confused than Susan Kemp. He was strongly attracted to her, and yet could not make out the very close relationship she obviously enjoyed with me. Like the other Wrens, Susan found Fleming fascinating, and the barbed exchanges which took place between them entertained the whole company. One evening, when she had the nerve to mention his reputation as a chocolate sailor, he agreed that he had been called that at the Admiralty, but struck back by asking, 'Would you like a bite?'

Quick as a flash Susan answered, 'It depends: are you milk chocolate or plain?'

In training Fleming had one psychological block – over the use of

109

firearms. He blazed away happily enough on the ranges, but until then he had never managed to bring himself to kill anybody: he had tried, but been unable to pull the trigger. Time would show what would happen when we got to Berlin.

Although based at Birdham, he spent some time with his 30th Assault Unit at Guildford, and a good many days in London, working with Morton on the strategic plans. There were many difficult decisions to be taken, or at any rate thought about, in advance. What would we do if our allies got wind of our plans, before the operation, during its initial stages, or during the actual escape down the Havel? What if Bormann proved difficult, or even dangerous, to handle? (That was relatively simple: our doctor, Jenny Wright, would quieten him down with a tranquillising injection.) What if the Freedom Fighters discovered who our prisoner was? What if our position became impossibly dangerous? Should we just kill Bormann and try to save our own skins? (The answer to this was an emphatic 'No'. The rest of us were expendable, but Bormann was definitely not.) Such questions were vigorously debated by our command group; once Fleming had made a decision, it was incorporated into his operational rules, which I was then formally 'requested and required' to carry out.

All through this training period elaborate precautions were taken to maintain Fleming's own cover and security. As far as the rest of the intelligence world was concerned, he was still on appointment to Commonwealth naval intelligence divisions in India, the Far East, Australia and New Zealand, or making occasional trips to Jamaica. There was no trace in any official document of the fact that he was leading a Most Secret operation from a base near Portsmouth.

Neither he nor I had any problem settling into the command structure Morton had devised. Acting like a commodore first-class on a warship, Fleming was in overall strategic command, but I, the operational commander, still ran the sub-section without interference. We had got on well from the start, but as the weeks went on our relationship deepened into one of real friendship and mutual respect. The sixteen-year gap between us seemed irrelevant, and in the evenings, at the pub, we spent many a cheerful hour trying to outdo each other with our respective genealogies. Fleming was descended from John of Gaunt on one side and the ancient kings of Scotland on the other, while my line went back through the Coutts banking family to Robert Creighton, Bishop of Bath and Wells in the seventeenth century, and thence to Red Comyn, who was slain by Robert the Bruce, and Charlemagne. On my McQuarrie mother's side I could trace the line to a great-uncle, Lachlan Macquarie, who had been Governor of South Australia, and finally to King MacAlpine of Scotland. Loud was our disbelief when we discovered that Red Comyn was our mutual ancestor.

For several weeks I remained puzzled by Fleming's character. Then one day I watched a film starring Leslie Howard as the Scarlet Pimpernel, and suddenly I discerned an extraordinary affinity between my commanding officer and the character on the screen. With his drawl, his arrogance, his upper-class attitudes and his snobbishness, Fleming was in many ways a typical Old Etonian; but gradually I saw that he was deliberately exaggerating these characteristics – perhaps out of shyness – as a kind of personal cover, and that underneath his slightly caddish exterior he was kind, helpful, determined and brave. In other words, he was a modern version of Sir Percy Blakeney, the foppish and apparently useless nobleman, of illustrious descent, with an inane laugh and a maddening drawl, who, in Baroness Orczy's novel, shows infinite guile and courage rescuing French aristocrats during the French Revolution. On the surface Fleming might appear to be a chocolate sailor, but underneath he was capable of leading the most dangerous undercover operations. He was the aristo leading Operation James Bond, and I was his henchman, a latter-day Sir Andrew Ffoulkes.

Full of excitement at my discovery, I got my sister to have a seal specially made, representing a small, star-shaped flower. When Fleming next had occasion to sign a memorandum at Birdham, I asked if I might imprint it for him. I lit a match, held it to the wick at the end of the bar of sealing-wax, and, as the molten wax dripped on to the paper, I pushed the seal into it.

Looking down, he muttered, 'Good God! Whatever gave you that idea?'

In fact he knew perfectly well. Until then it had never occurred to him that he was a reincarnation of Sir Percy Blakeney, but from the moment I brought out the truth, a new relationship opened up between us.

One evening after supper he and I settled down with glasses of brandy in front of the fire in the library, lying back on cushions piled on the floorboards. 'You bottle things up too much, Christopher,' he began. 'It's always better if you can let them out and talk to someone you can trust, someone who's become fond of you. So what about K-XVII?'

K-XVII! I hadn't heard the name since December 1941. The whole terrible episode had played through my mind when I sought out Churchill in the Hole in the Ground, but nobody else had ever mentioned it to me. Now, suddenly, here it was again. Before I could say anything, Fleming began to recite a stream of details.

'Five minutes after midday on 28 November 1941, Dutch submarine K-XVII, commanded by Lieutenant-Commander Besançon, approaches a position in the Pacific, latitude 43° 30′ north, longitude 155° 20′ east, approximately 280 miles north-east of Japan's Tankan Bay. There she sights a fleet of Japanese warships. They've been making a three-leg zig-zag course. Commander Besançon correctly calculates this to be a course-made-good – a direct track – of 088° (true). This will bring them to Hawaii and Pearl Harbour, eight hundred nautical miles ahead . . .'

I stared at him dumbstruck. How could he know all this? Then I noticed his fingers tapping on the floorboards. They were beating out the Morse for 'NC6'. As in the distress signal, SOS, there was no separation between the letters and the number, but I immediately recognised the rhythm of a familiar secret code: the call-sign of my naval controller on Operation SUBEND.

'Yes, Christopher,' said Fleming quietly. ' I was your controller. I was NC6. I pressed your button. But I didn't know you, or your side of the story.'

So I told him what had happened. I told him how I had witnessed the destruction of K-XVII and all her crew, whom I had come to know well over the previous few days. I related how fused canisters of cyanide gas and high explosive had been taken aboard at my direction, disguised as Christmas gifts of food and drink from Queen Wilhelmina and our Admiral, Submarines, Sir Max Horton. From the safety of a Berwick flying boat I had watched as the aircraft suddenly shuddered, and an enormous explosion vomited out great spouts of water, together with broken-up crates of stores, bits of men, oil and oddments of equipment. It was as if a colossal underwater creature had swallowed a submarine, chewed up its human and mechanical contents, and then been violently sick.

I wondered how long the oil would keep the sharks away. I wondered how many Dutch mothers and fathers would be left grieving over the loss of their young sons. Above all, I wondered what they would say or do if they knew that their valiant submariners had been sacrificed simply because the highest authorities in Britain and America did not trust them to keep their mouths shut.*

Now at Birdham, overcome by the memories, I could not hold back the tears, and lay there on the floor racked by emotion. Fleming was on his feet immediately. Quickly he brought me another brandy, and sat down beside me. 'Good gracious me, dear old fellow,' he said. 'Don't take it so hard, my very dear old chap.' Then, as if to help me recover, he revealed that he had not only helped direct the operation: he had also been involved in the cover-up afterwards. He told me he had been required to call on Queen Wilhelmina, who was living in exile near Reading, and explain to her what had happened, as well as to alter the submarine's records with Far East Naval Command.

Fleming's energy and intelligence became an inspiration to all at Birdham, not least because he took the trouble to get to know every man and woman, English, French or German, and to learn his or her background and interests. With his excellent German, he could talk freely to the Freedom Fighters in their own language, and so established a special rapport with them.

Under his acute yet benevolent leadership, individuals blossomed. One of Susan's ablest Wrens was Third Officer Caroline Saunders, a tall, sensitive red-head, all legs and arms, attractive overall but a bit angular, like an overgrown filly, and at twenty the same age as myself. Shorter and older (at twenty-six) but no less effective was Surgeon-Lieutenant Jenny Wright, who had freckles and brown hair. A trained Commando, she was also a serious-minded doctor, with an engaging habit of giving vent to sudden spurts of humour. On the signals side, we were much

* For the background to this incident, see Appendix.

indebted to Third Officer Penny Wirrell, who was Scottish, small and squirrel-like, with a pointed, inquisitive nose and mousey hair. A real professional, she jealously guarded every item of her equipment.

Among the Freedom Fighters, Israel Bloem was admirably backed up by his second-in-command, Captain Hannah Fierstein. Minute – barely five feet tall, with a doll-like figure – she always looked like a naughty schoolgirl, even though, at twenty-six, she was one of the veterans in the party. Not only did she have a degree in philosophy from the Sorbonne: she was also an ace at unarmed combat and weapons-handling, and as tough as anyone on the base. One day she achieved instant fame within the Section when Bloem whacked her, for not being as polite as he would have wished – whereupon she promptly snatched his cane and hit him back.

More immediately impressive was Lieutenant Christa Shulberg, who, in spite of her name, was not Jewish at all. Her six-foot frame, silver-blond hair and wasp-waist gave her the look of a Nordic Amazon, and she combined great strength and endurance with total femininity. Powerful yet gentle, decisive yet obedient, always thinking of others, she once distinguished herself particularly during a grenade exercise.

We were training with plastic Type 62 grenades, which you detonated by unscrewing a cap and allowing the weighted tape underneath to unwind. This in turn released a metal ball, which made an electrical connection and set off the detonator. One of the very young commandos, having unscrewed the cap, dropped his grenade and stood looking at it, frozen in panic. Had it gone off, it could easily have killed everyone present; but Christa flung herself face down on it, held the tape in position, and shouted at everyone else to scatter at the double. She then picked herself up, wound the tape tightly back into position and screwed the cap on again. Having carried the grenade slowly and carefully back to the armoury, she returned to her group and whacked the stuffing out of the offender – and then burst into tears and ran off. Later she put herself on report before Bloem for striking one of her people: and he, not knowing whether to whack her or recommend her for a medal, did both.

In the middle of February Bloem ordered four of his people, who were already in Berlin near the Grosser Müggelsee, to step up their efforts to make contact with local people and identify possible safe houses for when the main raiding party came in. They were also to reconnoitre the state of the waterways and report back to the UK, routing their radio calls through relays in western Germany.

At Birdham, information came in continuously, not only from Berlin, but from agents throughout Europe, both inside and outside the areas still held by the Germans. Fleming generally took the morning conference at which new intelligence was discussed, but often Morton himself presided: an office and bedroom were kept ready for him, and he frequently stayed overnight. Whenever he did, we were liable to be subjected to one of his ghost stories, which he told after dinner at length and with immense relish, blithely ignoring the fact that most of his listeners had heard the tales countless times before.

One favourite concerned a country house which he himself had taken, in spite of the fact that several previous occupants had committed suicide by jumping into the lake. Going to sleep there one night, he had an oppressive dream, in which something seemed to be coming at him very fast. Cornered, unable to escape, he woke up covered with sweat. An impulse made him walk along the passage to look at the list of the house's previous tenants – and he found that his own name had appeared at the bottom. He therefore called in his old friend the Reverend C. C. Martindale, SJ, to exorcise the evil spirit. When the priest pronounced the words, 'In the name of the Father, *go out!*' they heard a scream, followed by a splash in the lake – and after that there was no more trouble.

Sunday, 4 March 1945, was a black-letter day. By special messenger Susan received a Top-Secret, Priority-One package which emanated from an Austrian resistance group and contained a sworn statement by Hans Gerhardt, the student who had been in the Hitler Youth organisation, and had witnessed the torture and death of Patricia. His 24-page report gave the place, the date, the time, a full description of what had happened, and the ranks and names of the SS torturers.

Susan was horrified by the account, yet at the same time she was filled with admiration for Patricia's gallantry. In one way she wished she had never had to come to terms with such dreadful details, but in another she was glad, for Patricia's achievement was clearly set out, for all authorised personnel to see.

I too read the statement. Devoid of emotion, I wrote my own report and recommendations. There was one that any commanding officer would have had to make. I could never have imagined that one day I would sit quietly at a desk and write of my beloved girl, 'I have the honour to recommend that Second Officer Patricia Falkiner be awarded the George Cross'; but now I wrote those very words, proposing that she should receive the highest decoration for gallantry that could be awarded to a woman. I attached a copy of Gerhardt's statement to my report, and sent it off to Morton.

Privately, I told Fleming and Susan that when our operation and the war were over, I was going to ask Morton for a sub-section with which I could hunt down the Standartenführer and his group, all of whose names we now had. Fleming agreed that the SS murderers were war criminals of the foulest sort, and must be brought to trial.*

Next day, Monday 5 March, a German courier in Zurich made contact with Wren Third Officer Caroline Hurst, the outstandingly intelligent and attractive girl, who had won a double first at Cambridge. For the past year she had been serving in Spain and Portugal, where she had shown great enterprise and courage. Recently she had joined our Swiss sub-section, posing as a friend of mine, and now the courier approached her to suggest that I should again travel to Germany, to meet first Ribbentrop, and then Bormann, who had apparently shown interest in the Foreign Minister's proposals. The rendezvous was to be in Berlin.

The news fired the M Section into instant action. Morton, Fleming and I took less than an hour to decide that we should keep the appointment. But we also decided to launch a preliminary operation at once. Two days before we left, Operation JBV (for James Bond Vanguard) would drop into the Müggelsee by parachute, and the first M Section group would establish itself in Berlin.

---

* After the war M Section personnel did indeed hunt down the Standartenführer. They found him already under arrest, for other crimes, and in due course he was sentenced to death by special tribunal.

The party would include ten men and ten women of the German Freedom Fighters, five of them natives of the city. With them would go twenty Royal Marine Commandos some of them Special Boat Service and some mine-disposal specialists, as well as ten operational Wrens and Naval Commandos from the M Section itself – in all, fifty men and women, with twenty kayaks and allied equipment. Their initial task was to parachute safely into the lake, secure hiding-up positions and establish radio contact with Birdham.

Their way had been admirably paved by the two men and two women whom Bloem had recruited locally. Over the past month this resourceful quartet had surveyed almost every square yard of the Müggelsee, its islands, ancillary waterways, woods and surrounding towns; and they had taken a special interest in Rahnsdorf, a suburb of Berlin spread round the south-east corner of the lake, where the Spree flowed in through a maze of smaller lakes, channels and islands.

Hiding-places for kayaks and other boats abounded in this area, and it was there that the pioneers had made their best contacts among the local population, recruiting nearly fifty people who were prepared to give active help. They had also managed to find friends on one of the wooded hills above the north shore of the lake, where one particular house gave them not only a magnificent lookout position, but also a perfect site for the long-range radio the JBV party would bring out.

Reports from the reconnaissance group made it clear that mines and stakes were a serious problem, both in the Müggelsee itself and in the rivers and canals, many of which had been deliberately blocked by booms and other obstructions. The pioneers had done what they could to mark out the dangerous areas of the big lake, but they needed expert help to make further clearances. They had also cached the rations we had dropped, some for them, but mostly for our own people: we had sent in large supplies of tinned food for use on land, and smaller packs for loading into kayaks – corned beef, spam, sausages, baked beans, dried egg, dried milk, tinned fruit, rum, laxatives and so on.

The JBV group was commanded by Hannah Fierstein. Although personnel from the Freedom Fighters, the M Section and SOE were all used to having women in charge, the Royal Marine Commandos and the SBS were not; yet on this occasion nobody was put out, because everyone recognised Hannah's exceptional abilities, not just as an individual fighter, but also as a leader. Morton and Fleming had foreseen that the initial operation on the Müggelsee would entail much liaison with local people, and so would need an exceptionally delicate touch. There was no one better able to direct it than this small but immensely determined woman.

The party was scheduled to take off on the evening of Thursday, 8 March. At dusk the evening before, Fleming and I were taking our usual talking-walk round the edge of the grounds at Birdham when we heard someone crying in a small copse. There, curled up like a fluffy ball, was Hannah, wailing miserably to herself. Seeing us, she tried to run off, but we stopped her and asked her what was the matter. After a little gentle persuasion, she told us between sobs that the war had already claimed practically all her family. The SS had killed her mother, father and three sisters, and she had no idea what had happened to her two brothers. The weight of her loss had suddenly overcome her.

Talking about the tragedy restored her equilibrium, and as we walked back to the house together Fleming asked why she had gone all the way out to the perimeter woods. Her reply surprised and humbled us. As commanding officer of Op. JBV, she said, she thought it would be neither proper nor good for morale if she were to break down with her group around her. She had therefore gone off on her own to have a good cry and get the sadness out of her system, as any good Jewish mother or leader should.

The next night, 8 March, she led her group in the parachute jump into the Grosser Müggelsee – and she was the only one who died. The rest were guided in, safe from mines and stakes, by the waiting Freedom Fighters, but Hannah's parachute-release mechanism became jammed, and she was drowned as she struggled to free it. Her second-in-command, the redoubtable Christa Shulberg, immediately took charge, and within half an hour the entire party were safely hidden away in various small groups. Equally importantly, the high-powered short-wave radio was set up in the safe house on the wooded hillside north of the lake, and contact was made, through a relay, with Birdham. Op. JB was in business in Berlin. But it was a heavy blow to have lost one of our best hands at the very outset of the operation.

10

In the Ruins of the Reich

On Saturday, 10 March 1945, Fleming and I flew to Madrid and thence to Zurich. The second hop, partly across the northern Mediterranean, caused us no small concern. Far below us the Royal Navy was patrolling, and we knew full well how itchy a gunnery officer's trigger finger could become when an unidentified aircraft was sighted.

By then the Allies were massing along the Rhine, so that approaches to Berlin from the west were blocked, and a passage through Bavaria would also have been hazardous. Caroline Hurst had therefore arranged a car to take us to Vaduz, the capital of Liechtenstein.

The higher slopes of the Alps were still thickly coated with snow, but the valleys were clear, and there was scarcely any traffic on the roads. From Vaduz we were driven over the Austrian border into the province of Vorarlberg, where we met the same two officials from the German Foreign Office who had looked after us on our previous trip. Now they produced the Waffen-SS uniforms they had been keeping for us, and we changed into them, and I put my usual bandage across my face. Then they took us out to a military airstrip near Feldkirch, where two little high-winged monoplanes with open cockpits sat waiting.

Fleming and I stared at them in consternation. They carried Luftwaffe markings, with prominent black-and-white Balken crosses on the sides of the fuselage, and yet they looked strangely familiar.

'Lysanders!' Fleming exclaimed. 'But no, they can't be.'

His first impression was right: the planes were indeed Mark 1 Westland Lysanders, captured from the British at the time of Dunkirk. During the war we had used similar aircraft with outstanding success to ferry SOE agents into and out of France at night: their ability to take off and land in very short spaces, and to fly quietly at tree-top height, made them ideal for covert operations. The Germans evidently appreciated their merits, for they had adapted these two by fitting an extra seat into each rear compartment, close behind the original.

Fleming and I squeezed into one rear compartment, he in the front seat, I behind, with my legs either side of him. Our two escorts climbed into the other plane, and away we went, flying nose to tail along valley bottoms, with the hills towering over us on either side. Even though we had been issued with good leather flying suits, the journey was exceedingly cold, and the noise made conversation almost impossible. My main worry was that Fleming greatly fancied having a go with the .303 Lewis machine-gun mounted just in front of him. Mostly following main roads, and occasionally landing on one to relieve nature or collect fuel, we proceeded to Nuremberg and Zwickau at zero feet, only lifting to any altitude when we approached Berlin itself.

As we went up over the city, aiming to land at Tempelhof, we were amazed by the extent of the devastation wrought by British and American bombing. Hundreds upon hundreds of buildings had been reduced to skeletons: street after street was blocked by craters and heaps of debris. Smoke was rising, and a pall of death seemed to hang over Hitler's capital: I felt that the wrath of the Lord was finally being visited on Sodom and Gomorrah. Clearly, the place was in chaos, and we could see at a glance that a clandestine operation would meet little organised opposition.

What fascinated us still more than the ruins were the waterways that we had been studying so eagerly. There they all were: as we came in from the south-west, we could see the Havel, the Wannsee, the Spree, the multiple canals. Amid all the tangled ruins our proposed escape route shone out like a bright ribbon of silver. Fleming kept pointing and exclaiming as he recognised landmarks, but I was not particularly excited. Rather, I felt humbled by the realisation that the system of waterways – the backbone of our operation – was a natural phenomenon and the work of God. On a lower level, I was determined to remain absolutely cool, and not to become over-excited.

On the last turn before we went in we caught a glimpse of the Müggelsee – a big, pewter-grey sheet of water in the distance – and as we came in to land I thought of Hannah Fierstein. In the latest message received in England, Christa Shulberg had reported that JBV were doing well: they had made good contacts with the leaders of local anti-Nazi groups, and had their kayaks and weapons well hidden.

The state to which Hitler's empire had been reduced came sharply home to us when our pilot tried to land. Four times he went gliding in, and four times he had to power away, unable to find even the short space he needed between bomb-craters. Finally he put down on a track outside the airfield boundary, but as we were decelerating the starboard wheel dipped into a hole and the aircraft heeled over, so that the tip of our right wing was knocked off.

We scrambled out, cold and shaken but unhurt, and after a short delay we were picked up by an SS officer in a huge, battered, grey Mercedes, with numerous rips and holes in its canvas roof, which took us to the Foreign Office in Wilhelmstrasse, some three miles to the north. I had learnt the plan of central Berlin so thoroughly that I could have called all the turns to the driver – except that he kept having to make detours because streets were blocked by craters or rubble. A gangrenous smell filled the air. Much of this, I reckoned, was the legacy of the last mass bombing raid by the Americans, which had taken place on the night of 24 February.

There was practically no civilian traffic: just a scatter of military transport, mainly motorcycles with sidecars, carrying all sorts of cargo. But there were people on foot everywhere: old men, women and children with ancient perambulators and makeshift wooden boxes on wheels, searching pathetically for food, water and fuel. We wanted to stop and give them some of the chocolate we were carrying, but our driver kept going, so we called out and threw a couple of bars into the road. To our distress, people swarmed on to the windfall like rats, and in a second they were fighting for it. I felt we were on the road to oblivion.

The large and impressive government buildings in Wilhelm-strasse had all been damaged, but as we pulled up in a bomb-hole outside the Foreign Office, an unbelievably well turned-out SS officer stepped forward. His diplomatic gala dress, black breeches and highly polished boots seemed to have no connection with the devastation all round him; his bark of 'Heil Hitler!' and his cracking salute might have been in honour of some great victory. He escorted us along the side of the Foreign Office building, then across the remains of gardens in the direction of the Tiergarten, leaving the Führerbunker on our left, and finally down two flights of concrete steps to a set of steel doors.

At first we thought this was the Foreign Office bunker: only later did we discover that it belonged to the Party Chancellery, and was the personal retreat of Martin Bormann. Inside, it was like an air-raid shelter, with small, square rooms on either side of the corridors: some of it was bare concrete, and in some areas the walls had been plastered over with beige rendering. Big ceiling lights with circular glass covers cast a bilious glow, and the whole complex was pervaded by the ceaseless roar of an air-ventilation plant.

We were taken to a concrete cubicle with a couple of bunks, and shown what passed for a bathroom: a cell-like alcove, with a single cold tap above a handbasin, and a hole in the floor for a lavatory. After a half-hour wait, two SS men came and escorted us up into the Foreign Office itself.

Ribbentrop's office, once obviously grand and elegant, was a ruin. Most of the tall windows were cracked or blown out: the furniture was thickly coated with dust, and water dripped from a hole in the ceiling. Yet, like the guard outside, the Foreign Minister seemed oblivious of his surroundings, and was carrying on as if everything was perfectly normal, dressed in his usual uniform of black jacket and white shirt.

He looked pastier and thinner than when I had seen him last, but still he gave us a friendly welcome, and ushered us to a table on which some food had been set out: cold sausage, black bread and *ersatz* coffee tasting bitterly of acorns. With his retainers dismissed, he proceeded quickly to business.

'*Alles in Ordnung*,' he began. 'Everything is under control.'

Bormann, he said, had taken the bait. He had agreed to pay Ribbentrop the twenty-five million Swiss francs. He had also agreed to honour the deal initiated by Ribbentrop in Weinheim, whereby Herr Bond and I would receive £900,000, on top of the deposit of £100,000 already lodged in the bank in Zurich. But now time was swiftly running out. The Russian armies were approaching from the east. The question was, did we really have the resources to lift the senior Nazis out of the trap before it closed?

By prior agreement we both declared that, in the interests of security, we could not reveal our plans until it became absolutely necessary for our passengers to know them, in the last moments before the escape. Ribbentrop obviously thought we were prevaricating: he began to look uncomfortable, and asked if we could give him any evidence of our capability.

'Certainly,' said Fleming. 'I presume it's safe to go out of doors?'

'Of course,' Ribbentrop replied. 'But why?'

'We'll show you.'

Calling something to his secretary, the Foreign Minister walked out of his office, down a back staircase and out into the open. The guards on the door stared in surprise, but he ignored them and, at Fleming's suggestion, carried on into the middle of a bomb-site. There I connected up our transceiver radio and called, 'JBC to JBV, over.' Within seconds I got an answer. 'JBV to JBC,' came a woman's voice.

There followed a brief and deliberately unprofessional exchange of pleasantries, as if one lot of marauding and traitorous pirates were chatting to another.

'How's your sex life, Sarah?'

'Dying a natural death, thank you, darlin'. Everything's clapped up round here.'

'What, the natives?'

'Blimey, no. Your bloody randy mates. Hands like poxed-up treacle . . .'

This nonsense was something we had rehearsed beforehand, and now it went down well. Ribbentrop was not to know that our associates were only eight miles away, on the Müggelsee; nor could he be aware that so far only the vanguard of our operational group was in position. But the fact that we had people close at hand seemed to reassure him enormously, and he told us that Bormann would see us sometime that afternoon.

Back in our claustrophobic quarters, the two SS officers escorting us searched our luggage and removed our radios and side-arms. When Fleming objected, they said that everything would be returned before we left. Then they clanged the steel door shut, and we became secure prisoners of Nazi Germany.

For the first time, Fleming looked worried. Never before, he said, had he been locked up, let alone by an enemy. I, on the other hand, felt no sense of oppression. I had been imprisoned, chained up and generally knocked about so many times that I could hardly keep count. The conditions here in Berlin were a thousand times preferable to those I had endured in the castle at Cherbourg.

Watching my expression, and somehow reading my thoughts, Fleming seemed to take heart. 'At least it won't be anything like Cherbourg again,' he said.

'No,' I agreed. 'Nothing could ever be as bad as that.'

What I did not divulge was that this day – Tuesday, 13 March – was my twenty-first birthday. For one thing, we were in no position to celebrate; and for another, the date differed from the one down in the records as being the birthday of Christopher Creighton. Time hung heavily on us. Foolishly, we had brought nothing to read, and, in spite of the noise of the ventilation fans, we were reluctant to talk business, for fear that microphones had been planted in the walls. With nothing else to do, we sat about on our two wooden stools or lay on the bunks, talking nonsense. Luckily for me Fleming had for the time being given up smoking, after arguments with Susan and Jenny Wright, the doctor, about the harm it was doing him.

At last, sometime in the evening, there came a rattle of keys in the door and then a knock. In walked a middle-aged man, followed by a young woman. We both recognised our visitor immediately, for over the past weeks we had been staring daily at photographs of him: Martin Bormann. In one hand he carried a hefty wad of files.

He was short, thick-necked and almost bull-like in his solidity, with square, powerful-looking shoulders. His close-cropped hair, receding slightly from his forehead, was plastered down with grease, and over his left eye was a prominent, ugly scar. Bushy eyebrows shadowed eyes that were small and pig-like, admirably suiting the code-name we had given him; his nose was almost hooked, with a large bump on the bridge, his upper lip thin and cruel. I noticed that his fingers were short and stubby, and that the backs of them, like the backs of his hands, were covered with thick dark hair. Altogether, he gave an impression of unlimited strength and no little malevolence: a far more formidable character than his namesake in *The House at Pooh Corner*.

His manner, however, was perfectly civil. He spoke in a quiet voice, and after each phrase waited patiently for the girl interpreter to translate. Fleming did the same, reckoning that it might be useful to keep his own fluency in German under wraps.

Echoing Ribbentrop almost word for word, Bormann agreed that the war was lost. He too, he said, wished to escape to a refuge in which he would be safe. But, he said, he also had to make sure that nobody would start a witch-hunt and come looking for him. The world would have to believe him dead. To this end, a *Doppelgänger*, a double, would have to be found.

'You mean you don't have a double already?' Fleming asked in genuine surprise.

'*Keiner*,' said Bormann. 'None.'

'But surely the Führer has one?'

'Of course.'

'Why not you, then?'

Bormann replied that he could trust nobody – although he seemed to trust his young interpreter. In his present position, he said, he was the target of much petty-minded jealousy, and rivals would do anything to bring him down. Any talk of getting a double, or searching for one, would have been sure to attract unwelcome attention and suggest that he had devious motives.

'The question is,' he added, 'can you find someone sufficiently like me to pass muster?'

Fleming hesitated. He pointed out that we probably had little time in which to organise a search. All he could promise, he said, was that we would do our best.

'You realise,' Bormann went on, 'the man will have to be killed during our escape. His body will have to be left somewhere conspicuous, so that it is sure to be found. That means it will

125

have to correspond closely with mine – height, weight and so on – to stand up to a thorough post-mortem examination.'

'That should be no problem,' said Fleming smoothly. 'Equally, your safety in England is not in question. That is guaranteed. The only uncertainty is whether we can find a double quickly enough. We'll do our best, of course.'

Bormann seemed to accept this, and the talk moved on to the question of our payment. He reassured us that our agreement would be honoured. He had plenty of funds at his disposal, since he alone controlled access to all the Nazi assets overseas. 'Don't worry,' he told Fleming. 'I will see that the balance of £900,000 is paid into your account in Zurich as soon as I reach England safely.'

Before he left, Bormann handed over the package he was carrying. It consisted of four thick cardboard files slipped into an open-ended buff envelope, which had been done up with tatty white tape. It was a bulky package, three or four inches thick, and contained his medical and dental records, along with a collection of reports and photographs of himself. 'Take these,' he said. 'You'll need them. But be sure to bring them back.'

'Is everything here?' Fleming asked.

'As far as I know.'

Bormann then said a formal goodbye and prepared to leave; but at the last moment he turned back with a half-smile on his face and said, 'Next time we meet, Herr Bond, I shall dispense with my interpreter.'

Fleming was momentarily taken aback. Before he could reply, Bormann added: 'Every time I spoke during the past few minutes, I noticed that you understood everything I said before my assistant translated.'

With that he departed, leaving us uncertain as to who or what he thought we were. Did he believe we were true renegades and traitors, or did he know that we were intelligence officers? Either way, it seemed that he had decided to put his future in our hands.

Soon after his departure, our radios and weapons were returned, and we were allowed out into the air for exercise, and to signal our 'associates'. A call to the Müggelsee elicited the information that Christa and her people had made progress with their survey of the escape route, but that they had found the Spree blocked in many places by mines and other booby-traps. To clear a way through, they would need expert support parties. I assured her that help would be with them soon, and Christa replied that it felt very good to have us so close at hand.

Next day we set off for home by the same roundabout route that we had used on the way in: some genius of a mechanic had repaired the Lysander's broken wing, and we flew low-level back to Austria. Then we drove into Switzerland, and caught a full-sized aircraft from Lisbon to Croydon. On the final stage we were again travelling as Foreign Office couriers; during the journey Fleming had time to browse through Bormann's dossier, and he found out a good deal more about him, not least the fact that in earlier days he had been an enthusiastic horseman, and had once broken his collar-bone in a fall.

'That could be a tough one,' remarked Fleming thoughtfully. 'If anyone ever digs up what they think is Bormann's skeleton, they'll expect to find evidence of old damage on his clavicle, right side.'

During the flight Fleming nonchalantly revealed that my *alter ego*, Leading Seaman John Davis, had recently been discharged from the navy on medical grounds, after a term of detention carefully orchestrated by Morton. His fictitious transgressions had been legion – absence without leave, the wearing of improper medals, general indiscipline – and henceforth the young traitor would fade from his disreputable active service. Nevertheless, John Davis would continue with his activities as a double agent. Of course he would. As we droned northwards towards Cornwall I wondered who it was – some poor sod of an M Section member – who had been called upon to serve the detention for me in a naval prison.

11

Countdown

We arrived back at Birdham on Sunday, 18 March, and immediately went into conference. Time was running out. The Allies had begun crossing the Rhine ten days earlier, and were advancing swiftly eastwards. The Soviet armies had nearly reached the Oder in their westward drive on Berlin. It was clear that Germany could not hold out for more than a few weeks.

Our first decision was to reinforce JBV immediately by sending in another hundred men and women, including mine-disposal experts from HMS *Vernon*, to speed up the clearance of our escape route. To prepare the party was relatively simple, as our people were fully trained and geared up to go. Our much harder task was to find a passable double. Clearly, it would be best if the man was German, and Morton suggested that we would be most likely to find him in a prisoner-of-war camp. Susan Kemp at once questioned the morality of what we were attempting: was it acceptable to select a man, prisoner of war or otherwise, and by false pretences get him to volunteer unwittingly for his own certain death? The M Section had answers to most conundrums, but on this occasion the query was adjourned. Deception and double-dealing were the name of Morton's game.

I myself had solutions for our next two urgent problems: to secure the services of a top-flight dentist and a leading plastic surgeon, both of whom would be absolutely secure. Mr A. B. Aldred of 88 Park Street, Mayfair, was a leading dentist, and had looked after my family's teeth for as long as I could remember. How many times had I been taken to his surgery as a boy, quaking with anticipation? Besides, he had drilled out many people's lower molars, including one of my own, so that they would house L-pills. I had no doubt that he would work with total discretion on the teeth of our chosen prisoner so that they resembled, as closely as possible, the picture recorded in the dental records of Martin Bormann.

As for the plastic surgeon, in my early teens I had known a girl called Venora, whose father had been a close friend of my own father. Indeed, I remembered once having a bath with her, when I was twelve and she was six or so. It had been the custom in those days for children to call close friends of their parents 'Uncle', and this surrogate uncle of mine was now an air commodore, a Royal Air Force doctor working at the Queen Victoria Hospital, East Grinstead, where he had been doing wonders for terribly injured, burnt and scarred aircrew. His name was Archibald McIndoe.

Because Fleming and I were fully occupied with specialist training, Susan was put in charge of the quest for a double. Her moral scruples notwithstanding, she went straight to see McIndoe at East Grinstead, taking the Bormann dossier with her.

A tall, friendly, open New Zealander, McIndoe was not only a most skilful surgeon, but also a man of great warmth and enthusiasm. He roared with laughter when Susan mentioned the incident in the bath, and he seized on this bizarre new project with relish. He warned her that normally plastic surgery could not make one face look like another. Whatever changes he might effect, there would always be differences, possibly serious ones. On the other hand, a death-mask was never the same as the person's face in life, and this would make his task easier. If a reasonably similar double could be found, he might be able to manipulate the man's features so that in death they would resemble those of Bormann pretty well.

Having studied the Bormann dossier, particularly the photographs, McIndoe gave Susan detailed notes about the type of face he required, and she at once put secret inquiries in hand, not only in the United Kingdom, but also in Canada, where many German prisoners were being held. While a search was mounted in Britain, she herself flew to Toronto to look for possible candidates, and she had the authorities line up prisoners of roughly the right dimensions for her inspection.

Before anyone had been found, Fleming and I received an unexpected summons. On 19 March a signal arrived from Rheims, temporary home of Supreme Headquarters, Allied Expeditionary Force (SHAEF): General Dwight D. Eisenhower, the Supreme Commander, wished to see us immediately. This was a surprise: both of us had met Ike several times earlier in the war, and I had last seen him after the fiasco at Slapton Sands, the year before; but we could not imagine what he wanted from us at this point of the war.

In any case, a day or two later we flew to Rheims in an RAF aircraft, and were driven by American Military Police to the Collège Moderne et Technique, in which SHAEF was lodged. There were no hold-ups, and we were escorted swiftly to the second floor, where Eisenhower's Chief of Staff, General Walter Bedell Smith, met us on the landing, shook hands, and ushered us into what was obviously, in normal times, a classroom.

Eisenhower was his normal, friendly self: a bit podgy in the face, but vibrant, very much on the ball, and immediately impressive in his command of detail. Having given us coffee, he went straight to business.

'Okay, you guys, what are you up to?' he began.

'Oh, nothing in particular, General,' Fleming hedged.

'Bullshit, Ian! You fellas can't kid me.'

The hair on my neck rose as I heard Eisenhower say that, through some reliable source, he had heard of Churchill's plans for recovering stolen Nazi assets held outside Germany. When he mentioned the M Section and Operation James Bond in so many words, I felt that embarrassment must be written all over my face. Fleming, sitting beside me, remained apparently unruffled, but I sensed that he too was suffering from shock.

Eisenhower's tone, though not aggressive, was absolutely firm. He said outright that, where British interests were predominant, he did not trust Churchill or Morton. He wanted to be certain that, if we did manage to recover money, works of art or property, everything would be handed back to the rightful owners, rather than deposited in British or specifically Churchillian coffers.

We assured him that this was precisely what Churchill and Morton had pledged, and we gave him our word that we ourselves would do everything in our power to bring just settlements about. Eisenhower accepted our good faith, but pointed out that neither of us had the power to keep developments under control: however honourable our intentions, we could be overruled by higher authority. Since he, however, was Supreme Commander in Europe, final control over any operation in that theatre lay with him, and his word could be overruled only by a decision of the British and American joint chiefs of staff. Op. JB, which was very much a European enterprise, undoubtedly came within his jurisdiction, and he therefore ordered us to keep him informed of everything that we were doing.

To ensure a full flow of information, he told us, he had appointed a personal liaison officer to join the M Section for the duration of Op. JB. His choice was Lieutenant B. W. Brabenov, an intelligence officer with wide experience both in the field and in back-room control. He described this agent as a 'ball of fire', part Russian and part German, and able to speak both languages with the fluency of a native.

Little did we realise that Ike was pulling a fast one on us. But equally, we little knew what a priceless asset this Lieutenant Brabenov was going to be.

For the time being, we returned to England. Next day, when Churchill received Fleming's report of our encounter, via Morton, he exploded. What confounded cheek of Ike to suggest that he, the Prime Minister of Great Britain, was planning to petty-pilfer the Nazi coffers for his own advantage! Churchill was outraged that the Americans had got wind of the operation at all: because they had shown a tendency to blabbermouth secrets all over the place, he had done his best to prevent them hearing about it. As often happened, he vented his irritation on his intelligence chief.

Morton pointed out that for once it was not the Americans who had been blabbermouthing: someone on the British side must have passed the secret on. Churchill, who had been angrily awaiting his chance, leapt on that one.

'Precisely!' he growled. 'You're supposed to be my chief of security and intelligence. Now, if our most deadly secret has found its way to General Eisenhower, whose bloody fault is it but yours, pray?'

The Prime Minister then demanded a written explanation, on one page, of how the leak had occurred. But Morton, who had weathered such storms many times before, kept his head down and merely gave an enigmatic smile. Of course, it was he who had given the information to the Americans, believing that it would be best if they were in the know. A few days earlier, he had secretly briefed his opposite number, General W. J. 'Big Bill' Donovan, chief of the OSS, the Office of Strategic Services, and Donovan had passed word both to Eisenhower and to President Roosevelt.

Later that day Fleming and I got another surprise, not altogether welcome. Morton summoned us to his office in the Ministry of Works and told us that when we went into Germany to launch the final phase of Op. JB, two army officers would be attached to our party. Once we had landed, they would separate off on a special operation of their own, but they would require an escort of twenty of our most reliable Marine Commandos. Morton said he could not reveal what their mission was, but he made it clear that they were not trained Commandos, or even fighting soldiers. Nor, he also emphasised, was either of them cleared for any knowledge of Op. JB: they would join the Section solely to be trained, escorted into Germany, and delivered to the right place.

With that, he brought the two men in and introduced them. The first was Major Anthony Blunt, then aged thirty-eight: he wore the uniform of the Army Field Police, and said he was attached to MI 5. The second was Roger Hollis, wearing battledress and the insignia of a captain in the Army Intelligence Corps: slightly older than his colleague, he was described as a career officer in MI 5. Both men, Morton told us, were to come to Birdham and train with us for whatever time proved to be available.

Blunt was tall, but slim and frail in appearance. I immediately wondered how he would stand up to our violent training routines, never mind to the operation itself. Everything about him was scruffy: his hair was too long, his tie was slack, and his uniform looked as though it had been through a mangle. Fleming and I both took an instant dislike to him and felt that he was going to be a nuisance. Hollis, in contrast, was well-built and smartly turned out: he looked tough, and well able to fend for himself – although he coughed a good deal, as if he had something wrong with his chest – and he seemed a friendly, easy-going sort of person. The difference in the two men's attitudes was immediately summed up by the way they reacted to the news that they were about to come under the command of someone nearly twenty years younger than either. 'First class,' said Hollis to Morton. 'I'm sure I'll learn a lot from him.' Blunt, on the other hand, looked petulant and said, 'He's only a boy. What can he possibly teach me?'

At Birdham Hollis threw himself into our training heart and soul, but Blunt made no effort at all, and was constantly late for sessions or absent altogether. Within a day or two he had become an active nuisance, as he was disrupting our programme. Then, during a period of unarmed combat taken by our pretty little Scots wireless expert Penny Wirrell, he found himself detailed to be her opponent. His demeanour made it clear that he expected to finish her off in short order, but in fact the opposite happened: soon he found himself flying all over the place and landing heavily in the grass, usually with Penny on top of him.

A few minutes of this proved more than he could stand. Suddenly losing his temper when no bout was in progress, he kicked her in the back and punched her in the face. Instantly the instructor in charge yelled, 'STILL everyone! Everyone stand absolutely still!' – and it said much for the ingrained discipline of the Section that Blunt was not instantly demolished. I do not suppose he realised how close to total obliteration he was at that moment, or what might have happened if our young commandos had got their hands on him.

Instead, Penny put him under close arrest, and he was escorted before me by two officers, with Hollis in tow. When Blunt realised I was in charge, he started to bluster, claiming that I was not senior to him, and had no authority over him. Hollis tried to persuade him that, first, major and lieutenant-commander were equal ranks, but that the navy rank was always the senior; and that, second, I held command at Birdham by appointment, and therefore had authority over everyone in the sub-section, even someone nominally my superior.

I tried to continue with the hearing, but Blunt started to shout and protest. Then, as I ordered him to be quiet and pull himself together, he jumped forward and slapped me in the face, continuing to make insulting and insurbordinate remarks. I had no option but to keep him under close arrest and send him under maximum security to London. There, Morton gave him a severe reprimand and warned him that if he did not behave in accordance with the Army Act, he would be sent into custody under Rule 18b for an unspecified period (under wartime emergency powers, this meant detention without trial on the Isle of Man).

Blunt returned to Birdham slightly chastened; but behind the mission to which he and Hollis had been assigned, other factors were at work. These suddenly became evident with the arrival of a signal from the Supreme Commander, South-East Asia Command:

TO: LIEUTENANT-COMMANDER C. CREIGHTON. MOST SECRET.
IMMEDIATE. CYPHER CR3. HOLLIS/BLUNT OPERATION VITAL ME
AND MY FAMILY. PLEASE SUPPORT THEM UTMOST. BEST WISHES.
MOUNTBATTEN, ACTING ADMIRAL.

After consultation with Morton, I signalled back that I was in command of a first-priority, most-secret operation, to which Hollis had been giving full support, but Blunt none. With my message Hollis sent one of his own, confirming what I had written. But before our joint signal could reach Burma, I received another, from London, designated 'MOST SECRET, A 1, MOST IMMEDIATE', ordering me to report to Morton's office at 2100 hours the next evening.

Thinking I was in deep trouble, I took some essential documents with me, and made sure I arrived at the Ministry of Works building dead on time. As usual, I went in through the Parkside entrance, and turned right along the corridor to Room 60, where, to my surprise, I found two armed Royal Marine officers standing guard outside the door. After they had scrutinised my identity cards, I knocked on the door, and a quiet voice said, 'Come in.'

Inside, I found myself facing Admiral of the Fleet King George VI, who sat alone at Morton's desk in naval uniform. To come on the reigning monarch in that drab little room was certainly a surprise, but because, through my father, I had known the King as a child, and had danced with his daughters at Madame Vacani's classes, I was not put out. Already, during the war, I had come before him twice to brief him on operations in which I had taken part. We were both serving officers of the Royal Navy, with no favours asked, given or expected. As Prince George, he had served as a normal naval cadet, and had been subject to normal training and discipline – so much so that on one occasion a cane had been broken across his backside, and he had had to suffer the indignity of waiting for another one to be brought. As I had undergone almost exactly the same ordeal, and had discussed it with the him on a previous occasion, we were on easy terms, notwithstanding the vast difference in rank.

Thus I was not thrown by this sudden confrontation. I knew that as sovereign chief of the navy he liked to be treated as a normal senior flag officer by any other naval officer who came into contact with him. So now my reaction was simple. My cap went under my left arm. I stood quickly and silently to attention and said, 'Creighton, sir. You sent for me.' I followed this with a sharp nod of my head, keeping the rest of my body rigid: the Coburg bow, always used in court and service circles.

The King shook my hand, motioned me to sit opposite him, and told me he was sorry to hear I had been obstructive about Hollis and Blunt, who were working partly at his own request. 'Perhaps if I tell you, in strictest secrecy, what they're doing, you will understand better,' he said, not unkindly. I noticed the slight weakness of his Rs, but no trace of the stammer which had once plagued his public speaking.

He confided that he was worried about correspondence lodged in Schloss Kronberg, a castle near Frankfurt belonging to the Hesse family, of which Mountbatten was a scion. He believed that the collection included letters from Queen Victoria to her eldest daughter, the Princess Royal, who became Empress of Prussia, mother of the Kaiser. He also thought there might be letters from his own mother, Queen Mary, to her German relations. Since these documents were purely private, and concerned the family, he did not want them made public.

Worse, he feared other letters might contain embarrassing evidence that his brother, the Duke of Windsor, formerly King Edward VIII, had shown pro-Nazi leanings. Unfortunately, he said, there were valid reasons for believing this to be true, and he was extremely anxious that the correspondence should not fall into the wrong hands. Blunt and Hollis had been asssigned the job of finding the letters and bringing them out.

The King was manifestly concerned. I could see he did not want to believe what he had just admitted. When he asked me to explain what had gone wrong at Birdham, I showed him copies of the relevant signals, and of the report I had just written for Morton. Then, having laid out the facts, I submitted that Blunt's character was fundamentally unsuited to hazardous operations. From what I had seen of him, I judged that in a potentially dangerous situation, when guns were firing, he might well prove unreliable.

The King looked at me sternly for a few seconds and asked if I stood by what I had just said.

'Yes, sir.'

'Well?'

'I submit, sir, that you would not be well served by such an amateur in a professional wartime operation.'

It took some courage to say that, because I knew that Blunt had connections with the royal family. But by then my blood was up, and I requested permission to ask a question. When the King nodded, I asked if Blunt had made his complaint directly to him. The answer was 'Yes, he did.'

'With respect, sir, I submit that this in itself was a breach of military discipline.' I pointed out that, as the King was well aware, anyone in the services who wished to make a complaint to higher authority must channel it through his own commanding officer. In this instance the complainant had bypassed not only myself but Fleming and Morton as well.

The King smiled and nodded, but he also rebuked me for being headstrong, a charge I could not rebut. But before I left, he wished me the best of luck with Op. JB, which he said he had been following with the keenest interest.

Three days later, both Hollis and Blunt were withdrawn from Birdham – but not before another unnerving incident had taken place. Our main office, on the first floor of the manor house, contained various secret papers, among them details of Op. JB. The door was kept locked, and on it was posted a standing order, stating that no one might enter the room without authorisation from the sub-section commander, myself.

At 0100 one morning, Susan Kemp heard a noise in that area and came down, to find Blunt in the office, reading some papers. She immediately placed him under close arrest again, and had him held incommunicado, pending orders from Morton. Two days later he was taken away under escort and returned to his own unit. Because he had been cleared for security by MI 5, no further action was taken against him, but in our eyes this was a really serious offence. Striking an officer was one thing, but a deliberate breach of orders involving secrets was something altogether different. Only time would show whether any real damage had been done.

During these upheavals, the search for a double had been proceeding on both sides of the Atlantic, and it was in Canada that we struck lucky. Oddly enough, Susan found her man not in any of the line-ups laid on for her but, quite by chance, in one of the many groups sent out to work on farms near Toronto. He was standing in a row, digging, when suddenly he turned to look in the visitors' direction. Susan's companion, Jenny Lewis, instinctively pointed and said, 'Look! There he is – Piglet!' His name was Otto Günther, and he was quickly flown to England.

Meanwhile, two other possibles had been found in Britain. After careful physical examination, backed by X-rays, McIndoe and Aldred chose Günther, and the other two men were returned to their camps. Over the next two weeks our wretched victim went through one session of corrective surgery after another. McIndoe gave him a scar over the left eye to match Bormann's, which we saw from the records was the legacy of a road accident, and made one or two other minor adjustments. The surgeon emphasised that, although the operations were quickly done, it would be some time before the wounds healed completely, and before the scar tissue looked old. All we could do was hope that several weeks would pass before we went to action stations. On the dental front, Mr Aldred also did his best to make Günther match Bormann's records, removing a couple of teeth and inserting a bridge and extra fillings where necessary.

Both experts, however, warned that the match was still by no means perfect, and that a post-mortem examination might well bring giveaway discrepancies to light. It was at this stage that McIndoe made an inspired remark. 'We've done all the plastic surgery we can on the man,' he said, 'but why don't you do some on the records as well?'

It was a brilliantly simple solution. Two M Section officers from the forgery unit took charge of Bormann's records and, working closely with McIndoe and Aldred, adapted them to fit Günther in every particular. Some documents had to be doctored, others made up from scratch; photographs, dental charts and X-rays had to correspond exactly with our man's peculiarities, and the forgeries were no easy task, for the original papers were of all types and ages. Fortunately the M Section officers had highly skilled craftsmen at their disposal: many of them had until recently been residing, at His Majesty's pleasure, in leading correction establishments, and between them there was little that they could not create or fix. The doctored records were all, naturally, in the name of Martin Bormann, and we felt confident that if after the end of the war they fell into the hands of the Russians (or indeed of the Americans or the British), nobody would doubt that they were the genuine documents of Hitler's secretary. Furthermore, we felt sure that, for his own good, Bormann had collected together *all* his own records, and that no originals had been left behind in Germany. The only set available after the war – *our* set – would precisely match the body of the hapless Herr Günther, which we planned to leave behind us in the ruins of Berlin.

As to what Susan told Günther about his role, I did not care to inquire too closely; but it was enormously to her credit that she fought down her conscientious objections and gained his co-operation by falsely promising him special treatment now, and quick repatriation after the war.

During the preparation of Günther, there was a tense scene at Birdham when Fleming gave us our orders about the man's future. The three of us were sitting at the big table in the library. Fleming turned to me and said, 'I confirm. You are to abduct Martin Bormann from Berlin, with or without his consent, and escort him to England. Further, you will take all necessary steps to make it appear that Bormann died in Berlin while attempting to escape. You will carry out these orders by whatever means you deem necessary, notwithstanding any law or international convention.'

I muttered, 'Aye, aye, sir.'

Fleming then repeated to Susan that she had no discretion about what to tell the double, in order to obtain his co-operation: 'He is to believe that he will not be harmed.'

Very quietly Susan answered, 'Aye, aye, sir.'

Günther's fate was clear to us all. Moreover, I could see that it was going to fall to me to kill him.

The atmosphere in our little group had become unbearably tense, and suddenly, with a quite uncharacteristic show of feeling, Fleming stood up, extending a hand to each of us, and holding on tightly.

'Well,' he said, 'there it is.'

'Yes,' said Susan. 'It is, isn't it.'

In the first week of April we despatched our reinforcements to the Müggelsee. By the time they were all tucked away round the shores of the lake, JBV had a strength of over a hundred and fifty men and women; but Christa Shulberg had performed so exceptionally well in command that, far from supplanting her with some senior officer to take charge of the much larger force, we kept her in place and she was promoted captain. At her disposal she had plenty of people whose first language was German, and several with fluent Russian. With the reinforcements had gone a variety of uniforms to give cover in any foreseeable situation: SS, Wehrmacht, Soviet Army, United States and British Military Police, Royal Navy, and numerous women's uniforms, including German, Soviet and French, all manufactured or adapted by the M Section's tailors.

In reviewing our plans, we realised that in designating the advance-guard 'JBV' we had made a mistake, for over poor radio links the letters could easily be confused with 'JBC', the call-sign of our command group. To avoid potentially dangerous misunderstandings, we therefore renamed Christa's force 'JB7'.

12

Our Yankee Doodle Girl

For me, the arrival of Lieutenant B. W. Brabenov was one of the high spots of the operation.

Late in the forenoon of Sunday, 6 April 1945, a jeep scorched up to the main gates at Birdham. Its doors were emblazoned with the words UNITED STATES NAVY, and it contained only the driver, an attractive, well-rounded young woman with strikingly blond hair, cut very short. She wore a khaki jacket and skirt, and on her shoulders were the two gold stripes and star of a US Navy lieutenant. She also displayed above her left breast more medal ribbons than the entire company of the M Section could muster between them.

The Royal Marine Commando on the gate, who would have been unruffled if the enemy had attacked in numbers, was comprehensively taken aback by this apparition, which announced itself as Lieutenant Barbara W. Brabenov, from the United States Navy Office of Intelligence. Having checked the two identity cards she offered, the guard waved her through, and she roared off in the direction of the manor house, leaving him bereft of expletives.

Outside the front door she pulled up in the driveway, leapt out of the jeep, sprang to attention and cracked off a salute at the white ensign on the flagstaff. At her request, the guard on the door summoned the officer of the day, and when he appeared she jumped to attention again, saluted a second time and asked permission to come aboard. Since she appeared to be well aboard already, the officer was left as speechless as the man on the gate.

We soon realised we had a formidable recruit. We gathered that for the past six months she had been working in the UK and in recently liberated parts of Europe, under the direct orders of the chief of the OSS, General 'Big Bill' Donovan. Beyond that we did not inquire: one did not ask questions of that kind. That she was attractive and feminine, anybody could see at once: what took a little longer to emerge was that she was efficient, tough, disciplined and experienced.

She came from New York State, had a university degree, and, in spite of her Russian and German grandparents, sounded as normal American as blueberry pie. Her only drawback was a tendency to salute anything that bore a resemblance to a senior officer, indoors or out, with her cap on or off; but this weakness Susan soon cured by means of a tactful word in her ear, and Brabenov had the good sense to observe King's Regulations and Admiralty Instructions to just the right degree.

Strictly speaking, her appointment was that of a liaison officer, and her role was to watch, learn and report to Eisenhower. Such a task, however, was far too passive for someone of her fizzing energy. Before she had been at Birdham a day, she insisted on taking part in every phase of our operational training, and she threw herself into it with such gusto, application and high spirits that within forty-eight hours she had been accepted by all hands. Not the least of her charms was the fact that she seemed totally unaware of her own exuberant physique, and of the effect it had on men. When it came to weapons-handling, she was in a class of her own. With a .38 Smith & Wesson, at twenty paces, she could put bullet after bullet – as she herself gracefully expressed it – 'up a gnat's asshole', and she was exceedingly quick on the draw.

Almost the only chink in her armour was that she had never handled a kayak; but at Birdham we had some of the world's leading experts, Royal Marine SBS Cammandos, and soon they whisked her off to fast-flowing rivers in the Welsh mountains for white-water trials. Although she complained vigorously about certain physical problems – '*You*'ve never been rear-end-up in the rapids with your breasts hanging out' – she mastered her new craft in record time, and indeed wore out all the instructors. Whereas they had planned to give her a couple of runs through the rapids, and two or three practices at yomping (carrying) kayaks overland, to pass obstructions in the river, she wanted to do everything ten times, and she returned to Birdham elated, as skilful as most of the experts, if not more so.

On the planning front, she was a goldmine of knowledge and good sense, and she had the great merit of never pretending to know facts or subjects which she had not mastered. Such was her thirst for information, and so quick was she to learn, that in the classroom, also, she drove most of the instructors out of their minds with her curiosity and speed of assimilation.

A great one for letting off steam, she taught the Section a game called Cowboys and Indians, which proved an almost exact replica of the British game known as French and English. Two teams, red and blue, competed for seven flags kept in the base camp of each side's marked territory: the object, pursued under strict rules of engagement, was to capture all your opponents' flags without being captured yourself. The American variation was that, instead of running about on foot, one played the game on horseback.

Fleming and I agreed that it would sharpen up our reactions and fitness – but where were we to find the horses? As with most things, Brabenov had the answer: they were 'attached' to a nearby US naval base, where the officers had persuaded the local hunting fraternity to let them ride their horses at a nominal price. So we took to playing Cowboys and Indians crossed with French and English: Fleming and Susan Kemp captained the opposing teams, with Brabenov and three Wrens acting as mounted umpires. One game lasted for two days, having been continued on foot right through the night.

Yet games, exercises and training could not go on for ever. The time for action was fast approaching. By the second week in April Hitler's Reich was in its death throes: on the tenth the US 2nd Armoured Division reached the River Elbe at Magdeburg, a hundred miles west of Berlin, and Marshal Zhukov, the Soviet Commander-in-Chief, was only sixty miles east of the capital. But now it had become clear that the Western Allies were not going to advance beyond the Elbe for the time being: this meant it would be the Russians who captured Berlin.

The implications for Op. JB were equally clear. We had known for some time that we would be dealing with Germans, a few friendly, but most of them definitely not. Now we realised that we would probably have to cope with Russians as well: in all probability, we would have to make our way out of Berlin through an encircling cordon of Soviet troops. We knew they could be both unreliable and hostile, even to their own allies, and we saw that to have a fluent Russian-speaker in our snatch team would be a big advantage. There were already some Russian-speakers among the advance party, but now our thoughts naturally turned to Brabenov.

Before we could suggest that she join our operation, she herself volunteered. And yet, keen as we were to take her aboard, we had no authority to do so. Eisenhower had sent her to us as a liaison and intelligence officer, and no matter how highly he recommended her reliability, trustworthiness and fitness to be his personal representative, he had not cleared her to go into action. Fleming put the point to her, and as usual she had an answer: her boss, General Donovan, was coming to London. In fact, he was due to meet Morton there the next day. Was there a chance that we could invite both of them down to Birdham for dinner, so that the matter could be settled there and then?

There was no mystery about why Donovan was known as 'Big Bill'. He was a hulking great man, then just under sixty, and as chief of the OSS he held a position which almost exactly mirrored Morton's. Just as Morton answered only to the King and the Prime Minister, so Donovan answered only to the President, and not to any government department or service. The similarities between the OSS and the M Section were legion. Both had been formed to carry out unconventional operations and obtain information, to protect the security of their respective nations. Both habitually overrode the obstruction, hostility, red tape and bureaucracy of government departments. Each had under its roof a highly skilled and experienced secret intelligence and combat organisation, drawn not only from all ranks of every fighting service, but also from civilians in all types of work and from every social level. Both organisations had the means and the authority to carry out counter-espionage, sabotage, assassinations, propaganda

– everything the regular forces wished they could do, but were not allowed to.

Donovan himself was unusual: in the First World War he had commanded the 69th Regiment, the 'Fighting Irish', but then he had left the army and become a distinguished attorney. A southerner, a fervent Roman Catholic and a Republican, he was in many ways the exact opposite of his President, Franklin D. Roosevelt, who was a Yankee, a Protestant and a Democrat. Yet he shared with Roosevelt a passionate belief in freedom and decency, and he had become a most trusted agent, as well as a close friend, of the President.

Morton and Donovan were also old friends and partners. On the surface they seemed quite different: whereas Morton was quiet and dour, Donovan was brash and outgoing. But both were exceedingly capable, and behind their chosen façades they were united in their aims, and they had worked closely together throughout the war. Morton had told Donovan about Op. JB not just because he felt it his duty to do so: he also thought the American might provide practical help – as indeed he did.

Fleming and I knew Donovan of old. We had both taken part in operations for him, and, at separate times, had trained under him at Camp X, at Oshawa, on the north shore of Lake Ontario in Canada. So when he and Morton arrived at Birdham on the evening of Monday, 9 April, it was a reunion of old friends. Brabenov greeted her general with a smart salute, which he returned with rigid precision; but then formality collapsed. He gave his blonde agent a hug and a kiss, and they went whirling round the room to the springy rhythm of an Irish jig, provided by Israel Bloem on his fiddle. 'This is my best girl,' Donovan announced to us all as they came to rest. 'She's the tops.'

That evening the secret circle of the M Section dined together: Morton, Fleming, Susan Kemp and myself, with the two Americans, Donovan and Brabenov, as our guests. We were captivated when Donovan recounted some ridiculous episodes of secret intelligence work – and then, inevitably, Morton launched into a series of ghost stories, in most of which he claimed to have been involved himself. Having heard them before, I was not in the least scared, but the others were, especially when Morton insisted on turning out the lights and leaving just one candle flickering on the table. Donovan, good Irish Catholic that he was, crossed himself vigorously and asked whether the Cardinal Archbishop of Westminster approved of such spiritualism. Morton replied that not only had the Cardinal given his private approval but two of the stories emanated from him.

After dinner we adjourned to the library, and with the aid of the large-scale model we went through every phase of our abduction plan. On the night the operation began, JBC, the command group, would parachute into the Müggelsee and be received by the men and women of JB7. We would lie up in safe houses, and the next night we would proceed north-west down the Spree by kayak, taking Günther, our double, with us, escorted by a small section of Royal Marine commandos and German Freedom Fighters.

Our destination would be a point on the bank some twelve miles downstream, just before the Weidendamm Bridge, where the river flowed under Friedrichstrasse and turned southwards towards the big park known as the Tiergarten (the Zoo). There we would disembark, leaving the kayaks in the charge of our escort, who would return to the Müggelsee base. We ourselves would then make our way through the streets to whatever rendezvous the Germans had set – presumably the Chancellery bunker, just off Wilhelmstrasse.

If the Spree turned out to be impassable, we had two alternative approaches in mind: the Spree Canal, from which we would land alongside Museum Island, to the east of our destination, and the Landwehr Canal, on the opposite side of our target (the south-west), which we would leave at the point where it went under Potsdamerstrasse. The first of these three was our preferred choice, since the Spree was much the biggest waterway, and offered most scope for manoeuvre; but all were within about three-quarters of a mile of the bunker, and we should be able to walk that distance in fifteen minutes at the most.

Thereafter, we would remain in radio contact with our escort, and with the main back-up party. When the time came to leave, we would bring Bormann and Ribbentrop out with us, kill Günther at some point near the Chancellery, leave his body in a place where it was sure to be found, rejoin our kayak party, and proceed down-river with our two very important guests.

As we went through the details, Donovan made many good

points, asking particularly about clearance of the waterways. The answer, here, was that it was proving a tough job. Working almost entirely at night, the specialists from HMS *Vernon* had already removed more than fifty mines and other explosive obstructions from the Müggelsee, the Spree and the Havel towards the Elbe. In spite of the fact that they had infra-red night-vision equipment, the work was extremely hazardous: four men had been killed. It had proved impossible to clear or disarm all the mines that had been found: many remained attached to bridges or landing-stages, where they could be set off by impact, by trip-wire, or by remote-controlled detonators ashore. At least we now knew where most of these devices were; but the operational group would have to be exceedingly vigilant.

Mines apart, some of the waterways had been blocked with booms, and in numerous places collapsed buildings or blown-up bridges had created fortuitous obstructions. These latter should not cause us serious difficulties, as we could lift our kayaks out of the water and carry them over or round. As for the booms, our clearance parties had cut breaches in as many as possible, patching them up again so that they showed no sign of interference, but leaving them so that a gap could be opened in a minute or two for the passage of kayaks.

In two places downstream on the Spree our people had found large petrol tanks, with stop-cocks and pipes leading down into the river. Close by were crude yet efficient ignition-guns, clearly designed to set alight petrol released on to the water. Such devices were nothing new to us, for we knew similar arrangements had been made on the Thames in London, to incinerate anyone attempting to attack the city from the river. Yet in our case the idea had been to defend the capital against the enemy. In Berlin, it looked as though the Nazis had formed a desperate plan to stop people leaving Berlin in the moment of defeat. Had the devices been used, they would not only have destroyed all living creatures on the river: they would probably have burnt down what remained of Hitler's capital.

In laying our plans before Donovan, Fleming emphasised the chaos which, by all accounts, prevailed in Berlin. Public services – electricity, water, transport – had mostly failed. At night the city was pitch-dark, except for the light from burning buildings and gunfire flashes. Yet everywhere people were on the move, either scrounging food and fuel or seeking to escape before the Russians arrived. When we had to move through the streets at night, it should be easy enough to join the throng unnoticed.

'There's one other circumstance in our favour, General,' said Fleming by way of summing up.

'Oh yes?'

'Our reports indicate that the Spree's exceptionally low. We suspect that weirs have been bombed downstream. Whatever the cause, the water level is right down, and if there's a battle going on overhead, we should be well beneath it.'

As our discussions were ending Donovan took me aside and reiterated that Brabenov was quite the best agent he had, and he fully agreed that she should become one of the operational party. 'There something else, as well,' he added. 'She can act.'

'Act?' I was not sure what he meant.

'She should have gone on the stage – she can act the pants off most professionals. That could come in handy.'

Business over, we went to join our ship's company in the recreation room. By then everyone was in a merry state, and I could not restrain myself from going to the piano and launching into George M. Cohan's 'Yankee Doodle Dandy', with lyrics altered slightly to suit local conditions:

> She's a Yankee Doodle Dandy,
> A Yankee Doodle do or die,
> A real live lady from her Uncle Sam,
> And born on the fourth of July.
> She's a Yankee Doodle sweetheart,
> A Yankee Doodle precious pearl.
> Miss Yankee Doodle came to Birdham
> To join the Royal Navy,
> Barbara is that Yankee Doodle girl –
> Oh, Yes!
> Barbara is our Yankee Doodle Girl.

The place went berserk in the traditional Birdham manner. All round the room people hugged and kissed, and everyone joined in the pandemonium save Morton, who stood and watched in stony silence.

In the morning we entered Brabenov's name on the active list, and allocated her a pseudonym from A. A. Milne. When I announced that the only one left was Alice, a howl of laughter went up, for Alice is Christopher Robin's nanny. But for me the choice was exceedingly poignant, for Alice had been Patricia's code-name.

Our next three days were devoted to a parachute refresher course. The twenty-eight men and women detailed to go in as the command group included Bloem, nine of his paratroopers, ten Royal Marine Commandos and SBS, Brabenov, Kemp, Fleming and myself. The remaining four were Otto Günther, who had been under intensive parachute instruction for the past week, and three Wrens, one of whom, Caroline Hurst, had been specially recalled from Switzerland because she spoke both German and Russian.

Fleming, who had never made an operational jump before, was understandably nervous, but after he had twice been shoved out into space by Brabenov, he gained confidence remarkably. Anything, he said, was better than being pushed out of a plane by her.

With our parachute techniques polished, we were as ready as we could ever be, and our main concern was that we might over-train, becoming stale in body and mind. Then our worries were briskly cut short. On Friday, 20 April, word came from Berlin via Zurich that Fleming and I should arrive at the Berlin Chancellery on the 25th. We at once signalled back that we would be there, and issued orders for JBC to parachute into Berlin on the night of the twenty-third.

On the morning of Sunday the 22nd, Brabenov brought in a signal which read:

TOP SECRET A1 MOST IMMEDIATE FROM SHAEF. TO ALICE FOR POOH AND CHRISTOPHER ROBIN, OP. JB. CYPHER CR3. GOOD LUCK YOU BASTARDS AND REMEMBER I WANT FULL DETAILS DOWN TO THE LAST CENT. OKAY? IKE.

To which Fleming signalled back, all in one word:

IKEOKAYIKE.

13

Piglet's Sty

Most of our gear, including our kayaks packed up in kit form, had gone on ahead and had already been despatched to JB7. I had two changes of underwear, oiled long-johns, shoes, boat-shoes and Ursula jacket and trousers – special waterproof wear, named after a submarine – which had been adapted to resemble the outfits of Waffen-SS patrols, and could also be made to look like the top gear of Soviet waterborne intelligence by turning cap and jacket inside out. My cap had an SS badge on the outside, and when reversed it became a Russian fur cap, with the badge of a Soviet Special Intelligence Group. The Ursula jacket had zips and studs, army-officer-type pockets low down either side, two breast pockets, and several matching interior pockets for when it was turned inside out. Our plan was that, underneath this top layer, we would wear thin British uniform, so that if we were about to be captured we could strip off and escape being shot as spies.

Each of us carried a fighting knife, a Smith & Wesson .38 revolver, two 36 grenades, waterproof watches, underwater writing-tablets and life-jackets. The party began leaving Birdham at about two bells in the afternoon watch (1300 hours) on Sunday, 22 April 1945; but we did not all go in one group. We travelled in six or seven cars, leaving at intervals, and drove to the RAF base at Tempsford, near Bedford (had we all gone together in one coach, it would have been obvious to any observer that a whole unit was on the move). Günther was escorted by a Royal Marine

Commando sergeant, and had his head encased in a specially made one-piece white bandage, through which only his eyes, nose and lips were visible. In the peaceful environment of England the head-dress was glaringly conspicuous, but we had been assured by JB7 that in Berlin many walking wounded went about in just such bandages, and that in the ravaged German capital it would attract no attention.

At Tempsford we boarded a Wellington bomber of 161 Squadron and ranged ourselves along the sides of the fuselage, belting ourselves into low, flip-down seats, facing inwards. In a few minutes we were airborne and on our way to Braunschweig (Brunswick), which the Allies had overrun a week earlier. Because we flew fairly low, the air never grew very cold, but the roar of the engines made conversation impossible, and each of us was left with his or her own thoughts. I myself felt excited and happy, comfortable with our command set-up, and with plenty to keep my mind occupied.

At Braunschweig we were driven to a house commandeered from the Germans and quartered there for the night. I remember few details. It was a large house in the suburbs of the town, and a surprising level of comfort: hot baths, good food, proper beds. Next day we were not due to fly until after dark, so we sat about running through our routines yet again, particularly our alternative plan for using the Landwehr Canal if the Spree turned out to be blocked. Then, about 1900 hours, we were driven back out to the airfield and boarded our Wellington again.

By then Fleming was looking decidedly nervous. 'Aren't you frightened?' he asked as we went up the steps.

'Of course I am.'

'Why doesn't it show on your face, then?'

I couldn't answer that. I was as scared as anybody, for we were about to go into the heart of enemy territory without any fighter escort: the RAF flight planners had decided that a single bomber, flying low, would stand the best chance of escaping detection. The Luftwaffe, though greatly weakened, was still capable of launching fighter sorties; but our aim was evasion rather than confrontation, and we banked on covering the 120-odd miles to Berlin unobserved (the flight would take a little over half an hour). In particular, we did not want to alert an enemy reception committee on the ground in our target area. Our own forces round the Müggelsee were fairly formidable, but it would be by far the best if we could slip in without setting off a fire-fight.

As the pilot set course for Berlin, hopes and fears came crowding in on me. The members of JBC faced each other in the dim, red night-vision light. Susan Kemp was next to me on my left, Fleming and Brabenov directly opposite. Again the roar of the engines made conversation impossible, and my thoughts turned more and more gloomy. Except for the raid on the Irish U-boat base, this was the first time I had been on an operation with other people. Before, I had always gone alone, and now I could not get used to having so many others around me. Everyone I looked at, every young face I studied, was my responsibility, and mine alone. Even Fleming was now in my care. My word was law, and under the Articles of War disobedience commanded the death penalty. All the 150-odd men and women of JB7 already on the waterways, and now the twenty-eight in the command party, would immediately carry out any order I gave. Their health, their welfare, their lives – all were in my hands.

By what right was I in a position of such power? What special attributes did I have? As I searched my conscience, the mother of depressions settled on me, and my mind faded into oblivion, my small spark of originality snuffed out, my skills paralysed, my minimal courage ebbing fast. Again I looked across at Brabenov and Fleming. The seat next to them had been empty. Now it was occupied by someone I knew all too well, someone who had plagued me all my thinking years. It was my black angel, my angel of death.

The flashing of the stand-by lights brought me back to reality. The aircraft tilted slightly downwards. The engine noise eased. Later, we heard that the first our people on the ground knew of our approach was the rushing noise of an aircraft gliding in towards them.

In the belly of the bomber Fleming clipped on first, determined to lead the way. As the green GO light flicked on, he shot a glance at Brabenov. 'If you shove me,' it said, 'I'll have you court-martialled!' Then, for the first time in his life, he jumped out into operational action. Close behind him, I too paused for a split second. 'St Laurence, St Benedict and my dear God of Battles,'

I breathed to myself, 'we're going parachuting.' With that I was out as well.

Swinging in the murky air, I saw the north-eastern horizon flickering with flashes of artillery fire: the advancing Soviet army. They were certainly not twenty miles off, as the official reports had told us. Still closer at hand, the great mass of Berlin lay like a black blanket, pock-marked by fires. Straight beneath me, the surface of the Müggelsee gave off a dull gleam. But there was very little time to look around. All too soon I realised I was going to miss the water and land on the southern shore, so I brought my knees up, preparing to roll over on impact.

In the event, I landed half on the ground, half in a tree, twisted the release knob of my harness anti-clockwise, gave it a sharp hit and fell out of it. Then came a stab of alarm. Standing close by me, covering me with a gun, was a tall figure in SS uniform. In a flash of light I saw the red-and-black insignia on the shoulder. But before I could reach for my Smith & Wesson, the figure spoke – in a woman's voice.

It was Christa Shulberg, dressed to kill. After giving me a kiss and a welcome to her country, she spoilt things by saluting. The navy does not salute at night, and no regular officer can help being irritated if somebody makes such a basic mistake. I was therefore not as affectionate as I should have been. Having quickly checked that there was no opposition on shore, Caroline Saunders and I stripped to our underwear, dived into the icy water, and swam out to make sure that the pick-up by kayak was going to plan. After the loss of Hannah Fierstein, we were not going to spare one ounce of effort to make sure all our people were safe.

Everything turned out well. All were safely recovered. The parachutes were collected, rolled and tied up, loaded on to one of the two motorboats JB7 had managed to steal, and taken off to be hidden in a safe house. Back on shore, I towelled off, got dressed, and took passage in a motor boat across the lake to the north-eastern shore. Then we walked uphill through trees to the biggest house our Freedom Fighters had commandeered.

The house appeared to have been the holiday home of well-to-do Berliners. It was made of wood, and quite large, with a big cellar and two upper storeys. It stood on a hill about 200 metres from the north-east shore of the lake, east of Friedrichshagen and north of Rahnsdorf, and was surrounded by sparse woods. Our pioneers had done well to commandeer it and rig it out as a secure operational base. It made a good look-out point, and was an ideal site for the high-powered, short-wave radio which they had brought in, and which enabled them to maintain round-the-clock contact with the M Section control at Bletchley. Our people had made themselves comfortable with hammocks, bunks, bedding, water-heaters and cooking equipment, and they scrounged a good deal of fresh food from the surrounding area. The boys, as always when in a minority, found themselves pleasurably cossetted by a surplus of solicitous little mothers, and Susan was very moved by the atmosphere when she arrived.

We were given a rousing welcome, and a magnificent meal of corned beef, baked beans and fresh eggs somehow acquired locally, washed down by liberal shots of schnapps. Public electricity supplies had long since died, but a generator gave us light, and the girls had got things magnificently organised. They were cooking on primus-type oil stoves and bigger wood-burning ranges, and food and drink seemed plentiful. The radio link with England was working well, and our safe arrival was soon known in Bletchley. In an atmosphere of such high spirits and vitality, it was hard to believe that we were in the middle of a doomed city.

Behind carefully drawn blackout curtains we caught up on recent events. Some of our Freedom Fighters had made friends with local people, and found lodging with them, by pretending to be Berliners on the run from the advancing Soviets. Since everyone hated the Russians, it had been easy to find accommodation; and the result was that JB7 had gained control of many houses and facilities in the area. Better still, they had created havoc among the bands of Waffen-SS and other Nazis who were roaming the streets in a last-minute attempt to settle scores. The official report put in by Israel Bloem recorded over three hundred enemy killed, mostly with their throats slit and their eyes gouged out, some with their testicles ripped off. Many a Nazi made the greatest and last mistake of his life when he saw a couple of apparently innocent girls coming his way, and looked on them as easy prey. The GFF regularly patrolled the suburbs round the safe house, with two girls ahead as decoys and two boys following at a discreet distance. They deliberately frequented areas in which they knew unofficial SS were operating. The usual pattern was for the 'blacks' to accost the girls and start trying to rape them. At first the apparent victims would offer little resistance, but as soon as their assailants had exposed themselves, they would whip out their fighting knives and slice off their vital organs. Then they stabbed them in the eyes, behind the ears or in the jugular. Finally, holding aloft their bloody trophies, they would cry out, 'That's for my father (or mother, brother or sister),' and fling the severed parts on to the bodies, spitting on them for good measure. Far from being ashamed of such actions, they came back and happily reported them to Susan, who one evening went marauding with them.

Such was the revenge exacted by our Jewish people for the torture and murder of their fathers, mothers and families in the concentration camps. And so fierce was the atmosphere of hatred the Nazis had generated that after the war, to the consternation of Morton and Churchill, both Fleming and I countersigned Bloem's reports with the words, 'We fully approve of these actions.'

During the night, while the rest of us got our heads down, a small party ferried six kayaks across to the north-west corner of the Müggelsee and a mile down the Spree, where they hid them in a derelict shed, at a point just north of Vorstadt Ender Island. In the daylight hours of 24 April we had time to catch up on our own people's situation reports. Their most encouraging discovery was that disused railway tunnels and other subterranean pasageways ran from close by the Foreign Ministry bunker to the Friedrichstrasse station, a very short distance from our pick-up point by the Weidendamm bridge. If those underground escape routes remained open, our task of spiriting Bormann and Ribbentrop out of the bunker would be greatly simplified. (Everyone had been told that our mission was to lift two men from the centre of the city, but the identity of our pick-up targets was still known only to Fleming, Susan Kemp, Brabenov and myself.)

By 2030 hours we were ready to go. After a final check of our equipment – radios, weapons, forged passes, various uniforms, food – we made our way down through the trees and embarked in one of the motorboats, which took us across to our hide-out position in the derelict shed. There we transferred to kayaks. In the lead was the big, fair-haired Captain John Morgan, with me as his crewman. The second kayak was manned by SBS Royal

Marine Commando Sergeant David Jones and Günther, wearing his head-bandage. Next came Brabenov with her Commando, Sergeant John Rawlins, and then Fleming with Sergeant Peter Fletcher. The last two kayaks were crewed by Freedom Fighters, one man and one woman in each. We took the girls because we saw that they would be invaluable in any encounter with the police or SS: if anyone challenged us, who better to talk us out of a tight corner than two pretty young *Fräuleins*? At the very least they might be able to stop hostile forces opening fire on us by paddling over and going ashore for a parley – and any official who tried to arrest them would get a disabling shock.

For me it was a joy and a relief to be back in an operational kayak for the first time in more than a year, and to feel the little craft come alive in the water as John Morgan and I paddled off into the dark. Everything felt familiar, and without thinking I could put my hands on all the equipment stowed in its special pouches: tommy-gun, hand grenades, R/G lamps, compass, first-aid kit. A thick drizzle made visibility poor, and this suited us fine: the buildings along the river banks were dark, and the only light came from gunfire flashes, shells exploding and warehouses or factories on fire. The sounds of battle were staccato and irregular, but after a while they seemed to fuse into a continuous background noise. One kayak was in radio contact with Susan Kemp, now in charge at the Müggelsee command centre, but for inter-canoe communication we relied on Morse sent by our R/G lights, which, being infra-red, could not be seen by the enemy or picked up by direction-finders.

So it was that six kayaks headed north-west through the stricken city. We hugged the eastern bank, maintaining precise line ahead, and exactly three boat-lengths between canoes. We had twelve miles to go, and with the current in our favour John calculated that our effective speed should be between three and four knots. In other words, we should reach our destination between 0030 and 0100. I was glad to find that the Spree was a considerable waterway, often fifty yards and more across, since this gave us some room for manoeuvre. Also, as our scouts had told us, its level was very low, so that for much of the way we travelled between banks or walls ten or fifteen feet high, and this alone afforded a good measure of security, since the shellfire passed harmlessly over our heads.

For most of its length the river flowed through fully built-up areas; but at some points railway lines ran beside it – there was nothing moving along them – and early in our voyage we found ourselves passing Plänterwald and Treptow parks, an extensive area of woods on the port, or left-hand, bank. Already, in advance, we had assigned every significant landmark a code-letter, in alphabetical order: long study of our model at Birdham had ingrained them all in our memories, and as we passed each one we noted it on our underwater writing-tablets, prefixed by S for starboard or P for port. Then there were the numerous bridges: Waisen, Fischer, Kurfürsten, Kaiser Wilhelm, Friedrich (the names of several of these have changed since the war).

Gradually the river swung west, and after three hours we saw the shattered hulk of the cathedral loom above us to port. Our next landmark was the dome of the Bode Museum, also to port. Then we shot the Monbijou Bridge, and knew we were within minutes of the set-down point John had chosen, in the shadow of the Weidendamm Bridge.

There it was: an immense steel structure filling the sky ahead. John steered silently in to the south bank and came alongside a wall nearly twenty feet high, one and a half minutes inside the time he had set himself. Thanks to the hard work of our scouts, a rope-ladder was already in position. While John held the kayak steady, I wriggled into the straps of my haversack, whispered good-bye and climbed the slimy wall to the quay above. Below me, one by one, the other three kayaks slid in to disgorge their passengers and then disappeared silently into the darkness. Brabenov's pack was particularly heavy, since it contained, besides her own kit, the medical and dental records Bormann had loaned us.

Within minutes the last of the kayaks had sped away, leaving the river apparently deserted. In fact a stiff paddle faced our Commandos, for their orders were to go back upstream and wait at the Müggelsee base until we recalled them forward for the actual breakout.

Up on the quay, at street level, we felt much more exposed. The noise of shellfire seemed louder, the flashes of explosions brighter. Now, on top of our thin shirts bearing Royal Navy insignia, we wore our Ursula gear with Waffen-SS Special Waterborne badges and caps. The party appeared to be under the command of Brabenov, who sported the insignia of a Brigadeführer. With her leading, and our German-made sub-machine-guns at the ready, we set out westwards in line ahead along the street that followed the south bank of the river, keeping about ten yards apart, so as to present no single target. We had hardly started moving before we were assailed by a nauseating smell of rotting flesh: dead bodies were decomposing in every corner, in shell-holes, in ditches, in the gutters, under piles of masonry, and the air was heavy with the stench of death.

Other people were on the move, some walking fast, others running. The whistle and crash of incoming shells kept everyone on edge. In a few moments we came to Friedrichstrasse and turned left down it, to the south. Again we could navigate from memory, using the maps of central Berlin imprinted on our minds.

The first turn to the right, after the Friedrichstrasse station, was Georgenstrasse, and we took that. Just as we did so two men came racing past from the opposite direction. A burst of automatic fire from behind cut both of them down. Our party shrank back into doorways. One of the fugitives had been killed instantly, but the other started screaming, until another burst of fire silenced him.

Within seconds a five-strong SS vigilante group was on top of us. To have run would have signed our death-warrant, so we stood rooted. The red-haired officer in charge, seeing us there but not immediately discerning our identity, yelled out a challenge in German: 'Come forward and raise your hands!'

'*Scheisskerl!*' shouted Brabenov in an astonishingly loud, almost baritone voice. 'Shithead! How dare you speak to a senior officer without coming to attention and giving the Führer salute?'

The German hesitated for a moment, then saluted and blurted out, '*Heil Hitler, Brigadeführerin!*'

Brabenov, playing up magnificently, tore into him, demanding to know what he was doing, and what his orders were. When he claimed that he had been detailed to shoot deserters, she told him he was in the wrong place. He should be north of the river, she said, closer to the advancing Russians. *That* was the place for deserters.

'So,' she concluded, 'get going before I take your names and blast your backsides off!'

Again the man saluted. As his group began to shamble off,

Brabenov, still in character, turned to us and yelled, 'As for *you* three shitheads, you get moving, too!'

It was a bravura performance. But then, a moment later, we came on something that was too much even for our phenomenal Yankee Doodle girl. As we turned out of Friedrichstrasse into Unter den Linden, we found ourselves on top of a group of women and children who had just been hit by a shell. Most of them were dead, blown to pieces. Among them was a young woman whose head had been split in two. She lay in a pool of blood; but beside her exposed breast, still alive, was a tiny baby, only a few months old. It too was covered in blood, and the light from a blazing building revealed that one little arm had been severed at the shoulder. Blood was pumping from the wound, but with its dying strength the infant was still instinctively trying to reach for its mother and suck from her breast.

Brabenov went down on one knee. The baby seemed to hear her, and reached out its remaining hand in her direction. She picked it up, cuddled it to her and vainly tried to staunch its wound with a handkerchief; but within seconds its life had flickered away. Touching her lips to its forehead, she laid it beside its mother's body on the pavement, and, kneeling, made the sign of the cross, the baby's blood dripping from her fingers. (Fascinated, I saw that she made the sign in the manner of the Russian Orthodox Church, starting from right to left.)

'Oh God!' she groaned. 'This is too much. My people are fighting each other. My father and my mother – Germans and Russians.'

Then, in a second or two, she got hold of herself and was her professional self again, and we went on. Just short of the Foreign Ministry I stopped the group in a sheltering doorway and called John Morgan on my walkie–talkie. At 0107 hours I reported that we were within three minutes of Piglet's sty. '*Bonne chance*,' I concluded. 'Over.'

'Romeo JBC,' Morgan answered. 'God bless. JB7-1 listening out.'

That was the end of our communication for the time being. Once we were underground, JB7 would not be able to call us. They would have to wait until we came through to them.

14

At Close Quarters

By then the Foreign Ministry had been severely damaged. Not a window remained intact in the building, and big holes had been blown in its grandiose masonry. As we approached the entrance to the Chancellery bunker, behind the Foreign Ministry on the eastern edge of the Tiergarten, the guards brought their weapons to the ready, but evidently they had been told to expect us, for when Brabenov announced who we were, they called up a man to escort us down into the bowels of the earth. We found ourselves in the same air-raid shelter as before, but this time all four of us were put into a single cell-like room, and to our surprise no one relieved us of our side-arms.

Dumping our heavy haversacks, we surveyed our new accommodation. There was not much to see. The room contained four bunks with filthy old mattresses and a couple of grey blankets apiece. A bare wooden table and four chairs completed the furnishings; in an alcove screened off by a curtain were a washbasin with a single tap and, on the floor, two chamber pots.

When Brabenov discovered these, she reacted with her normal resilience and guts. Pretending to be thrilled, she held the pots out in front of her and cried, 'OK, you guys, who's sharing with me?'

Fleming and I burst out laughing. Günther did not understand what she had said until the remark was translated; then he too laughed, and claimed it was the nicest invitation he had ever had from a lady. When he clicked his heels and bowed, Brabenov returned the compliment with a mock curtsey.

On the table someone had laid out the bare essentials of a meal: cold sausage, black bread, soup, foul *ersatz* coffee and a primus stove.

'Whoopee!' exlaimed Brabenov. 'A feast!'

As I began to heat up the soup, Fleming brought out a flask and gave everyone a much-needed shot of brandy. The idea of spending days and nights in such a dungeon was hard to face; and in the early hours of the morning, as I lay on my bunk trying to disregard the roar of the ventilation system, I longed to be out in the freedom of the open air. Until we were on the river, masters of our own destiny, it would be impossible to relax. Soon after Günther had gone to sleep, he started to snore loudly, and the noise woke Brabenov, who came across and sat on my bunk. When I glanced across at the hapless man whom I would have to kill before the week was out, she somehow sensed my distress and held my arm.

'Maybe I should kill him now,' I whispered, 'when he's had a drink and is out for the count.'

The grip on my arm tightened.

'At least I'm in the right place,' I said.

'What do you mean?'

'With all the other mass-murderers.'

Brabenov had no more comfort to offer. Instead, she silently made her sign of the cross, and invoked help from somewhere else.

Morning confirmed that our quarters and living conditions were all too like those of a gaol. Breakfast of a sort was brought to us, but one of us had to empty our chamber pots into a bucket at the end of the corridor. Then we had nothing to do but wait for a summons from Ribbentrop.

This came at about 0930. Leaving Brabenov and Günther in our cell, Fleming and I went up under escort into the wrecked Foreign Ministry. The noise of shellfire, muffled down in the concrete-clad cellars, was far more menacing above ground, and the screech of incoming projectiles was disconcertingly loud. Standing on his dignity to the last, Ribbentrop was still using his old office, even though it was a wreck, with the windows long since blown out, the walls pitted by shell-splinters, the coverings of the chairs ripped up, and piles of fallen plaster on the floor.

His greeting was friendly enough, but I could see that he was under immense strain.

'Why don't you move down below?' I asked. 'If you stay up here, it can only be a matter of time before you get blown to kingdom come.'

'I'd rather that than cower underground with all that ill-bred, common scum,' he answered haughtily. 'And anyway, I shall be out of here tomorrow.'

'Really?' said Fleming. 'We're going that soon?'

'No . . .' For once Ribbentrop looked uncomfortable as he revealed that he had changed his mind. Instead of coming with us, he had arranged a passage out of Berlin through Count Bernadotte and the Swedish Embassy.*

'But Bormann is still relying on you entirely,' he said quickly. 'He will see you right. Indeed, he has already recompensed me handsomely for producing the Davis-Bond escape organisation.'

For a few minutes the Foreign Minister tried to make conversation, but his mind was clearly elsewhere, and soon he said goodbye. As we shook hands, I felt no emotion of any kind, neither contempt for this empty poseur, nor regret at parting with an old family friend. Rather, I was glad that we would not be encumbered with him on our passage down-river, and that we would be able to concentrate on the man we really wanted.

Before we left, I reminded Ribbentrop that, while we were waiting, we needed permission to go up into the open air and make radio contact with our people every few hours. To this he readily agreed, and he gave his guards orders that we were to be allowed out whenever we asked.

Down in our concrete dungeon we found Bormann awaiting us. He had been talking to Brabenov, but of Günther there was no

* Whether Ribbentrop was bluffing I do not know. In the event, he escaped from Berlin on his own, apparently in a light aircraft which took off from the main east–west axis. After trying unsuccessfully to ingratiate himself with Admiral Karl Dönitz, whom Hitler had appointed his successor, Ribbentrop disappeared, until he was arrested by British troops in Hamburg on 14 June 1945. Brought to trial at Nuremberg, he was sentenced to death in October 1946.

sign. When I asked where he had gone, Bormann replied that he had had him taken to other quarters, partly so that Günther would not see the person whom he was impersonating, and partly so that Bormann himself could get a good, surreptitious look at him. He agreed that the likeness was excellent.

'In that case,' said Brabenov, 'you had better have your records back.' She handed over the dossier of medical and other papers, explaining that they had been expertly adjusted to match Günther's particulars. Bormann opened one of the files and after a cursory look through it muttered, '*Ausgezeichnet*! Excellent!'

Our key question, of course, was 'When are we leaving?' But to this he would give no definite answer. It might be in two days' time, he said. It might be in five or six. Six days in this chicken-coop! The prospect appalled us.

'Why can't we go now, before the Russians block the escape routes?' Fleming asked.

Bormann replied that it was not the Russians who worried him, so much as the SS and the Nazi Party faithful. Already a number of officials had been shot while trying to sneak off: if he himself attempted to slip out at that moment, he would run a high risk of being detected. He judged it better to wait until confusion increased in the final paroxysms of defeat. Then, he said, every man would be looking to save himself – and that would be the moment to go.

'But why the hell,' said Fleming, a good deal irritated, 'couldn't you arrange for your double here, in Berlin, and save us a lot of trouble?'

Once more Bormann patiently explained that if anyone had seen him recruiting a double, he would immediately have come under suspicion of trying to escape.

As we waited, tension increased inexorably. From Bloem's intelligence reports, forwarded to us by JB7, we knew that the Soviet forces had now almost encircled the centre of Berlin: they were within nine miles of the Müggelsee and twelve of Hitler's last redoubt. Our own ears told us that the battle was intensifying: the muffled explosions of incoming shells were more or less continuous. It was clear that if we did not leave within the next couple of days, we would not leave at all. Waiting became more and more difficult – and until the end came, we simply had to endure. I think it was easiest for me, since I was used to life in submarines, and felt less claustrophobic than the others; but they both responded to our incarceration fully in character, Fleming by behaving most gallantly towards Brabenov, and she by retaining her normal ebullient cheerfulness. It was the bonds of friendship built up between us at Birdham, forged by discipline and training, that carried us through and overcame the difficulties of living at such close quarters.

Rough food was brought to us, and we cooked and ate what we could of it: from the mere fact that our rations grew ever more meagre, we could tell that pressure on Hitler's last citadel was increasing day by day. Every morning we emptied our chamber pots into the communal bucket. We invented ridiculous games, indulged in riotous horseplay, and laughed a lot. Six times in every twenty-four hours one of us went up into the open and contacted JB7 to exchange reports.

At 0930 on the morning of 29 April, Bormann appeared and asked for a detailed briefing. Sitting at the bare wooden table, we went through our plans, with several significant omissions. Brabenov interpreted as we described how our flotilla would proceed down-river, with everyone, including our passenger, wearing whatever uniform was most appropriate to the surroundings.

At first Bormann seemed worried. He knew how heavily the waterways had been mined and defended, and he doubted our ability to find a way down them. Gradually, however, his confidence grew as he heard how effectively our mine-clearance experts had been at work, and when I concluded, he remarked with a smile, '*Durch Berlin fließt immer noch die Spree.*'

'It's a line from a popular song,' Brabenov explained. '"Whatever happens, the Spree's still flowing through Berlin." He reckons it's a good omen.'

Bormann confided that he himself had done a good deal of canoeing as a hobby, and I lined up two chairs, one behind the other, so that we could simulate our seating positions in a kayak and have a little practice.

By the morning of Sunday, 30 April, it was clear the bunkers could not hold out much longer. Up in the open the shellfire was continuous, and our radio contacts told us that the Soviet armies were closing in from every direction, with special units assigned to capture the Reich Chancellery, only a few yards from where we were holed up. No food or water appeared that morning, and we were forced to breakfast off our own iron rations of hard biscuit and sips of brandy.

That afternoon, at about 1520, Fleming suddenly said to me, 'I cannot order you, and I am not ordering you, to kill Piglet's double.'

Brabenov came quickly over, and we all three stood in the middle of the room, holding one another's arms tightly.

Fleming went on in a low voice: 'You're the operational commander. Killing Günther is entirely a tactical affair. It doesn't come under my strategic rules of engagement. However, Lieutenant-Commander Creighton – Christopher – you will do everything in your power to ensure that Martin Bormann is brought safely out of Berlin and delivered into Allied hands on the west bank of the Elbe. You will carry out these orders in such a manner as to make it appear that Bormann died while attempting to escape – notwithstanding your personal safety, comfort, principles, *or those of any other person whatsoever*. You are requested and required to carry out your orders and rules of engagement without regard to the rank, status or occupation of any person, or the rules and covenants of any organisation, including the Geneva Convention, save M Section control. You are so charged under the Articles of War.'

'And the penalty for disobedience is death,' I responded softly.

'Something like that.'

That afternoon, when Brabenov and I returned from a radio session in the chaos above, the mood of our host had changed altogether. Bormann stood there accompanied by two armed SS officers, who had taken up an aggressive stance on either side of him with their revolvers levelled at Fleming. Now they covered me.

'*Was ist los?*' asked Brabenov evenly. 'What's the matter?'

Bormann raised a file he had been carrying under one arm, and when I saw on it the word ABWEHR I knew what was coming. In a well-rehearsed warning to my companions, I gave a sniff.

With Brabenov interpreting, Bormann began a quiet indictment. For some time, he said, he had been trying to gain access to the files kept by the late Admiral Canaris, former head of the Abwehr intelligence service, who had been executed by the SS for his anti-Nazi leanings. At last, said Bormann, he had succeeded in getting what he wanted, and this file – he brandished it – was mine. Clearly laid out in it, with full details, were my activities as a British double agent. The record showed beyond doubt that I was not a renegade deserter but an officer in the Royal Navy.

'What about *him*?' Bormann demanded, gesturing at Fleming. 'What about this friend of yours, the so-called Herr Bond? Is he Royal Navy also?'

I saw that both revolvers were pointing more or less at me. Small adjustments would have swivelled them to cover Fleming, but they were not pointing anywhere near Brabenov, whom the Germans were treating merely as an interpreter – a fatal error. Instead of answering, I gave another sniff.

In the time it took to blink, Brabenov had drawn her Smith & Wesson .38, swept back the hammer with the heel of her left hand, and fired two shots from the hip, disabling both SS men with bullets in their gun arms. In the confined space the crash of the two explosions was deafening, and a smell of cordite filled the room.

Before the Germans could recover from the shock, I too had drawn a revolver and levelled it at Bormann. After a moment he nodded his head to signify surrender. The SS weapons clattered to the floor. As the wounded men groaned and grasped their arms, he and his companions looked stunned by the speed and accuracy of our girl's marksmanship. Fleming and I were not in the least surprised, for we had witnessed it many times before at Birdham.

Then Fleming broke into fluent German to confirm that all three of us were naval officers, and that he himself was in overall command of an operation launched specifically to bring Bormann out of Berlin and transport him to Britain, where he would be given absolute asylum, and enough money to live in comfort and safety for the rest of his life. He could choose now: whether to die immediately, or to come with us.

For a few seconds our victim stared at us, his eyes switching from Fleming to myself and back. Of course we had no intention of killing him, but he was not to know that. For all he could tell, he was on the verge of extinction. Then he challenged us: 'In exchange for what?'

Fleming told him: in exchange for his full co-operation in

identifying and handing over all the money, gold, jewellery, real-estate deeds and other assets which the Nazis had secreted outside Germany, and of which he had control, and his absolute collaboration with British interrogators in revealing every detail of his life and times in the Nazi Party.

This time there was no hesitation. 'I accept,' he said. Then, once we had holstered our weapons, he went to the door, opened it, and shouted down the corridor. In a moment two officers from his own Chancellery staff came in, standing stiffly to attention and giving Nazi salutes. Bormann whispered something to one of them, whereupon they hustled the two wounded men out of the room. Their fate was clear to all of us: they had heard too much to live.

Bormann looked shaken. Fleming warned him that he had better be extremely careful from now on. We three were by no means the only people who knew of his plan to escape: the 150-odd members of the British special forces deployed around Berlin were well aware of what was happening, and the moment one of our four-hourly radio contacts failed to go through to our local headquarters, word of his treachery would be with the other Nazi leaders, not least Goebbels, within minutes. (This was not true, but it sounded dangerous.)

After a moment Bormann nodded his agreement. Fleming finished by saying, 'And I'll have that Abwehr file.'

There was another short pause before Bormann handed it over. Then he said, 'You have no need to worry. I shall keep my word.'

In retrospect, I thought Brabenov had taken an excessive risk in firing the two shots; but I did not mention it to her. When I gave the second sniff, I had intended only that she should distract the two SS men while I went in and disarmed them. I had not anticipated that her reaction would be so instantaneous. The sound of the detonations could have brought the whole of the Nazi headquarters down on us; but in fact nobody seemed to have heard them through the thick concrete and steel cladding – or, if they had, they had mistaken them for odd shots in the ever-increasing battle above ground. If Brabenov had missed, her bullets would have ricocheted about off the cement walls, killing God knows whom; but she was a true professional, and an ace at firing from the hip – or anywhere else – and she made no mistake.

With Fleming, myself and Brabenov trapped in the bunker, Susan was effectively in command of the whole operation – and nobody could have acted with greater skill or courage. That night she and her people came five miles down-river before beaching their canoes on the bank at the beginning of the Spree Canal, where it branched westwards off the main stream. They were still seven miles upstream of our pick-up point, but within easier reach. In her final radio message that night she reported that the battle was raging violently over their heads, but that the Spree itself continued to sweep majestically through the city, apparently untouched by the conflict. In my mind I could see the little boats slipping downstream in line ahead, at precise four-boat-length intervals, and vanishing into the shoreline shadows when she ordered them to beach.

Her flotilla consisted of twelve kayaks, two of which had been adapted to carry the heavy radio equipment needed to communicate with the M Section radio truck on the Elbe. There were four spare berths, for us three and our star guest. The plan was that when our departure was imminent, the flotilla should proceed downstream during the night and hide up as close as possible to the Weidendamm Bridge and the bunkers. Then, as we left, they would come out of cover and pick us up.

Our evening radio contact with the Müggelsee told us that the Russians were everywhere: but for the underground passages leading towards the Spree, we would have little chance of getting out. At 2030 hours Bormann came in again, to tell us that we would make our breakout the next evening, Tuesday, 1 May. The main Nazi group would not leave until then, he said, and he himself could not possibly go until they did.

For some time I had been wondering what had happened to Hitler, and when I asked, Bormann came back with the enigmatic reply, 'The Führer is dead.' He would not elaborate or say what had happened, but left us for the night.

It was a strange paradox for all of us. The war had lasted six years, and terrible atrocities had been committed. For months – years – countless people had been trying to exterminate the main perpetrator, Adolf Hitler. Now, apparently, he was dead; but his demise did not appear to have affected anything. The Soviets were still crashing and bashing their way into the centre of the city. People were still dying in their thousands. In a few hours we would be on our way, escorting the keeper of billions of dollars' worth of Nazi loot down the river to safety. But why? And for what?

We knew the answers to those questions perfectly well. We were not acting from motives of patriotism or high moral principles. We were not doing this for England or Uncle Sam. As usual, we were simply doing what we had been told to do: we were carrying out our orders. By tomorrow night we would probably all be dead, killed by our allies, the bloody, triumphant, murderous, raping soldiers of a repressive totalitarian regime – but before we were snuffed out, we would do our best.

After a while our enforced inaction allowed my mind to relax, and into it stole a thought I had been trying hard to suppress. I had hoped it would remain in my subconscious until the moment I was bound to act on it, but now it came surging to the fore: the fact that I would soon have to kill again.

Piglet's double had to die. Moreover, he had to perish within minutes of our leaving the bunker. Somewhere in the no man's land between the bunker and the river, I would have to assassinate him, leaving his body at a spot where it was reasonably sure to be found. One bullet through the heart was the solution on which we had agreed – a single shot, and no other injury that might impair his identification as Bormann. The gun that fired that shot could not be British or American, so we had settled on a 9mm Luger, which I had holstered with my .38 Smith & Wesson.

It was clear to Brabenov, if not to Fleming, that my black angel had returned. Sensing that depression and inner torment had suddenly flooded through me, she jumped up, fetched a packet from her haversack and handed each of us a bar of Hershey chocolate, an American favourite.

'I saved these for a special occasion,' she announced.

'Good-oh!' said Fleming enthusiastically. 'I love Hershey bars.'

I got up and put my hands on Brabenov's shoulders. 'Brabenov, *ma bien-aimée, tu es la meilleure.*'

'*Je t'en prie, mon brave,*' she whispered in her Anglo-American–Russian-German French. 'And but for your naval discipline, I'd kiss you.'

But Fleming had had enough, for obvious reasons. 'Sod the pair of you!' he exclaimed. 'I'm going to crash out.' Then he softened, and as we munched he muttered, 'Now we're all chocolate sailors.'

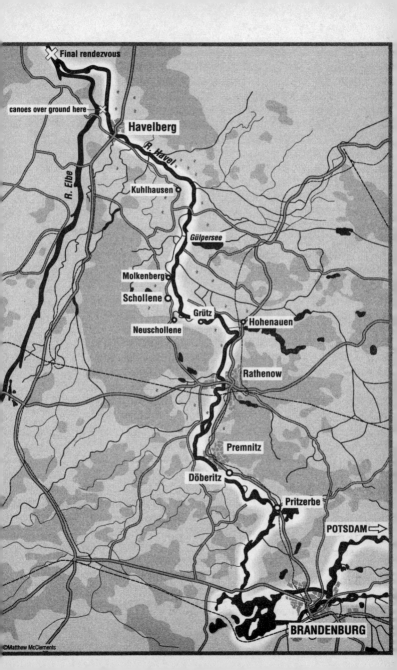

Sunken barge

Monbijou bridge

Weidendamm bridge

SPREE

Pick-up point

Marschall bridge

SPREE

Friedrichstrasse station

Georgenstrasse

Wilhelmstrasse

Brandenburg gate

Unter den Linden

Friedrichstrasse

Unter den Linden

Tiergarten

Foreign Ministry and bunkers

Reichs Chancellery and Führer bunkers

Wilhelmstrasse

©Matthew McClements

15

On the River

By the evening of Tuesday, 1 May, we felt as if we were on our marks at the start of a marathon race: with nights of strenuous effort ahead, and threats closing in from every side, we itched for the gun to go and launch us on our way. Bormann had confirmed that we would leave that night; but still we did not trust him. There remained a chance that he would double-cross us and make off on his own, using some other escape channel which he himself had devised. If he did that, the chances were that he would be able to enjoy the riches he had salted away, and live in luxury for the rest of his days. He could, if he wished, leave us incarcerated where we were, to die from hunger and thirst, or to be found alive by the Russians. This latter possibility bothered Fleming not one jot: if Soviet soldiers discovered us, locked in a cell and holding Royal Naval identity cards, with luck they would accept us as bona fide Allied officers detained by the Nazis, and hand us over to the British authorities in the usual way.

But Bormann knew that we were his best bet, and at 1700 I was let out of the bunker to make contact with JBPU, the pick-up group. As I climbed to street level, it was abundantly clear that Berlin had entered its death throes. The stench of excrement seemed to follow me up into the open air, for the main sewers had been blown open, and their stink mingled foully with that of rotting bodies. The noise of battle had risen to such awesome proportions that I sought out a hollow in some rubble which shielded me from the worst of the din, as well as from the shell-splinters and chunks of masonry that were flying through the air.

Susan Kemp, in command of the pick-up group, reported that she and her kayaks were hidden in the wreck of a barge, sunk in the Spree only three hundred yards short of the Weidendamm Bridge. The barge had been half-gutted by fire, but inside its scorched shell the party had slung their hammocks from the bulkheads and made themselves at home. I told her to stand by for action any time after dark, but warned her not to break cover until I ordered it.

For me, that was the easy part. Much harder was to order Christa Shulberg and the whole of the rear group to leave their well-established base on the Müggelsee and follow the pick-up flotilla down-river. They had only eight serviceable kayaks and two medium-sized motorboats to accommodate fifty people, but if they squeezed sixteen or seventeen into each of the boats they should be able to manage. Unlike the canoes, the motor vessels could not run silently, but by then the general noise level was so high that this did not seem to be a problem. At least they had plenty of fuel, privily siphoned out of the tanks filled to set the waterways on fire.

At 2100 I went up into the open again, taking Brabenov with me. When at last we got through to Christa, she had alarming news. She reported that four of her people had just been killed in action, a mile north of Vorstadt Ender Island. Two men and two women – Theo and Leon, Lisabeth and Sarah – had all been shot dead as they moved in to try to protect a group of Berliners from the Russians, who were looting houses and raping and bayonetting women and children indiscriminately.

As we stood in the shattered garden, buffeted by explosions, the report left both of us shocked, Brabenov especially. Again she was confronted by the fact that her father's kinsmen were slaughtering her mother's. As for me, I too felt my heart being torn apart. Help came from the rigid discipline instilled by the Royal Navy, the discipline that defies pain, fear, hesitation and doubt, and all basic emotion. To anyone who could take the savage punishments of Dartmouth and the M Section, to anyone who could survive the brutalities of the SS and the Gestapo in the prison at Cherbourg, this hail of shells on the heart of Hitler's dying empire was a picnic.

I know my face had gone blank. Brabenov had never seen me look so inhuman, and now, after a glance at me, she backed away. As I raised my microphone and spoke to Christa, I sounded matter-of-fact, official and totally devoid of emotion.

'JB7. This is JBC. Your report affirmative. You will disregard casualties and execute Operations Kanga and Christa immediately. JBC out.'

Brabenov stared at me again, and kept her distance.

Back inside the bunker, time dragged past. Preying on my mind was the fact that very soon I was going to have to murder the wretched Günther. To my shame, I still did not know what yarn had been spun him, or what he thought was going on in all this lengthy performance. My one consolation was that he did not seem worried: he was heading for extinction with the stolidity of an ox.

For the breakout, Fleming, Brabenov and I had decided to wear our converted Ursula waterproof jackets and trousers with Soviet Special Intelligence insignia, but with SS caps and greatcoats on top of them. Dressed like that, we stood the best chance of leaving the bunker area undetected, but we would then be able to throw off the coats when we reached our kayaks or if we ran into Soviet forces. In our haversacks we also carried naval uniform (British or American) and Wehrmacht greatcoats, suitable for private soldiers.

Just before 2300 Bormann at last appeared and announced that departure was imminent. Günther was brought in, still wearing his head-bandage, clad in the uniform of a Wehrmacht private and carrying a black leather coat slung over his shoulder. Bormann had already warned him that he would have to submit to a thorough body-search, and now he did so, apparently unmoved by the indignity of the proceedings. At our order he removed his clothes, and while Brabenov went carefully through them Fleming and I attended to the man himself. I was concentrating on my unpleasant task so thoroughly that it was only when I made my penetration into his anus, using his own dirty handkerchief as a sheath, that the terrible reality of what I was about to do again hit me. Here I was touching, searching, probing the body of a man whom, within an hour, I would have to kill.

Thank heavens, the search was soon over, and it yielded nothing at all on the man himself, and in his clothes only one unappetising sandwich, which appeared to have no filling between the slices of black bread. In a few minutes Günther had dressed again, and he was escorted out of our room.

Soon afterwards we put Bormann through the same process. This time our body-search revealed three glass phials of potassium cyanide strapped under his armpits, but we allowed him to keep them, as they did not give anything away. The contents of his pockets were another matter. Apart from some Reichsmarks and a few immaterial odds and ends, they included two crucial identity cards: his Nazi Party membership card, number 60508, and one describing him as head of the Nazi Party Chancellery and private secretary to the Führer. Last but far from least were his current diary and a large buff envelope, which was neither addressed nor sealed.

Opening the diary, Fleming flicked to the entry for that day, Tuesday, 1 May. It consisted of a single word: *Ausbruchsversuch* (breakout attempt). The buff envelope contained a sheaf of typed pages. Having skimmed through some of them, Fleming handed them without comment to Brabenov – and for the first time in our acquaintance our Yankee Doodle girl lost her cool.

'Jesus!' she exclaimed. 'You know what this is? It's Hitler's personal will. As far as I can see it names Martin Bormann as his sole executor.'

She asked Bormann if that was correct, and he nodded. We had made an extraordinary find. Even if this was only one of several copies, it was a document of the first importance, as it would undoubtedly support later claims for the recovery of Nazi assets in Switzerland and elsewhere.

A rapid discussion followed about who should take the cards, diary and testament. We had already decided that it would be best for Günther to carry no papers: if he were the real Martin Bormann trying to escape, he would obviously have nothing on him that could lead to identification. On the other hand, if a diary were found in his pocket, its presence might be interpreted as a last-minute oversight, and might help pin down the identity of the body. We therefore gave Günther the diary, and Fleming kept the rest of the documents.

As for Bormann, we had brought with us an identity card forged by the M Section which gave him a false name and described him as a junior Nazi Party worker. When Fleming presented it to him, he seemed content. We then explained that we ourselves would keep his real identity cards and the copy of the will, and stow them in one of our all-proof cases (which were protected against water, fire and blast), until they were safely in Allied hands.

Like rats on the run from a sinking ship, the Nazis were pouring out of their last stronghold. *Festung Berlin* indeed! The fortress was finally crumbling. The bunker corridors were full of people milling around, all talking at once, some screaming at the tops of their voices, as if drunk with alcohol or fear or a combination of both. It was easy enough to lose ourselves in this throng, but all the same our departure was carefully controlled, for it was vital that the members of our party kept in the right order. Even then, at the very end, we were anxious that Günther should not see Bormann's face, in case he suddenly realised what was happening and panicked.

Bormann led off, wearing a small pair of dark glasses, and with his cap pulled down over his eyes, and Brabenov by his side followed by Fleming and by the immensely tall figure of Dr Ludwig Stumpfegger, the Führer's doctor, who happened to fall in with our group uninvited. Behind them came Günther, in his head-bandage, with myself at his elbow. Altogether there seemed to be about twenty people in our group, weaving and jostling along, but so many of them had been wounded, and were sporting bandages of one kind or another, that our own disguises did not stand out.

Emerging from the bunker into the gardens of the Foreign Ministry, we walked across to the north side of the ruined Chancellery, and then down some steps into a series of deep tunnel-passages. Ten minutes later we came up into what Bormann thought was the Friedrichstrasse station, but it turned out that he had lost his way, and that this was only a suburban halt. Retracing our steps for some distance, we took another turning, and came up into the main station.

It was a moonlit night, fairly light anyway but given a surreal brightness by fires, shell flashes and streams of tracer. A heavy barrage was coming in over us from the north bank of the Spree, and what appeared to be Soviet tanks were firing towards us from just beyond the far end of the Weidendamm Bridge, only a couple of hundred yards west of our pick-up point. The noise was prodigious: fires blazed everywhere, and the air was full of smoke, which caught the light of the flames.

As we turned north up Friedrichstrasse, with Bormann and Stumpfegger still leading, I coaxed everyone to move faster, and manoeuvred them into the cover of two German tanks which were squealing and grinding slowly forward towards the bridge, now only two hundred yards ahead. Whatever else might happen, the moment had come when I must put an end to the wretched Günther.

As I drew my Luger from its holster, out of the corner of one eye I saw Fleming tactfully steer Brabenov a yard or two further from me. Then I clicked off the safety catch and lined up the barrel on the back of Günther's chest. The range was barely three metres: point-blank. My finger tightened on the trigger. 'Dear God,' I whispered, 'take me out of here. This cannot happen again.'

At that instant one of the German tanks received a direct hit right in front of us. With a colossal *bang* it exploded in a eruption of fire. The two men closest to it, Günther and Stumpfegger, took the blast squarely. One of them was blown into me, and all three of us rolled down into a deep bomb-crater. Inadvertently, the two Germans had shielded me from the worst of the blast, and although I suffered superficial cuts and shock I was not seriously hurt. Bormann, Fleming and Brabenov were also knocked down, but they were saved by the bulk of the second tank, which was between them and the explosion. By then we were very close to the bank of the river, and, after checking that Bormann and I were all right, Fleming went on ahead with Brabenov to contact our pick-up party.

Bormann struggled to his feet and joined me in the bomb-crater. By the light of the fiercely blazing tank, he peered first at Stumpfegger: the huge doctor was dead, although no injuries were apparent. It looked as though he had died of shock. Günther was also beyond help. From the fact that his arm was loose in its socket, it seemed that he had been hit by shrapnel in the right shoulder, and maybe elsewhere. We had neither the time nor the inclination to investigate further. But when I removed the head-bandage, his face emerged untouched, looking exactly like that of Martin Bormann.

Before I could make certain that he was dead, Bormann pushed

176

me aside, knelt down by the body, and quickly examined the face. Then he took something from his pocket and put his own face down close to Günther's mouth. Turning back to me, he shook his head and said, 'Dead.' Without a pause, he did the same for Stumpfegger. As he stood up, I fitted the one-piece bandage on to his head, and once more we were on our way. 'Thank God!' I thought. 'Thank God I didn't have to kill him.'*

On the south bank of the Spree we were dangerously close to the street fighting. Across the river, not much more than fifty yards away, tanks and running human figures showed hazily through the smoke and flames. Crouching behind whatever cover we could find, we came to the top of the river wall, where I found Brabenov and Fleming peering anxiously down through the haze of smoke. In the flickering, intermittent light, no kayaks were visible, and all we could see was the wreck of a huge barge which had sunk by the far bank.

'Where the hell's Susan?' snapped Fleming.

Brabenov flicked on her walkie-talkie. 'JB Pick-Up. Juliet Bravo Papa Uniform, this is Juliet Bravo Charlie. Over.'

There was a pause that seemed to last for ever. Then at last Penny Wirrell's voice piped up on the receiver: 'JBC, Delta Echo,** JBPU standing by. Over.'

'JBPU,' replied Brabenov, 'this is JBC. Pick up. Papa Uniform. Commence, commence, commence. Over.'

'JBC,' responded Penny instantly. 'Delta Echo, JBPU. Papa Uniform affirmative. Listening out.'

Crouching in the shelter of a ruined wall, we scanned the dark water for approaching canoes. Again, time appeared to stand still. Then Brabenov leapt to her feet, pointing across the river. 'Kayaks, sir. Green four-five!'

Our eyes swept forty-five degrees to starboard. Six little craft had slipped out from behind a sunken barge beside the far bank and turned directly towards us. Falling debris splashed

---

* What it was that Bormann took from his pocket I do not know. Someone has suggested that it was one of his potassium cyanide phials, and that he put it in Günther's mouth to make doubly sure he was dead; but I have no evidence for this assumption.

** The standard phrase meaning 'This is me'.

into the water near them, and shells whistled overhead; but the kayaks maintained station in rigid line ahead, precisely three boat-lengths apart.

The drop to the water was nearly twenty feet. As the boats came alongside, we let down a rope ladder, and a slim figure came scrambling up. It was Susan Kemp, who reported to Fleming with an urgent but totally unexpected order. He had been recalled to London immediately. No reason had been given, but he was to return upstream to the Müggelsee as soon as the escape party was safely away. At 0200 a Lysander would come in to land on the disused road along the south-west shore of the lake, and pick him up.

For a wild moment we considered the possibility of sending Bormann with him, but almost at once we dismissed it. Fleming and I – indeed, all members of Op. JB – were expendable, but Bormann was not, and the risks of trying to send him out by air would be infinitely higher than those of the river passage.

There was no time for any discussion or display of emotion. We were in the middle of a dangerous operation, and an order had been given. Fleming was recalled: that was it. Caroline Saunders had come downstream in one of the motorboats: in a matter of moments Fleming had gone down over the wall on a rope and was aboard it. As they pulled away, I called out, 'Good luck!' Fleming's reply was typical: 'Don't go and ponce up all our good work now, Christopher.'

With that he disappeared up-river, under the bridge to the east, with the erratic blaze of pyrotechnics continuing overhead. Bormann went down the ladder, secured by a bowline made fast round his chest and under his arms, held by two of our people up above. Once he was settled in the forward seat of our kayak, I went down to join him, and together we pushed off.

Susan led, with SBS Sergeant David Jones. Next came Brabenov with her Commando, Sergeant John Rawlins, then Bormann and myself. Behind us were Penny Wirrell and her wireless-telegraphy petty officer, Joan Marshall, with their short-wave radio equipment. Behind them came Surgeon-Lieutenant Jenny Wright, with Sub-Lieutenant Bill Webb from COPP. The last kayak was John Morgan's, with an empty seat that would have been filled by Fleming.

Hardly were we clear of the south wall when four more kayaks, led by Israel Bloem, came out from behind the barge and joined astern of the flotilla. Smoke, lurid with the glow of flames, drifted so low over the water that I could only just see Susan as she three times raised her right hand high above her head, with three fingers outstretched. Then she swung it down and ahead. All ten canoes moved into station behind her in line ahead, at three-boat-length intervals. Slotting together the two halves of our second double paddle, I passed it forward to Bormann, who immediately started to wield it expertly and with great power.

So the escape party of Op. JB headed downstream towards the Weidendamm Bridge. By now we had all shed our greatcoats, but for the time being we retained our SS caps, since, if we clashed with anyone, the opposition would most likely be German. Under the bridge was a long boom, set to prevent just such shipping movements as ours; but the Nazi authorities had not reckoned with the resourcefulness of the SBS or our mine-disposal experts from HMS *Vernon*. Near the north bank of the river our crews had privily cut away a section of the boom, and now the two leading kayak crews pulled this section out, so that our flotilla was able to slip through.

By then the Soviet tanks were almost on the river bank. Star shells and rockets exploded everywhere. Tank rounds screeched overhead. Sections of steel were falling from the bridge. Buildings collapsed as we looked up at them. In the glare of a thousand fires I watched with awe as Susan led her vulnerable convoy to the west and freedom. Later we heard from Sergeant David Jones that the sight of the great bridge above her head elicited the understatement of the operation. 'Bloody hell!' she remarked; and a moment later she was paddling clear.

I felt elated and content. Operational again in a war canoe, for which I had been thoroughly trained in COPP, I had the sense of coming home. My right hand went automatically to the pocket in which I knew chocolate would be stowed. I brought a piece out, and on impulse gave it to Bormann in the front seat; he put it into his mouth without losing a stroke. I was heartened to see that he appeared to be very strong: clearly his arms and shoulders were exceptionally powerful. From the start he did more than his share of work. In no time he was paddling like a trained professional, and before long I found that he could lift our loaded kayak almost single-handed. It seemed that our exercises in the bunker were paying off.

For the next two hours we slunk through the centre of the city, clinging to the north bank, which gave us cover from the attackers, even though we were under their noses, and proceeding with the utmost caution, yet as fast as we could, through the Tiergarten and past Charlottenburg. The Russians were perilously close on both sides, north and south; but luckily for us they were preoccupied with the land battle, and not thinking about people on the river. Many times we left the water, humping our kayaks overland to circumvent mines, deliberate obstructions or the ruins of blown-up bridges; but at every block we found a kayak team from the advance party waiting to help us through or round the obstacle. Broken sluices, bombed weirs, fast-running white water, huge sections of collapsed bridge – we negotiated or bypassed them all. At every stage our R/G equipment proved invaluable. Not only could one kayak communicate with another invisibly: through our two big infra-red sets we could also see in the dark, whereas the forces ashore – German or Russian – could see nothing at all.

Plenty of other people were travelling downriver with us; but all of them were dead. Several times our paddles bumped against something soft yet solid, and we saw a body floating beside us.

We knew it was essential to clear the centre of the city that night, for by the morning the Russians would be everywhere, searching for Nazi escapers, not least on the river. Yet as the sky began to lighten behind us with the approach of dawn, we had not gone as far as we would have liked.

By 0430 we had passed the big bend in Spandau, the point at which at which the Spree joins the Havel, and had turned south under the Charlotten and Dischinger bridges; but then, as we bore down the straight stretch towards the bridge at Pichelsdorf, we saw the kayaks ahead of us turning hard aport towards the eastern bank. Following on, I jumped ashore, made fast and scrambled up the shore, to find Susan apparently in a state of shock and unable to speak. Just ahead of her, part of the bridge had come down: a pile of tumbled masonry and fallen vehicles had blocked most of the river, and the current was surging in a rapid over some obstruction which had choked the remaining channel.

'It's bodies, sir,' called David Jones. 'A bloody great raft of dead bodies.'

'Secure alongside,' I ordered. 'Get some safety lines, and all hands available.'

'Very good, sir.'

In a moment John Morgan appeared with four of his men. When he saw what the block consisted of, he suggested that we should make an overland yomp round it.

'No,' I told him. 'It would take far too long. We've got to break it up.'

I tied a life-line round my waist, and two Marine Commandos did the same. Then we waded out until we were neck-deep in the rushing black water, neck-deep among the bodies of men, women, children, babies. It was one of the most horrific encounters any of us had ever known: we struggled to free the slimy, stinking corpses, bloated from immersion in the river, and all interlocked with wooden boxes and other floating debris. Thank God, the night was too dark for us to see individual faces. Once we had released a few key points, the jam began to break up of its own accord as the river swept the bodies away. I have never forgotten the sight of David Jones lifting a dead baby into the air and then, after a moment, allowing it to swirl off on the rushing waters.

Back on station, we passed under the remains of the bridge and through a small lake beyond it. Then we went through another narrow neck, and found the waterway widening into a huge expanse that stretched 1500 metres away on either hand. From our study of maps and models, we were expecting this change; yet the night was still so dark that we could not see exactly where we were. It was only when the flashes of gunfire receded into the distance to starboard that we realised we were on the Havel lake.

As the lake widened out still further, our tactical outlook changed. On the rivers there had been many shadows thrown by the banks, by buildings along them and by the remains of bridges: the glow of fires and the flashes of gunfire in the background had served to shroud the surface of the water in gloom, so that our kayaks would hardly have been visible even to people looking for us. Out on the expanse of the Havel, we felt more exposed and vulnerable. The chances of being spotted seemed much greater, even though we were a good distance from the Russians on the west bank; and it was imperative that we reached our lying-up point, six miles further south, before daybreak.

Our fragile flotilla forged on, hugging the eastern shoreline. No lights showed from the land there, and we knew that we had come level with the beginning of the Grunewald, the huge, forested park studded with the country homes of well-to-do Berliners. Susan Kemp took up her position in the van alongside Bloem and set a fast pace. Already we had paddled some eleven miles without a stop, except to make necessary diversions round obstacles, and the night was beginning to seem desperately long. Bormann, however, was showing enormous reserves of stamina: he paddled away strongly, and – as far as I could tell through his head-bandage – seemed friendly and co-operative. From time to time he turned round to ask in monosyllabic English if I was all right, and to pass me some brandy and chocolate from his own rations.

In general our communications were functioning well. Individual kayaks kept in touch with one another by R/G light, but two of them had been fitted out as main radio stations. Aboard each were a signals officer and a load of heavy equipment, the short-wave radios and accumulators carefully stowed so that they could not shift and puncture the skins of the canoes. Two thin masts, flexible and collapsible, had some seventy feet of aerial deployed between them, and this enabled us to maintain contact not only with JB7, following down behind us, but also with the M Section radio truck, which had come up behind the advancing British forces to the west bank of the Elbe, now only seventy miles ahead. By this means every stage of our progress was quickly relayed to Bletchley and the M Section control. Also, we heard from Caroline Saunders that Fleming had got away safely by Lysander at 0300. Her own group, she reported, had started down the Spree and proposed to lie up for the day on a small island in the Rummelsburgersee, an inlet leading off the north bank of the river. 'God protect our little fleet,' she signalled.

Over the Havel the sky was lightening, and we upped our stroke-rate. As we were signalled on by one of our own forward patrols ashore on the tip of the Schildhorn, a north-pointing promontory with a small inlet beyond it to port, I flippantly signalled to Susan, 'Come on, Cambridge.'

We had considered the Schildhorn as an emergency stopping point, and, as the flotilla streamed past, one of the boats requested permission to land: a member of the crew had been taken short. Susan refused peremptorily. From basic orders or previous operations, every one of our people knew that they had to make their own arrangements inside their kayak. Messy and unpleasant as it was, to urinate or even defecate inside one's clothes was sometimes tactically inescapable. To help contain our bodily functions, we all – men as well as women – carried supplies of tampons.

Soon after we had left the Schildhorn promontory behind, a tremendous glow began to grow ever brighter far out on our starboard bow. Gatow airport was a raging inferno, with the din of battle echoing out to us across the water, and fresh explosions shooting giant sheets of flame into the sky. As we looked in that direction, the surface of the lake became tinged with blue and orange, and the tops of the wavelets flickered white. To port, in contrast, the land was still pitch-dark: it gave the impression of open country, but we knew it was still the Grunewald.

The noises of battle grew fainter as we passed inside Lindwerder, a small island only fifty yards off-shore. (*Werder*, Bloem had told me, means eyot, or river island.) Now, we knew, we were within a couple of miles of our haven for the day, Schwanenwerder, or Swan Island, a bulbous peninsula jutting out some half a mile into the lake.

Paddling on, we reached it as the light was strengthening. Susan signalled the rest of the flotilla to follow and headed in towards the causeway, only twenty yards wide, which joined the peninsula to the mainland. Another of our forward groups was standing by to help us bring the kayaks ashore and hide them in the bushes. Within sixty seconds of the first canoe running on to the beach, all had landed and been hidden.

As we came to shore, the sun was just breaking above the horizon into a clear sky, harbinger of a glorious spring day. Through a haze of exhaustion I saw that a sandy beach swept away into the distance, backed by a solid wall of trees just coming out into their first and freshest leaf. Here indeed was the playground of pre-war Berlin; but now the sun was rising over the fall of the Third Reich – and in the far distance to the east, above the Grunewald, we could see a pall of smoke towering above the ruins of Hitler's capital.

The peninsula was about six hundred yards long and three hundred across, and its low hills were covered in woods, which gave ideal cover. Weekend houses and cabins were dotted among the trees, most of them fully occupied, not only by their owners, but also by an influx of squatters who had sought out a place of comparative safety in the hope of escaping the brutal Soviet incursions which seemed sure to follow. Our German Freedom Fighters had paved the way for us, making friends among the local population, and when we arrived they turned out in force to greet us, offering us places to sleep for the day and putting their meagre rations at our disposal. We responded in kind: soon we were enjoying a royal breakfast of sandwiches, porridge, tea, coffee and brandy, and we handed out tins of food like corned beef, which we had in abundance. Together with Brabenov, Kemp and John Morgan, I went round having a cheerful word with all our people, making sure that everyone was fit, and that there were no candidates for the sickbay. In fact everybody was in the highest spirits: most of them looked tired from the strain of the long voyage and the days and nights of waiting, but morale was tremendous. Wherever I went, I was offered food – so much so that Bloem asked someone if they were trying to kill me by over-feeding.

Soon after breakfast two signals came in. In the first Caroline Saunders gave the good news that JB7 was safely laid up on the island in the Rummelsburgersee, and hoped to reach the Wannsee, where we were, during the next night. The second, from M Section (Elbe), reported that Fleming was safely out of Germany and on his way to London.

As the sun climbed and gained warmth, people stripped off and began giving each other splash-baths, some of the girls washing the boys, and vice versa. Then, having checked our guard-positions and made sure that the watches were fair to everyone, all those not on duty tried to settle down and sleep.

That proved less easy than expected. Tired as I was, my mind was fizzing with the exhilaration of being in the open, on the move, and also with thoughts of the perils that lay ahead. With Fleming gone, the balance of command had shifted. Susan Kemp had firmly taken command of the flotilla, and was now second in command of the whole operation: she was developing into a first-rate leader, and I was happy to leave the immediate control and organisation of our little convoy to her. Brabenov was another power-house, with her expert knowledge, her readiness to help, and above all her high spirits laced with courage. Bloem, too, was utterly dependable: without him and his enterprising boys and girls, we would have got nowhere.

Yet now the burden of overall command fell squarely on me. At the very moment when I needed him most, Fleming was no longer there as guide and mentor. From now on every decision I took would be mine and mine alone. Apart from everything else, it was my direct responsibility to safeguard Bormann. My orders were to keep him under close escort: he spent the day handcuffed to a Royal Marine sergeant, and I had ordered the guard to shoot him dead if there was the slightest chance of his falling into Soviet hands.

For the time being, that possibility seemed remote: the morning passed without incident. But my anxieties were increased by another signal which arrived at midday, warning us that the Russians had captured the Potsdam Bridge, the next bridge ahead of us downstream. Poring over our maps and charts, we saw that Potsdam was widely spread out on both sides of the river: we considered the possibility of leaving the river and making a wide overland detour to the south, bypassing the bridge, but it was clear that any such scheme would present hazards of its own.

The minutes of that glorious May day ticked slowly past. Looking out to the south-west, we could see the wide expanse of Pfaueninsel (Peacock Island). Somehow I remembered that during the Olympic Games of 1936 Goebbels had given a phenomenal party there. Striving to outdo the other Nazi leaders in ostentation, he had entertained two thousand guests to supper and a firework display so violent that it turned some of the visitors' thoughts uneasily to the prospect of war.

Now the Pfaueninsel was again under intermittent bombardment, this time from Soviet armour, which had advanced into the suburbs of Kladow, on the western shore of the Havel. During the afternoon a Junkers sea-plane came in to land on the Wannsee, close to the big island. We speculated that this might represent a last-minute attempt to lift a high-ranking Nazi to safety, and sure enough, two small boats, one a motor yacht, the other a gaff-rigged yawl, came out, apparently to make contact with the pilot. No sooner had they appeared than the Soviet gunners took up target practice on both. The motorboat headed away at full speed and made good its escape. The Junkers took off, also unscathed. But the slow-moving yawl was less lucky: a direct hit blew it to pieces, and it went down, so far as we could see, with all hands. For us professional sailors, at action stations and highly trained in search-and-rescue techniques, it was terrible to have to stand by and watch helplessly as people drowned in front of our eyes. The incident shocked us, and made us all too well aware of what would happen if one our kayaks were hit by a Soviet shell.

Then in the evening, as we were beginning our preparations to move on, there came a highly unwelcome development. This time it was Brabenov who received a signal, direct from General Donovan. The gist of it was that the American intelligence authorities had run a check on Major Anthony Blunt and had come up with disturbing information. They had discovered that in 1936, while a student at Trinity College, Cambridge, Blunt had belonged to a secret society called The Apostles, which was not only overtly homosexual but also vehemently Marxist. Further, that same year he had joined the Communist Party, and he was still a member. (None of these facts had been reported by Blunt when he joined the Field Security Police: nor had MI 5 or any other British security service uncovered them.)

Looking thoroughly alarmed for once, Brabenov went straight to Kemp and asked what papers Blunt had been caught reading in the office at Birdham. The answer was: 'The plans, diagrams and notes for the abduction of Bormann down the Berlin waterways.' Susan added that every British check on Blunt had proved negative, and MI 5 had advised that, whatever he had seen at Birdham, there was no security risk.

Now this was manifestly untrue. After a quick discussion, I had to accept the strong likelihood that the Russians knew all about our operation, and were lying in wait ahead of us. What should we do?

Again we considered the possibility of avoiding the Potsdam Bridge by going overland to the south. Such a trek would be physically difficult, and if we met Soviet forces on land, we would be hard pressed to spin a convincing cover story. Obviously the Russians would search us thoroughly, and our equipment would arouse their worst suspicions. The overland route did not seem worth the risk.

On balance, the river offered us a better chance. For weeks we had exercised in our cover-role – that of a Soviet kayak group in search of important Nazis trying to escape down the Havel – and we had the uniforms and passes to support the deception. Better still, we had Russian-speakers in the form of Brabenov and Bloem who should be able to talk their way through any guard-point. We reasoned that, if we could succeed in bluffing the first Russians we met, news of our progress might be passed on down-river in Soviet radio reports, clearing the way for us by chain reaction right through to the Elbe. In addition, we somehow had to hold the route open for JB7, who were at that moment preparing to skim down behind us.

Our discussion brought up another problem. Kemp, Brabenov and Bloem all favoured waiting for the JB7 flotilla to join us. They wanted to stay where we were through the coming night, of 2–3 May, in the hope that our rear party would catch up with us before dawn. Then, the following evening, we could all proceed down-river together, so that we would only have to deceive the Russians once at each bridge or guard-point. It was surely hoping too much to think that we could slip kayak parties past the Soviet strong-points on two successive nights.

I saw the point of what my officers were saying, and shared their anxieties about the safety of JB7. Nevertheless, I knew we could not wait. However strongly we wished to bring all our own people out intact, our main task had to come first. My orders were to transport Bormann to the Elbe, and the operation had to take priority over all other considerations. Every moment we waited – never mind a whole night – would increase the danger and reduce the chances of success. In twenty-four hours' time the Russians would be more strongly entrenched, and more certain of themselves. It followed that we must press on, and that JB7 must take their chance behind us.

Soon everything was decided unanimously: we would leave as soon as darkness fell, and stick to the river, challenging any Soviet forces we met. A signal went off to M Section (Elbe), and we began to prepare for departure.

Again I found myself wishing that I had the benefit of Fleming's experience and wisdom. In his absence, I was wavering. Perhaps, after all, I should send Bormann overland with a single, German-speaking escort. If the pair were intercepted, the Russians would probably accept them as displaced German civilians and let them go: they had identity cards to support such a claim. With luck, they would be able to make their way across country to the Elbe, where M Section officers would meet them.

Meanwhile, the rest of us could go on down-river, confront any Russians we met and tell them the plain truth, that we were escaping British personnel. We had papers to prove this, too. But if we did that, we should have to ditch all our weapons, radios, spare uniforms and identity cards, and approach any strong-point unarmed, having already signalled M Section (Elbe) and the US Supreme Command, requesting them to warn the Russians to expect a genuine British escape group, and to let us through.

On the other hand, I had orders to keep Bormann under close escort within our group. To let him go off with one officer would be an abrogation not only of duty but also of loyalty to my companions, especially after all we had been through.

As I struggled with the various permutations, and dusk was falling, the gunfire from across the lake suddenly increased in intensity. The new barrage rumbled up from due south-west, the precise direction of the Potsdam Bridge, four and a half miles downstream. To me, the thunder on the horizon was the order for which I had been unconsciously waiting. I have already said that in the navy it is an unwritten law that a captain cannot go far wrong if he steers towards the sound of guns. Now I had the order for which I had been longing – and I would obey it wholeheartedly. I would steer for the Potsdam Bridge and the Soviet guns.

As the dusk settled on us, I wandered through my group. Everyone was having a wash, making ready their gear, cooking an early supper. I paced quietly among them, pausing to stop and talk to almost every man and woman in the team. All seemed alert, confident and friendly to me, even though I was younger than most of them. They did not know that I was about to lead them into point-blank range of the Russian armour, which, if things went wrong, could annihilate our soft-skinned flotilla in a few seconds.

I walked on and on, slowly round and through my people, and then – as I always did at moments like this – found myself a secluded spot among the bushes by the shore. As I knelt down facing the water, I became aware that most of the men and women not on watch had followed. Now they too knelt down all round me, and what I would have whispered, I spoke out loud, not just as a prayer for us all, but to instil courage and hope in myself, and to hide the terror in my heart:

> Dear God of St Laurence, St Edward the Confessor and St Benedict, guardian saints of our abbey at Ampleforth; and our God of Battles; and St Christopher, patron of all travellers . . . Protect us and watch over us, your humble servants, on this long and hazardous journey. Help us to evade, and if necessary destroy, our enemies. Amen.

Out of the corner of my eye I saw Bormann standing with David Jones. A moment later he took a step forward and knelt down with our group.

> Dear God of Battles! [I continued] Our Jesus Christ of Nazareth and Judea, who is Our Father, who art in Heaven . . .

Too late, I remembered that the Russians were supposed to be our allies and friends, rather than our deadly foes. But the words had been spoken. Our prayers went out over the calm water, and we prepared to launch the canoes again.

16

Comrade Colonel Natasha

W e moved off in small, staggered groups at 2000 hours, when full dark had fallen, taking the south-west route across the Wannsee, but slipping through the narrow channel inside the Pfaueninsel. There was an alternative and less exposed route by way of Kohlhasenbrück, but this would have meant shooting two extra-narrow bridges, one of which carried the main road to Potsdam and so, we presumed, would be guarded.

Now everyone in the party was wearing dark grey-green waterproof gear, with the caps and insignia of Soviet Special Intelligence, and we all carried apparently genuine Soviet papers and identity cards. For the time being the guns had fallen silent, but from our advance scouts we received intelligence that the Russians were now very active in Potsdam, and had installed searchlights on the bridge.

Because our next contact would almost certainly be with Soviet forces, I had changed our order of approach and put our Russian-speakers at the front. In the lead, now, was Brabenov, wearing the insignia of a full colonel of Soviet Special Intelligence, and behind her came Bloem, dressed as a lieutenant-colonel, each accompanied by a Russian-speaking Commando. Our plan was not to try to slip under the Potsdam Bridge unobserved, because that would have been reckless in the extreme; rather, we had decided that Brabenov should confront any guards we found and try to bluff us through. Further, we reckoned that our best tactics would be to make our presence known in an obvious, international manner, without waiting to be caught in searchlights.

As the Havel narrowed, once again becoming more river than lake, the current picked up, and we coasted with it, paddling only enough to steer and hold station. Then at last we swept round a bend and saw the bridge ahead.

It was dark. No lights shone down on to the water. We were still four or five hundred yards off when Susan signalled to the whole flotilla, 'Hoist battle ensigns.' Every other kayak had a bamboo pole or wireless aerial specially prepared for this moment, and now within a minute the Soviet red naval ensign, together with its miniature hammer and sickle, had been hoisted close-up above half our boats.

The river became quite narrow, and it offered nowhere to hide. We all had Thompson sub-machine-guns ready on our laps, and grenades to hand, but only in the last resort did we mean to use violence. Watching from my own kayak, third in the line, I waited till I judged the moment right, and then sent out the order with my R/G lamp: 'Alice away.'

Brabenov flashed back, 'Alice, affirmative.'

As she swung her canoe in towards the starboard bank, her crewman, Sergeant John Rawlins, fired his Very pistol. A red-and-white flare arched up over the bridge, and within seconds the Russians responded. Searchlights blazed on, flooding the surface of the river and catching us full in their glare. In a few moments Brabenov had reached the bank, jumped ashore, and called out in Russian, through a loud-hailer.

'*Rebyata!*' she roared. '*Lads!* Send down your senior officer to meet me.' Her voice was harsh, her manner all arrogance and aggression: as she waited on the bank in her usual stance – feet apart and hands on hips – she radiated the impression that anyone who displeased her would find himself in dire trouble.

When a Soviet captain came forward, she announced herself as Comrade Colonel Natasha Andreyevna Serova, and told the man she was leading an NKVD patrol in search of escaping Nazi criminals. Further, she was acting on the personal authority of Marshal Zhukov, the Soviet Supreme Commander. To prove what she said, she brought out her identity cards and pass, which had apparently been signed by Zhukov. Before the captain could ask her anything, she let loose a torrent of questions about the state of the river downstream and the disposition of any German forces still offering resistance.

Hardly giving him a chance to answer, she then bombarded him with a volley of orders. He was to let other Soviet units downstream know she was coming. He was to make sure they had all relevant information ready for her. He was to stand by, the following night, to help and escort through the bridge the second half of her own party, which consisted of two motorboats and ten more kayaks. Finally, he was to keep his eyes skinned for Nazi war criminals: if he found any and arrested them, he would be sure of immediate promotion.

With that, and a curt 'Carry on', she jumped back into her own canoe. In unison she and her crewman flicked their kayak round. The glare of the searchlights picked up the little Soviet red ensign which fluttered cheekily from the tip of her radio aerial. Still fully in character, she waved her arms like a Russian cavalry officer ordering the charge and shouted at us, '*Nu, poplyli dalshe!* (Paddle on!),' and '*Davaite! Davaite zhe!* (Shift yourselves!).

The rest of us heaved a huge collective sigh of relief as we followed her downstream beneath the bridge.* After a moment I looked back. The searchlights had swung round to keep us illuminated, and guns were trained on our backs. But Susan skilfully and unobtrusively led the flotilla close to the south-west bank, and as soon as we reached the point at which the river turned slightly to starboard, we were in the shadow of the few buildings that still stood.

But we were not safe yet, for although the river widened out for about three-quarters of a mile, it then closed in again to only seventy-five yards and headed directly for a second bridge, which, from our charts, appeared to carry the railway. As the Havel narrowed, so the speed of the water increased, and we did not need to paddle except to maintain steerage way.

---

* Later, when Kemp and I wrote our reports on the operation, and I made my recommendations for honours, Morton showed them to the Prime Minister. Churchill immediately remarked that, whatever military decoration Brabenov deserved, it would be even more appropriate to nominate her for an Academy Award.

Huge wharves and skeletal buildings, warehouses and cranes loomed high over us. But all was eerily dark and quiet. We could hardly see each other, and it therefore seemed unlikely that a Soviet patrol would spot us. We fairly flew under what was left of the bridge and shot out into more open water by the peninsula of Hermannswerder. Then again we entered narrows, and our speed picked up once more, until we emerged into a wider stretch and veered off to the south-west, towards Kaputh. Once again my God of Battles had shepherded us through.

That night we made another ten miles, and reached our planned lying-up spot on an island in the lake at the southern extremity of the Havel's flow. Guns could still be heard in the far distance, but our immediate surroundings were deliciously safe, tranquil and pleasant. Radio contact told us that after an uneventful passage down the Spree JB7 had reached the Wannsee safely and tied up on the site we had used, helped by a small party left behind to assist them. Congratulating them on their progress so far, we signalled that they must not relax: on the contrary, they must redouble their vigilance. We also warned them of the Soviet block on the Potsdam Bridge, and advised them how best to handle it.

Four times more on the short passage to Brandenburg we were challenged by Soviet units: at Ketzin, Göttin, Saaringen and in Brandenburg itself. But every time Brabenov carried the battle of words to the Russians, overwhelming them with questions and orders before they could ask her anything. Then, after navigating the Brandenburg lakes, we went out of them in a northerly direction, back into the confines of the Havel river, which in comparison seemed dangerously narrow. Here a few Germans were still holding out in pockets of resistance: we heard occasional gun-battles break out, but the defenders' attention was focused on possible attacks from the land, and we slipped by in the dark without trouble.

As we paddled on to the north, past Pritzerbe and Döberitz, the voyage became one of the happiest experiences any of us could recall. Our idyllic cruise down the river could only have been improved if we had been travelling by day. As it was, the nights were warm, with temperatures a couple of degrees above the seasonal average, and only twice did it rain heavily, both times during the day, when we were snugly encamped, most of us under groundsheets slung between two upturned kayaks. Our only loss was that we saw practically nothing of the spring countryside through which we passed.

The further we went, the more our journey took on the aura of a school outing: all ranks and ratings, regardless of sex, ate and slept together, and everyone helped look after everyone else. Yet the star of the party was undoubtedly our prisoner. When afloat he worked as hard as anyone, or harder, but when he came ashore he was severely burdened by the restrictions we deemed necessary. Not only was he still wearing the hot and heavy head-bandage: on land, he was constantly handcuffed to an escort, even when eating his meals, asleep, or relieving nature.

Then, as we began to feel more secure, we decided we could change his lot for the better. As far as we could tell, none of our people knew what Martin Bormann looked like; but there was just a chance that someone older, like Israel Bloem, might recognise him. If that happened, it might cause a lot of trouble, and we felt we must not take the slightest risk. (It was not inconceivable that one of our Freedom Fighters, motivated by hatred of the Nazis, might have killed him.)

We therefore decided that we must keep him disguised; but two of the girls, Magda and Rachel, seeing his discomfort, spontaneously produced a couple of balaclava-type face-masks made out of a dark-blue towel. They had cut generous spaces for eyes, nose and mouth, and left much of the back open, so that the new head-dress was far cooler and more comfortable than the old. The towelling soaked up sweat, and one mask could be washed and dried while the other was being worn. At the same time, we decided to dispense with the handcuffs, and although when ashore Bormann was still kept under close surveillance by a rotating duty watch of one officer and one senior NCO, his comfort and well-being improved dramatically.

By then everyone had found that our prisoner was a friendly individual with a helpful disposition, and he had established himself as an integral member of the group. Not knowing his real name, the girls had christened him Friedrich, or Fred, to which he was soon answering cheerfully. I myself was surprised by his apparent good nature. Briefings had suggested that Bormann was a tough, cruel schemer, but here, on his own and in enemy hands, he behaved impeccably, never complaining or losing his temper. Because we shared a kayak, it was I who saw most of him, and I found him not only obedient, co-operative and brave, but a source of great strength. He was amazingly powerful – twice as strong as I was – and he picked up kayaking faster than any naval recruit I could remember. He even organised some of the yomps round blockages; and he did it with such good sense that nobody, not even the Marine sergeants, resented it. After a while we came to depend on him for certain jobs, and because he was twenty years older than most of us, the girls – particularly the GFFs – treated him as a father-figure. His nickname was used with affection and respect, and on many non-operational matters people would seek advice from him first.

Once we were well down the Havel, the off-duty watches would sit around and listen while he told stories of the crazy Wittelsbach dynasty of Bavaria. One day he recounted the saga of Sisi (otherwise Elisabeth, Empress of Austria) who used to ride horses at midnight with her cousin, mad King Ludwig II. One night, he said, her husband, the handsome young Emperor Franz Josef, pursued them out into the waters of the lake at Neuschwanstein; and when, some time later, Ludwig was found drowned in the Starnberger See, near his castle of Berg, Sisi sat on the shore of the lake weeping – just as we were sitting on the bank of the Havel.

By the morning of Tuesday, 8 May, we had covered two-thirds of our route, and were only about twenty-five miles from the confluence of the Havel and the Elbe, where British and American forces were waiting. Having travelled northwards past Grütz, Schollene and Molkenberg, we turned east into the Gülpersee, a lake two miles wide, where our scouts had identified a good lying-up point in the marshes.

Just before dawn we carried our kayaks ashore and moved into a makeshift camp prepared by our advance party. Then, after all necessary checks had been made, watches closed up and personnel seen to, Penny Wirrell, the chief signals officer, came to me with what I could only describe as an extraordinary expression on her face. A signal had come in which seemed to make no sense. It was an order from the Admiralty, sent not

specifically to us but to 'All Ships'. It read simply, 'SPLICE THE
MAINBRACE'.

Everyone in the Royal Navy knew that the instruction no longer
referred to the hemp link between main and mizzen mastheads.
Rather, it meant a double issue of rum for all hands. This raised
a problem, for we had no rum, only powdered milk and lemonade,
and a small supply of brandy reserved for medicinal use, of which
Dr Jenny was not prepared to issue a single drop; in any case, we
could not divine why the Admiralty had ordered such widespread
celebration, which usually signified a great victory. We held our
breath until the mystery was solved by another signal, this time
from our own chief:

GERMANY HAS SURRENDERED UNCONDITIONALLY. HOSTILITIES
WILL CEASE MIDNIGHT TONIGHT 8 MAY. YOU WILL NOT RELAX
ONE IOTA BUT WILL DOUBLE YOUR VIGILANCE AGAINST SOVIET
FORCES. YOU STILL FACE GRAVE HAZARDS AND YOUR OPERATION
MUST SUCCEED. GOD BLESS YOU ALL. GOD PROTECT THE FLEET.
GOD SAVE THE KING. MORTON.

I collected all hands not on watch, warned them not to cheer
or make any noise, and read the message out. At the news
my people leapt up and down silently and embraced everyone in sight, including me. Then they raced off to the watch-
keepers, to spread the news and embrace everyone on duty.
Morton's warnings of danger could not dampen their high spirits, and, within reasonable limits, we managed to splice the
mainbrace.

JB7, still a day behind us, received the same message and were
beset by the same problem, of having no spirits with which to
celebrate. But soon they signalled us to say that they had solved
their difficulties by the expedient of the girls giving the men two
hugs and kisses instead of one. Brabenov immediately wanted to
know how the boys had reciprocated. Of what had *they* given two
helpings?

Those were no ordinary days and nights. A feeling of heady
exhilaration prevailed, but relationships between the sexes generally remained light and vivacious. The girls never complained
of being harassed by their brothers-in-arms; on the contrary, they

held them in special trust, and the men saw themselves as the girls' protectors.

But then, on the night of 8–9 May, as we left the Gülpersee and paddled northwards down the Havel, we became aware that, at the very moment when the war was officially ending, the Russians were closing in on us once again. Now they were on our right, to the east: we saw fires and heard shouts and screams, some of them from women, as well as the occasional burst of small-arms fire. From the noise, it seemed that some Soviet units were camped right on the bank of the river.

This made stealthy progress still more imperative. Gliding silently forward, we hugged the western shore; but in places the river was very narrow, and often we were forced to pass within yards of Soviet soldiers, most of whom – judging from their raucous voices – were drinking heavily. Several times during the night, to avoid confrontation, we had to leave the river altogether and hump our kayaks round through woods and marshes until we were clear of the position. It was heavy, exhausting work, and it cut down the distance we covered during the hours of darkness to only five miles.

By a combination of hard toil and good fortune, we had avoided any contact; but after exchanging ideas with our advance party, we decided to lie up for the next day a couple of miles south of the little town of Kuhlhausen, beside one of the many tributaries which twisted down to the Havel from the north-east. There we found what seemed to be a perfect campsite: a small, wooded island in a marshy lake, joined to the mainland by a causeway only a few feet wide. There seemed no reason why any local should visit the place, and after our labour during the night we looked forward to a good sleep.

At first everything went well. We made contact with JB7 and with M Section (Elbe), cooked a meal, washed, and checked our weapons, after which all those not on guard settled down. But then at midday gunfire and shouts from close at hand made the officer of the watch bring the whole unit to action stations. Within seconds every yard of the island's perimeter was covered.

Soon we could hear the screams of more than one woman, calling for help, and the drunken, aggressive shouts of men. With the babel of noise rapidly approaching our hide-out, we waited silently, looking across the causeway to the woods beyond.

A few moments later two teenaged girls staggered out of the trees, glancing back in terror at their pursuers. The younger of the two looked in a bad way: her face was bruised and bleeding, her dress ripped, and blood was running down one leg. We saw at once what had happened: a Soviet army unit had arrived in the area, and in accordance with standard practice its men were trying to rape anything that wore a skirt.

The pursuing drunks burst out of the trees and sighted their quarry trapped on the water's edge. The girls turned as if they were going to jump into the lake, the only chance they could see of escaping. Then one of them spotted the causeway: scrambling across to the end of it, they ran over to our island and into the trees.

At a quiet command our people seized them and held them firmly from behind, clamping hands over their mouths to prevent them crying out. A whisper of 'Freunde' in their ears stopped them struggling, and within a few seconds they had been bustled silently out of the way, deeper into the undergrowth.

By then the Russians had reached the far end of the causeway: a captain, with a sergeant and three other-ranks in attendance, their caps pushed back on their heads. Having looked glassily about, they lurched forward on to the island.

Suddenly, to their consternation, they found their way blocked by two women and a man in the uniforms of Soviet officers. Brabenov moved up to the captain and slapped him three or four times hard across the face, shouting out in Russian that his disgraceful conduct would be reported to Comrade Marshals Zhukov and Stalin. She began her usual story – that she was hunting for Nazi criminals, and instead had found Soviet ones.

The soldiers made an effort to pull themselves together, and stood to attention; but the captain was intoxicated enough to think that he could take advantage of the situation. From our hide-out in the trees, we could see him considering his position, and thinking over the possibilities. He fancied that only three opponents stood between him and his quarry. 'Two women and one small man' was written all over his face.

Lurching towards Brabenov, he demanded proof of her identity;

but before she could bring out a card he suddenly drew his revolver and swung it, to pistol-whip her. Encouraged by his show of aggression, his men launched themselves to attack Kemp and Bloem.

Before the Soviet soldiers had taken two paces, all four had been knocked silently senseless. As we moved to help Brabenov, she waved us away and faced the officer alone. With surgical precision she side-stepped his revolver and sprang clean into the air so that the full weight of her body delivered a vicious karate kick into his vitals. The man doubled up with a howl of agony. But Brabenov did not stop there. As he fell forward, clutching his testicles, her right hand streaked out and caught him under the chin. Using his weight and all her own strength to pivot her palm up over his face, she drove her two outstretched first fingers deep into his eye-sockets. With a scream he fell to the ground, clutching his hands to his face, his whole body twitching. Watching him dispassionately, Brabenov stepped back and stood still as a statue. Then she took a handkerchief from her pocket and wiped the blood off her fingers.

The man on the ground gradually ceased struggling. 'Get Jenny to look at him,' I said.

Surgeon-Lieutenant Jenny Wright, doubling in the section as commando and specialist technician, was already examining the German girls, and by the time she came to the end of the causeway the Soviet captain was beyond help. Jenny took one look at him and announced, 'He's dead.'

Now we were stuck with a problem not of our own making. We had five Russians soldiers on our hands, one dead, four bound and gagged. Obviously we could not set the survivors free, to return to their unit and report what had had happened. Equally, we could not leave them on the little island when we left, for sooner or later their colleagues would come looking for them, and a pursuit would start. There was only one sure way to silence them, and I was profoundly grateful when Bloem suggested it.

'Kill them all,' he said. 'It'll look as though they were caught by one of the last Nazi outposts.' Then, as if he had read my thoughts, he added, 'Don't worry, sir. We're used to this kind of thing. Leave it to us.' Little did he he know that I was used to it too.

Exactly what Bloem and his Freedom Fighters did, I never asked.

I merely specified that the Russians should be disposed of some distance from the island, so that even if search parties did come looking for them, they would not be in our area when Christa Shulberg and the rest of JB7 came down-river at the end of that night. A small detachment marched the prisoners away over the causeway and disappeared into the woods on the mainland. They certainly never fired any shots, which might have attracted attention. The deed was done silently, probably with knives.

On the island, we were stuck with the two injured German girls. It turned out that they were sisters; their mother had been raped and murdered by Soviet soldiers, their father killed on the Russian front. Both girls had been raped, and although the elder had only superficial injuries her sister was in a bad way: she had lost a lot of blood, and urgently needed hospital treatment.

If our luck held, we should reach the Elbe within thirty-six hours. Dr Jenny asked if we could take the girls with us, so that we could get them into a field hospital at the first possible moment. It would be difficult to rearrange the kayak crews, even though we had a spare boat, but in my view there was only one thing to do.

'Read them in,' I said, and I walked over to John Morgan to discuss the new crewing.

Brabenov, very subdued, asked Susan what 'read them in' meant. Susan explained that it was an old navy phrase, a way of saying, 'They're coming with us.'

'He really does care, then,' said Brabenov.

'Much too much,' Susan replied.

When the party returned after disposing of the four Russians, Brabenov was officer of the watch, so that it was to her that Bloem reported details of his disagreeable but essential mission. I watched from nearby as he moved off into the bushes. Left alone, Brabenov suddenly turned away and clutched at her face. Tears poured out through her fingers, and her whole body shook. She knelt down and rocked back on her haunches, bowing her head almost to the ground as she sobbed bitterly. Then she raised her head and made the sign of the cross, as always the 'wrong' way round.

Walking up behind her, I lifted her to her feet and wrapped my arms tightly round her. She responded gratefully, and her convulsions slowly subsided.

'Come on, Yankee Doodle Girl,' I whispered. 'The Elbe beckons.'

During the next night, that of 10 May, we came within seven miles of the big river, after many overland passages to avoid rampaging Russian forces, and to circumvent the blown-up bridges and sunken vessels that frequently blocked the Havel. It was tough work, not least because we had to carry the younger girl, who, though not in immediate danger, was too weak to walk far.

By 0300 on the morning of Friday, 11 May, our eight kayaks were back on the river and proceeding north-west towards the darkened town of Havelberg. Because Brabenov had spearheaded every other approach to Soviet guard-points, I decided it was only fair to give her a break, and I put Bloem in the lead instead. Thus two canoes containing him, one of his lieutenants and two GFF girls ran down towards the medieval fortress of Haveberg, which rose out of the middle of the river, with streams passing it on either side and bridges linking it to the banks. Even with the prevailing tension we all wished that it were daylight so that we could have had a proper look at this historic citadel. Bloem and his party hugged the starboard bank of the stream that ran north-east of the fortress while the rest of us hung back in the shadows of the south-western shore opposite.

Somebody saw Bloem's kayaks approaching. Powerful lights snapped on, catching the two little boats in their glare. A man began shouting in Russian from the street beside the river. Bloem shouted back, trying to emulate the brazen confidence which had stood Brabenov in such good stead; but for some reason he did not carry conviction. The guards ignored his replies and ordered him ashore.

The moment his kayak touched the bank, I knew he was in trouble. Brabenov whispered urgently to me, asking permission to go to his aid, but I refused. The Russians had not yet spotted us, the main part of the flotilla, since we were beyond the range of the lights, and still in shadow. If we made any move across the stream, our presence would immediately be revealed – and our overwhelming imperative was to get Bormann through these last bottlenecks undetected.

I am sure Bloem realised this. I am sure he made a deliberate effort to draw attention away from the rest of the party. Suddenly both kayaks spun round and headed fast upstream, away from the lights. The Russians shouted out a last challenge, and, when the canoeists did not respond, opened fire with machine-guns and a twelve-pounder. Both boats, together with their occupants, were blown to pieces.

I passionately longed to open fire with our tommy-guns and avenge the deaths of our comrades; but I knew that any such action would probably be suicidal, and I forced myself to whisper an order that sent us slinking on down-river, under the south-west bridge, totally protected from the Soviets on the other side of the great fortress. I was shocked and outraged by the terrible, last-ditch tragedy. Israel Bloem, who had done such wonders for me; Israel Bloem, who had become a close personal friend; Israel Bloem, who played his fiddle masterfully with only six fingers: this marvellous man had been killed before my eyes, three days into the peace – and not even by the enemy, but by our alleged allies. Dead, too, were 23-year-old Lieutenant Jacob Cohen and two German girls, Magda and Rachel, aged eighteen and nineteen. I felt sick with the sense of loss.

But there was nothing for it but to carry on. By 0400 we had caught up with our advance party, who were waiting for us some two miles north-west of Havelberg, at a point where the Havel began running parallel with the Elbe. The confluence was still five miles ahead, but the big river was less than two miles directly to port, and, rather than risk any more confrontations with the Russians, I decided to reach it overland.

My plan was that all personnel should trek across the low ground between the rivers, carrying four kayaks with them, together with their weapons and all their personal gear. The rest of the boats were systematically searched for any item that might betray our identity, then holed, weighted down with stones from the shore, and sunk. While we worked at the scuttling, we went through to JB7 on the radio and told them on no account to try to navigate through Havelberg. Rather, they were to stop at least three miles upstream on the south-west bank and scuttle their motorboats in deep water. Then they were to hide up in camp and maintain radio silence until we called them in the morning with a plan for bringing them out. I did not tell them of the disaster that had befallen us, because I knew it would only cause extra anxiety.

As we slogged across country through the dark, my mind was full of Bloem and his colleagues, and I struggled to come to terms with what had happened. I knew that he and they had given their lives to save the rest of us – and I had sent them to their deaths by recklessly deciding to change a routine which over the past few nights had proved immensely effective. I tried to persuade myself that if I had let Brabenov carry on as usual she might have pulled off yet another triumph. On the other hand, it was possible that information emanating from Anthony Blunt had at last percolated through to the right quarter; and if it had, she, too, might have come to grief.

The loss was hard to bear; but it steeled my determination to bring our marathon journey to an end without further casualties. I would do everything in my power to prevent another death: I would go to any extreme to protect the rest of my people. I resolved that as soon as I had handed Bormann over to the authorities, I would return upstream and bring JB7 back to safety. The Bolsheviks would not get a single one of them.

On our way across country in the dark, we again made radio contact with the M Section special group which was awaiting us on the south-west bank of the Elbe, and confirmed that we were in the final stages of our approach. Morton himself was there, I knew: he would not have missed this rendezvous for anything.

Meeting no one on the cross-country route, we reached the bank of the big river in only forty-five minutes, just as dawn was breaking. Quickly we launched our four remaining kayaks and pushed out into the stream, the line of canoes flanked by swimmers wearing life-jackets and keeping close company. In the lead kayak was Susan, with the elder German girl, followed by Bormann and myself, Brabenov and Wirrell, and, in the last canoe, Dr Jenny with the second German girl. Swimming alongside were John Morgan, Sergeants David Jones and John Rawlins, Sub-Lieutenant Bill Webb, Wren WT Petty Officer Joan Marshall, a petty officer Naval Commando and four GFFs, two men and two women.

As we hit the powerful current, it swept us bodily downstream, and we were content to go with it. Kemp requested permission to hoist battle ensigns, and in a few minutes little white ensigns were secured close-up on our wireless aerials. Brabenov, not to be outdone, hoisted an 'Old Glory', the battle ensign of the US Navy, which she had been saving for the occasion.

Down the wide stream we swept in rigid line ahead, with our

swimmers holding station on either hand. Soon we saw our old friend the Havel flowing in from the right, a blaze of silver under the brightening eastern sky, and half a mile further downstream we sighted a temporary jetty made of wood and steel lattice-work, erected by British and American forces.

Journey's end! We secured our kayaks alongside at the precise time indicated in our last signal, and I had the honour to lead our party ashore. There to greet us were two senior M Section officers, and Morton himself. In the background stood the little convoy of two cars and three fifteen-hundredweight trucks assigned to them by the British Army. Morton was clad in his inevitable uniform of dark suit, bowler hat and rolled umbrella, which, as he stood to attention, he held erect like a sword.

I began walking towards him, to report; but then I turned back and saw that most of my people in the command party were ecstatically greeting their colleagues from the advance group on the shore. Some, however, were handing over the German girls to the doctors and nurses of an American army ambulance.

'Miss Kemp!' I called.

Susan came to attention and saluted.

'Attention in the group, if you please.'

'Aye, aye, sir!' She saluted again, then turned and called out in a loud voice, 'Group will come to attention! JB Group . . . SHUN!'

As one, the men and women of Operation James Bond sprang to attention where they stood. With that, I turned to Morton and saluted: 'I have the honour to report, sir, that your orders of 21 January have been carried out. Your prisoner is ready to be handed over into your custody.'

Morton had acknowledged my salute by doffing his bowler, in accordance with the regulations governing an army officer out of uniform. Now he replaced it, thanked me, and introduced me to Lieutenant-General William H. Simpson, commanding general of the US 9th Army. Simpson told me that, although he did not know the purpose of our operation, he had heard that it had been successful, and he congratulated me.

When I handed Bormann over to the waiting Commando escort, he shook hands with Brabenov, Morgan and myself, thanking us effusively for looking after him so well. He then waved to the rest of the operational group, and Morton was astounded to hear several of them call out warmly, '*Auf Wiedersehen*, Fred!'

'Fred?' spluttered Morton. 'Fred? What on earth is this about?'

For the Head of the M Section, the final straw came when Bormann and I embraced. This was too much. Not only was it contrary to every conceivable standing order of the army and navy: it was also the most ridiculous behaviour, totally unacceptable. Morton reacted by resorting to one of his favourite tricks: he simply turned his back and pretended he was not there. But in fact, at the moment of hand-over, he was standing only a yard from Hitler's secretary.

As our Very Important Passenger reached the cars, he turned back and gave me a naval salute, which, to Morton's renewed fury, I returned. Thus at six bells in the morning watch (1100 hours) of Friday, 11 May 1945, the main objective of Operation James Bond was accomplished; but when Morton, ever the devout Catholic, suggested a prayer of thanksgiving, I declined. My colleagues supported me: our minds were with our people trapped on the Havel in Soviet-occupied territory, and a prayer of thanks would have been both premature and presumptuous. On the other hand, a prayer for the safe deliverance of JB7 – that was another matter. So we all knelt in the mud on the bank of the Elbe, and once again Brabenov made her sign of the cross, back to front, as usual.

17

A Cutting-out Action

I had hardly been back on my feet for half a minute when Penny Wirrell rushed up with a priority signal from JB7, who had broken wireless silence to report that a Soviet battalion had crossed the Havel and was setting up camp within six hundred yards of their position. Our rear party was surrounded, with only one narrow outlet to the river as an escape route. I ordered Penny to make the signal, 'WITH YOU BEFORE THIS DAY IS OUT. CHRISTOPHER ROBIN.'

Oh for my motor torpedo-boats at Ramsgate! I turned to my group and raised my voice. 'People! Every man jack and girl of you, search downstream and find boats – any boats – to get us back up the Havel.'

There was a chorus of 'Aye, aye, sir!' and a volley of salutes as all fifty of them moved off at speed. For the next half-hour they searched frantically for a means of returning up-river. We needed a form of transport which would not only be practical for cutting out JB7, but which would not elicit loud protests, or even active opposition, from the Russians, or indeed the Board of Admiralty.

Like conjurors, Susan Kemp and Brabenov once again did the impossible, returning from a reconnaissance with a co-operative American sergeant in his jeep. Downstream they had discovered three landing-craft, personnel, moored against a section of prefabricated Bailey bridge. LCPs were not the sort of craft which spewed out tanks or troops on to beaches, but were more command vessels, and looked like very large motorboats, with interior cabins and other refinements. They were quite fast and manoeuvrable, and had been properly commissioned as navy warships.

Three LCPs were exactly what we needed, and I was glad to find that Susan had already roused up the flotilla leader. He turned out to be Peter Wild, an RNVR lieutenant, who appeared at the double and saluted. His orders, he said, were to assist the British and American armies by providing whatever river transport they required, and he had been detailed to report to the nearest command post, or to the senior naval officer in the theatre. There could be no doubt that, in an army-oriented command, the SNO was me; I therefore took the flotilla formally under my command, and told its leader and boat commanders what we intended to do. Further, I said that I, three of my officers and ten SBS Royal Marine Commandos would join the ships for a short passage up-river.

The only person not happy with our proposed arrangement was Morton. When he heard that we intended to go back up the Havel in British warships, he was considerably alarmed. He wished everything to be done through proper channels, and told me that, through the British general officer commanding the area, I should obtain permission from the local Russian commander to enter Soviet territory.

'I just came *down* the Havel without any,' I said, struggling to conceal my irritation.

'That was entirely different,' he countered. 'Officially, you weren't there.'

'I'm going to get them out, Uncle Desmond. I'm not leaving my people up a Communist creek with no fucking paddle, no matter how many court-martial guns may fire across Pompey harbour.'

Morton saw how determined I was; but he had the last word by saying that if we proposed to act without permission, he would turn his back and not be there.

When Brabenov came aboard the flotilla leader, she caused a sensation. In her bedraggled uniform of a Soviet colonel, with her short blond hair dripping, she saluted American-style and only just stopped herself asking permission to come aboard. The officers and ship's company were mesmerised. Our problems increased when Susan Kemp appeared in uniform, since, as the flotilla leader respectfully submitted, it was strictly forbidden for Wrens to be aboard a warship on operations. I quickly assured him that Kemp had special knowledge, and that I would take full responsibility.

At 1130 hours the three LCPs set out across the Elbe, proceeding upstream into the Havel and Soviet territory. Royal Navy white ensigns were worn at the flagstaff, and courtesy ensigns of Soviet Russia and the United States at the starboard yardarm. Kemp and I wore our Royal Naval battledress, somewhat crumpled after two weeks in our haversacks, and our Marines were also in British operational gear. We were glad to find that each boat had a passably serviceable Oerlikon gun – and I fully intended to use them if the lives of JB7 should in any way be threatened.

For those of us who had been travelling entirely by night, it was an uplifting experience to ascend the river in broad daylight. We felt that the sun shining on the water and the fields had finally stripped away the confusion and horror of war.

Another signal from JB7 confirmed that they were hidden in a thick wood some twelve miles upstream. Having got precise grid references of their position and plotted them on our charts, we confirmed that we would be close to them that evening, and would tell them our plan when we had checked out the area.

We had gone only four miles up the Havel when we were challenged from the bank by a Soviet patrol backed up by two tanks and two or three mobile gun-carriers. Those guns deflected sharply in our direction as the crews loaded and rammed home their shells, followed by small, bolster-like cartridges. The breeches slammed shut. The gunners each raised an arm, signalling that they were ready to fire. On the other side of the Havel another large formation of Russian troops was deploying.

A Soviet major in the armoured party called out to us to stop. We had no option but to obey, and the three LCPs hove to close by the bank. The major demanded, none too pleasantly, to know what we were doing in the Soviet zone. He had no record of any permission being given for British vessels to navigate the Havel. For a moment I wondered what damage our Oerlikon guns could inflict on this powerful detachment of the Soviet army before we were blown to kingdom come. Then suddenly Brabenov seized the initiative by leaping up on to the bows of the flotilla leader and blasting off over a loud-hailer her well-worn spiel about searching for Nazi war criminals. (In the exchanges that followed, Susan interpreted for the rest of us, *sotto voce*.)

'You must come alongside, Comrade Colonel,' replied the major. 'I need to see your papers and call my command headquarters.'

Brabenov hit her most imperious note. 'Silence, you son of a Siberian wart-hog!' she bellowed. 'How dare you order a colonel about? My orders from Marshal Zhukov give me complete priority. You damned infantry had no river transport to offer me – but fortunately, as you can see, the English navy, and their King, have kindly lent me three boats. And instead of being ashamed and helpful, you mongrels of the steppes attempt to block our way!'

The major was reduced to a state of confusion as Brabenov browbeat him with a volley of orders. When the LCPs moved off, he came to attention and saluted, looking totally crushed.

Our target area was barely nine miles upstream, and I did not want to arrive until close to dusk. We therefore proceeded in line astern at a very slow speed until, turning with the river, we saw the magnificent sight of the fortress town of Havelberg standing out in half-silhouette against the evening sky. As we navigated the north-eastern stream round the stronghold, where Bloem and his comrades had lost their lives, the boats dipped their ensigns, the officers saluted, and all the James Bond personnel said a prayer.

By then Soviet soldiers were on the rampage along the south-west bank of the river, so close to the trapped JB7 party that our people could see them smashing their way into houses and hear the screams of their victims. Together with her GFF colleague Tachin Nielsen, operational Wren Petty Officer Mary Conyers lay flat on her stomach in the undergrowth, watching the river downstream. Tachin was shocked and frightened by events on the bank, but Mary concentrated intently, and at around 1800, as dusk was falling, she detected the sound of engines approaching. A few seconds later she picked up our flotilla in her binoculars, and whispered excitedly to Caroline Saunders, who was on the other side of some bushes, 'Boats from downstream, ma'am. Wearing the white ensign. Range two cables. They're LCPs.'

'Thank you, Mary,' replied Caroline evenly. 'Stand by to receive and secure the line. Tachin, make the code-signal by R/G.'

Putting her transmitter to her eye, Tachin flashed an infra-red signal downstream at us, and immediately we had our mark.

It was part of my plan to tie up alongside the bank on which most of the Russian units were stationed, the one farthest away from our people's camp. In keeping with the Royal Navy's long tradition of cutting-out actions, we did everything slowly, so as not arouse suspicion that we were being furtive and trying to avoid contact with Soviet patrols, who watched us intently from both sides of the river as we approached. The sound of rifle-bolts being opened and closed clattered across the water.

I had marked Tachin's signal by reference to the third tree beyond a low hedge, and asked Peter Wild to steer straight for it. As he reached it, he turned hard aport and swung across the river, to come alongside the opposite bank, while Russians kept us covered from both sides of the stream.

As I hoped, their interest was focused on the leading boat, which was closest to them, and none of them noticed a small, quick movement on the port quarter of the last LCP in the line, where SBS Sergeant John Rawlins was standing ready with a line. When his boat turned, and its quarter came closest to the south bank, he hurled the end-coil of rope on to the shore, where willing hands seized it, hauled it in and made it fast. As the boat moved across the river, Rawlins and a couple of helpers paid out the line, weighting it at intervals, so that it would lie on the bottom and not foul any Soviet craft that might come past.

Our ploy worked well. Soon we were tied up alongside the north-east bank, with the flotilla leader ahead, the other two LCPs abreast behind, and all three facing downstream. Within half an hour a heavily armed Soviet patrol pulled up on the shore. The armoured cars and personnel carriers disgorged a major-general and six other officers, who came aboard bristling with suspicion and hostility, backed by overwhelming firepower.

Brabenov stepped forward and saluted. 'Colonel Natasha Andre-yevna Serova, of Marshal Zhukov's Special Intelligence Unit, at your service, sir! Welcome aboard, Comrade General. These English friends are helping me search for escaping Nazi criminals.'

Brabenov's appearance had its usual effect. The Soviet general had obviously not seen an attractive woman for months, let alone one with curves like hers. He was completely non-plussed, and followed her into the cabin as if hypnotised. As he went below she grabbed my arm and whispered, 'Now what?'

'Enchant him! Titillate him! Seduce him!. Get them all tight – anything to keep their attention off JB7.'

We began to ply our visitors with rum, and soon the general was promising full co-operation in our hunt for absconding Nazis: he asked only that Brabenov be sure to recommend him to Comrade Stalin for whatever assistance he managed to provide. Brabenov, for her part, sustained her role brilliantly, and as the rum took effect, the general became more and more distracted by his own efforts to fondle her irresistible backside.

Our impromptu party went swimmingly. As I had hoped, our guests stayed and stayed, and the drinking, lewd jokes and phoney cameraderie went on until well after dark. At about 2100 Susan and I went up on deck for an unobtrusive survey of the shore. A large number of Soviet soldiers stood on the bank near us, alert and heavily armed. Their officers and NCOs looked extremely unpleasant and dangerous – and they were watching our every move. Two tanks sat motionless with their guns levelled in our direction and their commanders on the turrets. From across the river more Soviet troops were gazing at us, and I noticed with some concern that they were within yards of JB7's marker.

Raucous shouts and laughter welled up from the cabin. The Home and Forces radio programme launched into 'Alexander's Ragtime Band'. What marvellous cover! Surely no Soviet soldier, however mean-minded and suspicious, would believe that any hanky-panky was in progress, with such cheerful music swinging out, and a comrade general on board.

It was time to move. With countless Soviet eyes on me, I raised my right hand to my lips, and opened and shut my mouth as if yawning: our signal for action stations. Susan, Peter Wild, the duty watch, Brabenov at the hatchway, Sergeant Rawlins on the after, outboard LCP – all saw it and reacted. Within moments, helped by two other commandos, Rawlins had hauled in the cross-river line until all the weights were resting just below the surface. Having secured it aft on the outboard LCP of the two rear boats, he raised his arm to tell Susan he was ready. She already had her R/G transmitter trained on JB7's position at 55° magnetic, and now she sent her invisible signal to Caroline Saunders on the far bank.

As Caroline received our signal she repeated it quietly to Christa Shulberg: 'G for go, ma'am.'

'Thank you,' Christa replied. Slowly she turned and in a firm whisper addressed her party: 'All right, people. Absolute silence. Slowly, and in precise discipline, JB7 will withdraw. And it's *now*!'

One by one the fifty men and women slid into the water and hauled themselves across on the now-taut line, which prevented them from being swept downstream. From the bridge of the flotilla leader I could see their heads, dark blobs in the water – but then I knew where they were. I prayed that no Soviet eyes would pick them up. If anyone did spot them, and started offensive action, I would order my Oerlikon gunners to open fire instantly. I would then go quickly below, take the Soviet general hostage, and proceed downstream with him bound to the mast, illuminated by a searchlight, and my Smith & Wesson held to his head. I almost prayed for the furore and the courts martial that would follow. I could see myself standing in the cabin aboard Nelson's *Victory* in Portsmouth, with my sword on the great table, its tip pointing at me to signify my guilt. I could hear myself saying, 'My people are safe. My conscience is clear. My soul is safe. At last I have done something to be proud of.'

Needless to say, no such drama came to pass. Everything turned out simple and easy. The last man over the river cut his end of the rope free and followed the rest; then, as he reached the boat, he pulled the line in and stowed it aboard, hoping that he had obliterated the final traces of occupation.

The members of JB7 were silently distributed through the two rear LCPs, lying flat on the deck or cooped up in lockers and engine-rooms, all fighting back their natural exuberance at being so effectively cut out. Everyone remained still, ready for any order or action. Then Kemp brought me a signal which purported to order me back to British headquarters on the Elbe. With profuse apologies, we told our guests that, alas, we must leave, and the Russians reluctantly disembarked, the general needing some assistance from Brabenov and myself. Our visitors were duly piped ashore by the bosun's mate, who nearly ruptured himself with his efforts not to laugh.

The LCPs let go and proceeded downstream in line ahead, restricting their speed to a leisurely pace, again to avoid suspicion. Even so, with assistance from the current we made some ten knots

– but during the two hours it took us to reach the Elbe, we stood to at full action stations, with all weapons ready. My last signal to base read: 'JBC TO M CONTROL. JB7 CUT OUT. AWAIT YOUR FURTHER ORDERS.'

For once Morton betrayed his excitement by allowing himself an emotional response. He sigalled back, 'OWL TIGGER AND POOH TO CHRISTOPHER ROBIN. WELCOME HOME OUR VERY DEAR PEOPLE. GOD BLESS YOU ALL.'

The LCPs came alongside the Bailey bridge. I cleared the lower decks, and the whole JB7 group came up. The rest of our command group, who had not seen them for ten days, were waiting ashore, and rushed to greet them on the jetty in a storm of hugs and kisses.

The warm night air was full of joy and excitement – but suddenly we all fell silent, and Christa Shulberg quietly spoke the names of their brothers- and sisters-in-arms who had died in the course of Operation James Bond. They were Israel Bloem and his three GFF commandos, two girls and a boy; four more GFFs lost when they tried to stop Russian soldiers raping civilians near the Müggelsee; Hannah Fierstein; and the five mine experts from HMS *Vernon* who had helped clear the waterways – fourteen casualties in all. But someone had been forgotten.

'Patricia Falkiner,' said Susan.

For a while we stood still and silent. Then, at Susan's request, Brabenov said a prayer. Her choice was surprising, but completely apt: the 'Battle Hymn of the American Republic'.

'Mine eyes have seen the glory of the coming of the Lord,' she began, but she had hardly reached the end of that first line before everyone – men and women, Jews and Gentiles, Germans and British, and a considerable portion of the American 9th Army – took up the hymn in full song, and our voices went out over the waters of the Elbe.

Just as we finished, a top-secret, A 1 Most Immediate signal arrived for me from the Special Operations department of the Admiralty. 'YOU ARE APPOINTED LCP FLOTILLA 21 IN TEMPORARY COMMAND,' it read. 'YOU WILL AT YOUR DISCRETION ATTEMPT CUTTING-OUT ACTION FOR PERSONNEL STRANDED NORTHWEST BANK HAVEL. YOU WILL NOT RPT NOT ENGAGE RUSSIAN FORCES.'

To which we could only add, 'Amen!'

18

Final Twists

When we returned to Birdham, Fleming was back in Germany, successfully completing the operation for which he had been whisked away from us in Berlin. This was to recover the archives of the German navy from Tambach Castle, and we belatedly discovered the reason for his precipitate departure: the admiral in charge of the records, knowing him from of old, had demanded that he attend in person. When Fleming rejoined us at the beginning of June, he was cock-a-hoop that things had gone so well; although he admitted that in comparison with Operation James Bond the expedition had been insignificant.

He brought with him some of the Kriegsmarine documents he had carried off, among them records of the U-boat refuelling bases in Ireland. Of burning interest to me were details of the base in Donegal we had blown up in October 1940, and of the two U-boats we had destroyed there. I not only observed but took part in the forging and doctoring of these records to show that no such base ever existed, and that the missing U-boats had been sunk elsewhere, at some other time. (The result is that, today, German naval historians deny that any U-boats were ever based in Ireland.)

Now Fleming's main task, directed by Morton and Donovan, became to implement the transfer of the Nazi assets in Switzerland and elsewhere to the beneficial control of Great Britain and the United States. Bormann kept his promise without demur: he was flown to Basle under escort and provided the necessary signatures; Morton and Donovan succeeded him as signatories, and for the time being the funds remained where they were, in the same banks. The initial transfers were completed before the end of June.

The success of our abduction, and the recovery of so much stolen property, prompted British and American secret circles to initiate several similar operations. Morton set up a new sub-section charged with the task of carrying off other prominent Nazis whose knowledge or expertise might benefit the West. Whether or not they were considered war criminals made no difference: if they co-operated, their slates would be wiped clean, and any offences disregarded. They would be well paid, and settled in a foster country as legitimate immigrants, with the chance of becoming British or American citizens.

Since the aim was to press former Nazis into service, we named the operation after Andrew Preston, the man who, it was once said, owned the entire Royal Navy, so many men had he rounded up into service. (Sailors talk of being 'in the Andrew'.) So we called it 'Operation Andrew', and Susan Kemp was placed in charge, using personnel that included agents of the OSS. Its success was startling, one prize catch being Wernher von Braun, a war criminal by any other name, but more important to the Americans as the genius behind the development of the V1 and V2 rockets.

At Birdham I was brought back into direct contact with our own star prisoner when Fleming ordered me to liaise on the crucial task of adapting Bormann for life in England. At first he was housed in the comparative luxury of a secure wing at Birdham, and there over the next few months he was intensively debriefed in a process which yielded a report of eight hundred pages, each page initialled by the protagonist and his interrogating officers. In this priceless historical document Bormann told his own story, and that of the Nazi Party, from the 1920s until 1945.

The debriefing yielded fascinating insights into his relationship with Hitler. When questioning started, Bormann's attitude to his former leader was respectful. He referred to him as 'the Führer', and appeared to take him seriously as a commander. Later, however, he began calling him 'that stupid old fool' and other names still less flattering.

As Bormann told his story to M Section officers, all over Europe the hunt for him was on. In the autumn of 1945 the International Military Tribunal assembling in Nuremberg published and broadcast notices throughout Germany, in four successive weeks, announcing:

Martin Bormann is charged with having committed Crimes against Peace, War Crimes and Crimes against Humanity ... If Martin Bormann appears, he is entitled to be heard in person or by counsel. If he fails to appear, he may be tried in his absence ... and if found guilty the sentence pronounced upon him will, without further hearing, and subject to the orders of the Control Council for Germany, be executed whenever he is found.

In order that he should *not* be found, it was obvious that his physical appearance, his demeanour and even his voice would have to be changed as much as possible. After several conferences on the subject, Morton decided once again to call in Archie McIndoe; but this time total security was of such paramount importance that the plastic surgeon was required to work at Birdham, where a wing was transformed into a makeshift hospital, and nurses were recruited from within the M Section and the GFF.

The cumulative effect of several operations was subtle but impressive: the shape of Bormann's ears was changed, his lips were thickened, the backs of his hands made less hairy by skin-grafts, his fingerprints altered, part of the bump removed from his nose, and the scar on his forehead extended. Once the patient had recovered, he underwent a period of training and rehabilitation, at the end of which he both walked and spoke quite differently. He deliberately cultivated a stammer – supposedly an after-effect of war – which in time became entirely natural, and could be used as a means of warding off unwelcome questions: if necessary, he could appear to have become tongue-tied and unable to answer.

By mid-summer 1945 most of my former colleagues had left Birdham, and the place was a ghost of its former self. Having settled in, Bormann was free to move around the main house unsupervised, and one evening he appeared in the big recreation-room while I, as usual, was playing the Bechstein. Seeing him, I stopped, whereupon he took my place and began to play loudly and violently, but quite well, until suddenly he slammed down the lid of the keyboard and stood up. It was as if he had wanted to show me that he, too, could perform, but then had abruptly lost patience.

The last time I saw him was during his recovery period, in July, when I was about to leave Birdham to go on a specialist training course. I went up to his suite of rooms and found him alone. By then he spoke a good deal of English, and I told him I had come to say goodbye. We stood looking at each other for what seemed a long time. Then we shook hands, and suddenly he once again embraced me. It was a strange moment for a 21-year-old. The man who held my shoulders had been an enemy, and, by all accounts, a vile war criminal. At that very moment his former cronies were being tried at Nuremberg, and he himself was being hunted half across the world. Yet at the time none of these things seemed to matter. My only thought was that this man had gone through extreme danger with the rest of us, showing no mean courage, and had played an unselfish part in our escape from Berlin. I therefore hugged him in return, put the face-piece back over his head for the last time – and suddenly Martin Bormann was gone.

At almost exactly that date, soon after the Japanese surrender, on the secret directive of the new Prime Minister, Clement Attlee, and with the approval of King George VI, Morton appointed another special sub-section to hunt down the remaining Nazi loot. Although nearly 90 per cent of the assets had already been recovered, with Bormann's help, those outstanding still amounted to billions of dollars' worth, and a world-wide search was called for.

The Soviet Union was naturally not asked to participate in Operation Midas Touch, but the new sub-section received almost unlimited authority, and it was backed by France, Belgium, Denmark, Holland and, of course, the United States. The American OSS was actively involved, and command was given to the newly promoted Lieutenant-Commander Barbara Brabenov. The other half of her command team was Second Officer Caroline Saunders, who had so distinguished herself alongside Christa Shulberg, directing JB7 on the Müggelsee and down the Berlin rivers. What these two women achieved cannot be described here. Suffice it to say that their success was immense, and resulted in the recovery of about half the assets still outstanding.

With Bormann recovered from his operations, the next problem was to furnish him with a more permanent home, and to this end two girls from the GFF were enlisted to act as his surrogate daughters. Since Germans were finding employment hard to come by, the two were glad to take the job of looking after him and fielding awkward questions from strangers – although naturally they did not know the identity of their pseudo-father. The place chosen for his domicile was Highgate, in north London, where many German immigrants already lived, and there the artificial family of three was installed in one of the M Section's houses.

For a few months the arrangement worked well, but then events and pressures combined to force a move. Bormann himself, deprived of friends, had nobody but the two girls to talk to, and he became increasingly neurotic. Two psychiatrists who saw him in February 1946 thought that he was on the verge of a nervous breakdown, and recommended that he should be taken to live in a country village, where he could get to know members of a small community. At the same time, the foreign intelligence agencies – the French in particular – who were searching for Bormann got a sniff of something; and although they had no idea where he was, the trail seemed to lead towards London.

Deciding that he must be moved, Morton entrusted the task of creating a safe new environment for him to Susan Kemp, whom he temporarily recalled from Germany. From previous experience she knew full well that any stranger arriving in a rural community would immediately attract attention, and if the newcomer was obviously foreign, nothing would check the locals' curiosity. The trick, if she could achieve it, would be to bring in the stranger with maximum prior publicity as a friend or relative of one of the best-liked families in the village.

Luckily Susan knew just such a family, in the form of Captain Peter Grant, RN, and his wife, Marlene Schuler Grant. Marlene, an Austrian who had come to England as a student during the 1930s, was a close friend; she had served in the Wrens and the family's joint naval background made them ideal for the task. Susan knew they could be trusted completely.

After discussing the idea with Morton, she made discreet inquiries, and reported that her friends would help. The position seemed ideal. During the war Marlene's parents had stayed in Austria, where they had joined the resistance, but both had been killed; now, Susan saw, the father could be profitably brought back from the dead. By a curious but useful fluke, his Christian name had been Martin. Morton liked the idea: he called in Peter Grant and was impressed by him, and was further reassured by his old naval reports, which were excellent. The Grants were therefore asked, in the strictest secrecy, to house, feed, look after and guard an immigrant of some importance – although of course the man's identity was never revealed to them. Naturally they would be well recompensed.

With preliminary agreements in place, Susan launched into action with what, inevitably, was known as Operation Piglet. In Highgate Bormann was apparently taken ill. An ambulance, owned and driven by the M Section, called and took him away, ostensibly to the local hospital, but in fact back to the secure wing at Birdham. His alleged daughters stayed on in the house long enough to announce to neighbours the sad death of their father; but three weeks later they too moved out and returned to Birdham.

Next Susan arranged for Marlene Schuler Grant to receive the glad news that her father had not been killed after all: he had just been found in a hospital for displaced persons, which he had entered soon after escaping from the Germans at the end of the war. His health was poor, and he had trouble speaking; but the Grants at once invited him to come over and live with them as soon as he was well enough – probably in five or six months' time. The news quickly went round the village, and celebratory parties were held.

A week later Marlene left home, ostensibly to visit her father at the hospital in Salzburg, seen off with the good wishes of friends. In fact she drove straight across country to Birdham, where, a couple of hours later, the Marine Commando guards saluted smartly as she came through the main gates, once again in the uniform of a second officer, WRNS. Susan had already explained the plan to Bormann, and now, tongue in cheek, she introduced him to his long-lost daughter, before handing over to Marlene and Penny Wirrell, late of Op. J.B.

There was no difficulty about finding Bormann a new name: obviously he must become Herr Martin Schuler. Over the next four months, Marlene visited Birdham twice a week, and in the course of long conversations made him familiar with every facet of her father's life, behaviour, likes, dislikes and so on, endlessly rehearsing incidents from the family's past. In particular they talked about religion. Martin Schuler had been a Catholic, and clearly Bormann had to pose as the same; but so strongly was he attracted by the ideas and beliefs of this religion, which was new to him, that after four months he was received and baptised into the Catholic Church. (When Morton, an ardent and intensely conservative Catholic, heard about this conversion, he was, for the first time in anyone's experience, literally speechless.)

During these preparations the security authorities became uncomfortably aware that agents searching for Bormann were beginning to look in the direction of the United Kingdom. MI 6 therefore mounted several elaborate exercises in deception to lay scent-trails elsewhere. In the autumn of 1946, for instance, rumours were put about that a small force of former SS men was holed up in an inaccessible redoubt, high in the Alps near Berchtesgaden, guarding some important person. Gradually the stories gained strength, claiming that the Nazi chief in question was Bormann, and in the end an American aircraft bombed the redoubt. The defenders were flushed out, and one of them, who was captured by Allied troops, confirmed that the man they had been guarding was Hitler's former secretary. The survivors took to the road in a small convoy, with military vehicles fore and aft, and a saloon car in the middle. For three days they drove southwards through Austria and Italy, closely followed by a British war crimes investigator, who became intensely excited, thinking he was about to pull off the coup of a lifetime. To his chagrin and mystification, however, his controlling officer repeatedly denied him permission to arrest his quarry – something he could easily have done, especially on one occasion when the Germans had pulled up in a village square, for a visit to a public lavatory, and he got a clear sight of the man he thought was Bormann, only a few yards off. Yet time and again, when he asked for fresh orders, he was told to follow but to make no contact.

After a pursuit of over a thousand kilometres, the convoy

reached the Italian port of Bari. There, at the dock gates, the Carabinieri let the German vehicles through, but closed the barrier in the face of the British, who saw the three vehicles hoisted aboard a ship in cargo nets the moment they reached the quay. The vessel's markings had been obliterated, and in a few minutes it sailed, showing no lights. Inquiries suggested it was bound for South America – and thus was created an indestructible rumour that Bormann had slipped out of Europe.

Meanwhile, in England, five months elapsed before Susan decided that everyone was ready for Herr Schuler to reappear from the dead. Then in August the Grants went off, apparently to Austria, and returned a few days later, on a Friday, with Marlene's long-lost father. The reception was cordial but quiet, for the villagers knew that they must treat the old man gently. Nevertheless, in due course they began to call, and before long Herr Schuler had met all the local luminaries, who liked him well enough.

Over the past few months Marlene had also been busy on another front. Before the war her parents-in-law had run a riding school in the village, and for some time she had been hoping to start it up again. Now she bought new horses and recruited new staff – three young men and three young women – who got things going admirably. Soon there was a brisk demand for lessons, especially from local children, and the school received the approval of the Institute of the Horse and the Pony Club.

When old Herr Schuler felt better, he said that he too wished to ride, and it turned out that he was a proficient horseman. Besides, he liked the young instructors, and felt secure with them – as well he might, since they were all Commandos and members of the M Section, led by Penny Wirrell. On the receiving end of their radios were sections of Royal Marine Commandos, at a base only minutes away. The fact that over the months instructors came and went, changing places with other young people, worried nobody.

So Martin Schuler fitted in to his adopted village. People liked him, and for nearly ten years he was a respected figure in the community. Then in 1956 word went out that he had fallen ill and died, and a funeral was held in the village churchyard. Even I, who had been so intimately involved in snatching Bormann, was led to believe that his life had ended before the age of sixty.

As for myself, in July 1945 I was staggered when Morton sent for me and told me I was to go on appointment for special training to become an actor. At first I thought I had mis-heard him, and then, when he repeated it, I said, 'You can't be serious!'

'Why not?' Morton snapped back. 'That's what most intelligence agents do – act. You've been acting almost from the day you entered my Section, if not before.'

'You've got natural talent,' added Fleming. 'But you need to learn the trade properly and have the rough edges ironed out.'

'Just so,' echoed Morton. 'Then you may be of some real use to us.'

'You're going to RADA, the Royal Academy of Dramatic Art,' Fleming told me, 'and to the Old Vic.'

To my everlasting shame, I had not the remotest idea what the Old Vic was. (RADA, however, I *did* know about. Three months earlier, unbeknownst to me, Morton had entered my name for it, apparently for cover purposes. After returning to England in May, I went to some classes, and it was at RADA that I met Roger Moore, who later ensured my initiation as a director with Warner Brothers in Hollywood, and who by an extraordinary coincidence became James Bond on screen.) I had to take Fleming's word that the Old Vic was the world's leading theatre company. Nevertheless, on the morning of Thursday, 16 August 1945, Brabenov and I, both in civilian clothes, stood in St Martin's Lane, in the heart of London's theatreland, and gazed across at the New Theatre, emblazoned with posters which announced:

THE OLD VIC THEATRE COMPANY IN REPERTORY

HENRY IV PARTS 1 & 2, OEDIPUS, THE CRITIC

UNCLE VANYA,　　　　ARMS & THE MAN

Laurence Olivier, Ralph Richardson, Sybil Thorndike

Brabenov was astounded. 'You're going to train with *that* lot?'

I nodded with an excess of forced humility.

'How the heck did you swing it?'

'Fleming fixed it with two of his pals, ex-Fleet Air Arm Lieutenant-Commanders Laurence Olivier and Ralph Richardson.'

Brabenov let out a loud yell. 'You goddamned son of a bitch! I wanna come too!'

'Listen!' I tried to placate her. 'On that river trip of ours you showed you didn't need any damned lessons in acting.'

'Sodding bullshit!' she replied.

We walked to the stage door, opposite the back of Wyndham's Theatre, and, after confirming our dinner date for that evening, I disappeared inside. As I went I clearly heard her say, 'Once more into the bloody breach, I suppose.'

By then the 'shred, doctor and forge' unit of the M Section had almost completed its task of expunging every trace of Operation James Bond from the face of the earth (except within its own records, of course). Churchill's original order to Morton had left no room for manoeuvre: not the slightest hint of the operation must ever leak out, the Prime Minister had decreed. The manipulation of records had to be carried out in such as a manner as to make it seem impossible that any such operation could have been mounted. Op. JB had to become a myth, the Operation that Never Was.

One of the prime objects of the cover-up was to safeguard Ian Fleming himself. Whereas anyone who stayed on in the navy would to some extent be protected by the fact that he or she was still in the service, Fleming, a wartime-only sailor, was about to return to civilian life. There he would become much more vulnerable to possible reprisals, and if the smallest whisper got out that he had been involved in an operation which recovered billions of Swiss francs' worth of Nazi loot, his days might well be numbered.

Extended cover was therefore put in place to show that during the duration of Op. JB, from early January to early May 1945, he had been either in the Far East, liaising with the intelligence divisions of the Commonwealth navies, or else in Jamaica, where he had visited Sir William Stephenson (head of British intelligence in the Americas; he was also known as 'Intrepid' or 'the Quiet Canadian') at the end of February. So thoroughly was the deception planned that, after returning to England briefly at the beginning of January, and being appointed to command the operation, he returned to the Far East for a few days later in the month. Thereafter, in the intervals of training at Birdham, he put in occasional appearances in Room 39, his old billet at the

Admiralty, and of course at Guildford, the new home of his 'Red Indians', the 30th Assault Unit.

What happened to me thereafter is another story for another day. Suffice it to say here that I found a happy home in show business, as actor and director on the stage, in films and in television. But I was still working with the M Section, and from the Cold War years two operations will always stand out in my mind. One concerned the state visit to Britain of the Soviet leaders Bulganin and Khrushchev in 1956, and the other took place in Czechoslovakia between 1966 and 1969. Until I retired from the world of secret intelligence in the early 1980s, the Section always came first, and this kept a tight rein on my artistic activities.

In 1995 my first-rate general practitioner decided that I should have been awarded a war pension. Having examined my records and assessed the stress I had suffered, he even predicted what my level of compensation would be. Old and influential friends persuaded me to apply, and when I did, I was declared to be 40 per cent disabled, the award being back-dated to March 1945. I was granted a generous, five-figure sum and a weekly pension, much in line with what the doctor had predicted, the amounts being based upon physical injury and the trauma which resulted from having to kill undefended and sometimes quite innocent people.

Of course I never lost interest in Piglet, and in the spring of 1947 I was much amused by the appearance of the book *The Last Days of Hitler* by Hugh Trevor-Roper, a former intelligence officer commissioned by the British authorities to reconstruct the Führer's final moments. One object of the exercise was to allay the anxieties of the Soviet leader, Stalin, who had developed an obsessive suspicion that Hitler had escaped and was still alive. Indeed, one Soviet report suggested that Bormann and Hitler had left the bunker together.

Having interviewed several of the people who had been present in the bunker at, or almost until, the very end, Trevor-Roper came to the conclusion that Hitler had committed suicide alongside his long-term mistress and wife of two days, Eva Braun, and that Bormann had got away, by some unspecified route, after the breakout on the night of 1–2 May 1945. One detail of Trevor-Roper's text which fascinated me was the fact that Bormann had set out with a copy of Hitler's private testament in his pocket, and that this had never been accounted for. I can reassure the author that it now rests safely with M Section's security control. It was characteristic of Morton's secretiveness that he, who certainly knew about Trevor-Roper's mission, and could have answered many of his key questions in a moment, never gave him the slightest help towards establishing the truth.

The international search for Bormann continued unabated throughout the 1950s and 1960s, interest flaring up whenever there was a report that he had been sighted. In his book *The Murderers Among Us*, published in 1967, the ace Nazi-hunter Simon Wiesenthal wrote:

Hitler's chief deputy has been the subject of more rumour, legend and controversy than any other Nazi leader . . . No other prominent Nazi has been declared dead and then revived so many times.

In 1964 an editor of the German magazine *Stern*, Jochen von Lang, made contact with Artur Axmann, the former head of the Hitler Youth, and went with him to the bridge near the Lehrter station, in central Berlin, where he claimed to have seen Bormann and Stumpfegger lying dead on the night of 1–2 May 1945. Fresh inquiries suggested that the two corpses had been carried several hundred yards to an amusement area known as the Ulap Fairground, and there buried. In July 1965 a major excavation in that area failed to reveal any human remains; but in December 1972 a new excavation, carried out as the preliminary to a building project, turned up two skeletons close to the site of the previous search. In due course the Frankfurt Court of Appeals, which had taken charge of the official hunt for Bormann, issued a report stating that the skeletons had been 'proved with certainty' to be those of Bormann and Stumpfegger, and that the search for Bormann was officially terminated.

This new investigation convinced Simon Wiesenthal, among others, that Bormann really had died during the last night of the war. Yet many observers remained sceptical, not least the Welsh surgeon Hugh Thomas, whose book *Doppelgängers*, published in 1995, re-examined events in the Führerbunker during the final days of the war. By comparing the accounts of survivors in detail, he showed that all their stories contradicted each other in some degree, and that none of them could be trusted: for one reason or another, none of the witnesses was telling the whole truth. Similarly, after careful medical, dental and forensic analysis, Mr Thomas concluded that the slightly burnt body of a woman found by the Russians outside the bunker could not have been that of Eva Braun: the teeth in no way matched those of Hitler's companion, the blood group was wrong, and the dead woman had not taken cyanide, but had been killed by a blast of shrapnel in the ribs. About the corpse identified by the Russians as that of Hitler, Mr Thomas was less certain: the dentition more or less matched that of the Führer, but there was one suspicious feature, in that the left foot and bottom of the left leg had been burnt away, as if to conceal some defect Hitler had not possessed, while the rest of the body had been only lightly scorched.

Mr Thomas also cast grave doubts on the alleged discovery of Bormann's skull in Berlin: indeed, he dismissed it as 'forensic fraud'. Among other discrepancies, he pointed out that the skull was caked with red-brown clay – a substance not found in Berlin, where the subsoil is sand. He agreed that the teeth in the skull closely resembled the dentition logged in Bormann's records, but showed that further fillings had been made since the last entries in the charts. In other words, no matter whether the records studied by Mr Thomas were those which the M Section had doctored, or some others, it was clear that the man the German authorities claimed was Bormann had lived on after 1945, and could not have died in the exodus from the Bunker. Mr Thomas concluded from his own wide research that Bormann went to live in Paraguay, that he died there in 1959, and that his remains were secretly returned to Berlin, where they were re-interred under the Ulap Fairground, until a tip-off led to their discovery. The burden of his painstaking evaluation was that the Bormann mystery had still not been satisfactorily solved.

Although I knew that much of what I had done must remain secret for the forseeable future, as time went by I began to hope I might be able to tell at least some of my story. On making discreet inquiries, I received guarded encouragement from the highest level. On 4 March 1952 Lord Ismay, who had been chief of staff to Churchill during the war, sent me a warm personal letter in which he wrote,

'I sincerely hope that soon it may be possible for your story to be told, and for you to receive the public acclaim which you so rightly deserve.'

In October 1954 Churchill himself – once again Prime Minister – wrote me a letter which I still find intensely moving:

10 Downing Street,
Whitehall.

MOST SECRET

Dear John,

Lord Ismay told me of your wishes but I am afraid that it is still impossible for anything to be done and you must not now speak of these matters. When I die, then, if your conscience so allows, tell your story for you have given and suffered much for England. If you do speak, then speak nothing but the truth, omitting of course those matters which you know can never be revealed. Do not seek to protect me for I am content to be judged by history. But do, I pray you, seek to protect those who did their duty honestly in the hope of a future world with freedom and justice for all.

Yours vy sincerely,
Winston S. Churchill

Fleming and I kept in touch intermittently. He left the navy with the avowed intent of writing novels, but eight years went by before his first, *Casino Royale*, appeared in 1953. Naturally I was delighted to find that he had named his fictional hero James Bond, and it was no surprise for me to discover that the chief of Bond's secret-service department was called M. From time to time I mentioned to Fleming the possibility that I might one day try to tell the true story of our joint operation, and in the autumn of 1963, with money pouring in from Bond novels and films, he wrote me a characteristically generous letter, which he sent in a fat registered packet:

16 Victoria Square
London SW1

14th October 1963

To: Commander 'James Bond', R.N.

He has always been my very dear friend and wartime comrade-in-arms, John Ainsworth-Davis.

The enclosed contribution comes with my grateful thanks and vivid remembrance of our Operation 'James Bond', in which 'Piglet', Martin Bormann, was clandestinely transported from wartime Berlin to England via the German waterways in April/May 1945. This eventually resulted in the recovery of some 95% of the Nazi assets plundered from occupied Europe, which had been deposited in neutral countries, mainly Switzerland.

Without any doubt, you and your operation were my secret inspiration for all that followed; a secret that I have never revealed to anyone else. It gives me great pleasure to tell you now.

I have missed you, and your bloody piano.

As ever,

Your most secret friend,

Ian Fleming.

If you do go ahead with a book on the subject, you may use this note any way you will. Publish it, if it helps.

The 'enclosed contribution' was £20,000 in big, white £5 notes. Although Fleming did not say so, I knew he meant the money to go to the survivors of the operation, and I was glad to share it out.

Less than a year after writing that letter, he was dead. Later, when I began to mention in confidence that he had been involved in Op. JB, people asked why he had never spoken or written a word to anyone else about it. Even to put that question indicates a failure of understanding. As his wife, Ann, used to remark, when it came to wartime intelligence work, Ian was 'an oyster', and simply did not discuss secret matters with anyone outside the service. In his biography of Fleming published in the autumn of 1995, the author

Andrew Lycett made the ludicrously naive remark that when, on 30 May 1945, Fleming wrote to a girlfriend complaining that he had had 'no devilry for too long', this proved he could have taken no part in 'the hunt' for Martin Bormann. On the contrary: that kind of flippant answer was Fleming's normal means of deflecting tiresome inquiries. He knew full well that during the war a serious breach of the Official Secrets Act could have carried the death penalty, and that even in peacetime he could have been arrested, court-martialled, cashiered and sentenced to at least five years' imprisonment for talking out of turn. His career and life would have been ruined. Small wonder that a man of such professionalism and discipline never blabbed.

For me, one major regret has always been that my father never knew the truth about my wartime service. He died at the beginning of January 1976, still believing I had been a renegade and traitor with a criminal background – for he was so indiscreet that nobody in authority had dared to enlighten him about my secret operations. After the war the M Section did nothing to improve my character references: on the contrary, they went out of their way to enhance my supposed villainy, adding psychopathic tendencies, gambling, bad debts and finally bankruptcy to my list of failings. This policy paid off on several occasions, not least in 1967 at the Barrendov Studios in Prague, where, under cover of an international film production, I was on an intelligence operation. When the KGB and the Czech SSS (secret police of the notorious Eighth Department) opened my mail – as they always did – and read threatening demands from creditors, they dropped their well-founded suspicions of me, and I was able to continue my undercover work.

The fact that my father and stepmother were kept in ignorance caused much grief to my mother and my sister Jennie; but post-war events proved that it was just as well. On three potentially danger-ous occasions Britons working for the KGB, the SSS and Odessa (the secret society of former members of the SS) came digging for information about my background; but my stepmother's scathing reports – apparently confirming every word of my old records – persuaded the inquirers that I could not possibly be a secret agent: the British Intelligence Services did not employ bankrupt, psychopathic, criminal traitors. It helped that, by then, my father vehemently denied that he had ever known Ribbentrop: if the former ambassador's name ever came up in conversation, he would exclaim, 'If ever I'd got anywhere near that bastard, I'd have killed him!'

The fact that my father could not know the truth about me remained a source of embarrassment and sorrow to Mountbatten. Years earlier, when my father appealed to him for help over my career, Lord Louis had written back a cover letter saying that, alas, my character was so bad that there was nothing he could do. When my father died, the long-term deception was evidently still weighing on Mountbatten's mind, for he wrote two more letters, the first to me, the second about me.

In the first, a personal note, he reminisced about my father. The second letter was to Susan Kemp, who had devoted her entire career to the M Section and moved steadily up through its ranks, becoming an Assistant Deputy Director in 1951, Deputy Director in 1955, and Director – M in person – from 1965 until her retirement in 1980. So secret was it, in Mountbatten's view, that on 21 January 1976 he drove over from Broadlands to her home and declared that he intended to set the record straight. Using our original code-names from A. A. Milne – Owl for Morton, Tigger for Churchill, Kanga for Susan and Christopher Robin for me – he dictated a five-page memorandum headed MOST SECRET, in which he outlined my career in covert operations.

'I shall certainly recommend that it's time for the curtain to be lifted on C. R.'s intelligence career,' he began. 'For some time I have wanted to confirm in writing his service in the Royal Navy under a cover name, and the various operations in which he was involved with the Morton Section.'

Having stated that he had known my father, Jack, at Christ's, Cambridge, Mountbatten recalled how he had cheered him on at the Antwerp Olympics, together with the Duke of York and Prince Henry. He said that he himself had several times met Ribbentrop at our house at 69 Harley Street, and that he had 'assisted' my entry into the Royal Navy under a cover-name. He then gave brief résumés of my earlier operations, before coming to Op JB:

In January 1945, C R was promoted Acting Lieutenant-Commander and appointed in Command of Operation James Bond, under the executive command of Commander Ian Fleming, RNVR (Sp). With Operational WRNS 'Wrens', Royal Marine Commandos and German patriot fighters, he abducted 'Piglet' from Berlin and using the German waterways brought him safely down the Spree and Havel to the Elbe and the British Forces on the North West bank.

Piglet had the key to the vast Nazi wealth held in Switzerland. Operation James Bond made possible the subsequent release of those assets for the people to whom it belonged or for the general good of the occupied territories from where it had been plundered.

At the end of the memorandum Mountbatten gave me permission to publish anything he had written, but only after he himself had, as he put it, 'gorn off'. As things turned out, he died in 1979, murdered by the IRA; but another twelve years passed before I saw this document again. The reason was that he gave it to Susan Kemp, instructing her that it should be held in safe-keeping along with other secret records of the M Section. He also asked her not to let me have it unless she thought I really needed it, and she in her wisdom withheld it.

For me, M Section documents had long been a matter of concern and controversy. One day in the late 1960s I went to see Morton at his home, told him I wanted to write a book about my career, and asked if I could have access to some of his papers – whereupon he completely lost control. Jabbing a finger in my direction from across the drawing-room, he damned me as an ignominious traitor and a son of Satan. He disowned me, and, in his own phrase, 'retired' from being my godfather. If I were to publish any such book, he boomed, he would tear the First World War bullet from his heart and hurl it at me with all the force that God had employed in destroying the Philistines.

I never saw him again; but a little later he burnt all his papers. Historians and politicians bewailed the loss of this priceless intelligence archive, covering the years 1920–60, and including details of Operation James Bond. When Morton died in 1971, the world assumed that he had taken his secrets to the grave.

That was certainly my impression – until 18 April 1991. That morning Susan Kemp telephoned for a chat about how I was getting on with the draft of my book, records or no records. We had scarcely begun talking when she came out with the startling but welcome news that she and the M Section's photographic experts had copied every one of Morton's records long before he had his bonfire, and had placed the copies in the safety of the Section's security control. (A doctor who gave him a routine check-up claimed that he had detected a dangerous irregularity in his heartbeat, and while Morton was in hospital for three days of tests his people raided his archive). Susan told me that I could have restricted access to some naval reports, but that I might not take any away or make copies: handwritten notes only. She also reminded me about Mountbatten's letter and memorandum.

A week later she picked me up and we drove into the Surrey countryside. In the course of a walk she confirmed that security control had agreed to provide me with further information about Bormann's final years. Then, after lunch in a pub, she drove me to a country town and parked outside the cemetery. We walked up a path to the Roman Catholic section and stopped by a patch of mown grass.

'Do you like conjuring tricks?' she asked.

'In a graveyard?'

'Why not? You're standing at Piglet's grave.'

She told me that, far from dying in 1956, Bormann had lived on in England until 1989, and then had been buried here. For a moment I was so startled that I did not believe her. But then I looked at her and decided that she was not joking. After a while we returned to the car and drove back to her house, where she showed me Mountbatten's letter, and I read again how concerned he had been that the true story of my naval service had never been told.

What I did not realise was that, even after all those years of service, I myself was still being used by the M Section in their schemes of disinformation. It was not until the spring of 1996 that Susan at last revealed to me the truth about Bormann's final years – and highly disconcerting it was to find that I, who had been involved in the preparation of disinformation schemes for much of my life, had myself fallen for one, and had been actively encouraged to follow a planted trail.

In July 1960, somewhere in the south of England, a man who called himself Peter Broderick-Hartley jumped on to a moving bus just after it had come round a corner, and so by chance met Johanne Nelson (generally known as Hanne), a Danish woman whose British husband had died a year earlier. He sat down beside her and they fell into conversation. He said he was a civil engineer; in fact he was a con-man and fantasist with a criminal record and a known propensity for fastening on to vulnerable women. Unknown to his new contact, for the past eight years he had been employed, trained and supervised by the M Section, which had cultivated him as another Bormann double.

The two began an affair. One evening, after a few drinks, Broderick-Hartley suddenly began speaking German, and carried on for half an hour, 'revealing' that he was Martin Bormann. He spoke passionately about Hitler, about Eva Braun and Goebbels, and about his own life in Germany. When at last he stopped, Hanne asked in English, 'Why are you telling me all this?' He seemed surprised, and said, 'Oh, I thought you were German.'

No Nazi herself – her family had Jewish antecedents – Hanne was at first alarmed by this outburst, because she believed that her lover really *was* Bormann: certainly he bore an extraordinary resemblance to Hitler's former secretary, and he had the same powerful, squat build. Yet by the time that Broderick-Hartley claimed to have played a major role in the Third Reich, she was so much in love with him that she suppressed her feelings of anxiety and guilt.

The two never cohabited, because Broderick-Hartley was living with a housekeeper, Hilda (whom he also referred to as Amy Gant). Nevertheless, he and Hanne spent much time together, and on 1 August 1961 she bore him a daughter, Vanessa. Soon afterwards he again told her he was Martin Bormann; when she said she did not believe it, he took a used envelope, rapidly scribbled a signature, and said, 'After all, you are now part of the Bormann family.' Although the signature was not a perfect match, it convinced Hanne.

For years Hanne wore an engagement ring, and naturally she would have much liked to live with the father of her child; but this was never possible because Hilda had such a hold over him – something that Hanne could never quite understand. As she soon discovered, her lover held extreme political ideas. He claimed that all Germans, not only himself, were Nazis at heart, whatever they professed outwardly.

In general, he said, his aim was to recreate the old Nazi movement in the form of a National Socialist Union in Europe. This could be achieved only if the other countries surrendered their identities and agreed to be ruled by Germans. First Europe, then the whole world, would be administered by a Nazi government in Berlin, where there would be an Upper House of German politicians, and a Lower House for representatives of other nationalities. In this new world-empire only German would be spoken, 'but people would soon get used to that', even in America. For all the obvious flaws in his character, Hanne saw him as 'a most brilliant man', with the ability to put Germany back on its feet.

In spite of his grandiose claims, his own behaviour was frequently puerile. On visits to London he pointed out Jews and made loud, derisive comments about them, saying that they should have been eliminated years ago, and that they would not escape next time round, as their names were all in the computer: 'They shall be liquidated one and all.' When he and Hanne walked along London streets, he would often barge a person of Semitic appearance off the pavement, saying 'You bloody Jews! Hitler should have exterminated the lot of you.'

This unreconstituted Nazi was a good rider, and often went to the races; he also enjoyed other typical English pastimes, and liked to dress in tweeds as a country squire, although he despised the British in general. He typed well, and kept a powerful radio transmitter – 'as big as a table-top', according to Hanne – which was frequently in use, sending and receiving messages.

He had a taste for caviare and champagne, and indulged his sybaritic tendencies as far as he could while ostensibly living a middle-class existence. His long-term frustration emerged in his claim that he 'owned a first-class ticket for life, but was unable to use it'. Referring to himself as 'the Third Man', he complained that he was always under surveillance – and this was certainly true, as M Section personnel were permanently on hand to keep an eye on him.

He and Hanne continued to meet intermittently over the years, and in 1984, five years before his death, they drank champagne and had dinner 'in a fine Chinese restaurant near Hyde Park'. Again he asked Hanne to marry him, and she, still admiring him, was sorely tempted to accept. But, thinking of her own Jewish antecedents, she declined his offer. When he died on 20 June 1989, he was buried in the unmarked grave I had seen, and she did not attend his funeral.

It was work on this book that put me in touch with Hanne. I met her in May 1995, when we had lunch at a small hotel in Sussex. Because one aim of the meeting was to make sure that she was genuine, I had arranged for M Section's security control to vet the venue and put full security in place. During drinks, holding it cleanly at the base, I picked up a glass my guest had been using, and passed it to a waitress, who in fact was one of our girls, so that the fingerprints could be checked. Twice more during the meal we repeated the procedure, and some thirty photographs were taken, several of them close-ups. Within twenty-four hours security control confirmed beyond any doubt that this was the woman with whom Broderick-Hartley had been associated.

Still – though I did not know it – my own section was playing me along. For several months thereafter I was greatly excited by my belief that I had at last stumbled on the truth about Bormann's latter years.

I knew that during the early 1950s suspicion and rumour about Bormann had been rife throughout Europe, with many fingers pointing at England. I also knew that after the end of the war several *Doppelgänger*s had performed well in Italy, Germany and other countries. What I did *not* know was that in 1952 the M Section had found a strikingly good replica of Bormann, in the form of Peter Broderick-Hartley, on their own doorstep, and had decided to make use of him also. The idea was that, if ever anyone seemed to be coming uncomfortably close to the truth, the British authorities could produce the resident double and say, 'There you are. Of course he looks like Bormann, but in fact he's got nothing to do with him.'

As I say, I knew nothing of this when Hanne showed me letters, written by her lover in English, and numerous photographs of him in England. His resemblance to Bormann was astonishing: the same broad cheekbones, the same hairline. But neither Hanne nor I – at that stage – realised that, to achieve the likeness, he had undergone extensive plastic surgery. Nor did either of us know that he had received long training in his role as Bormann's *Doppelgänger*, and that most of the letters apparently from him had been forged by M Section experts.

But the more I thought about Hanne's story the more I believed that her lover really was Bormann. She herself certainly did, and I do not blame her. Nevertheless, I was never totally convinced. There was something about the photographs which jarred: even given the fact that Bormann also had undergone plastic surgery, I could not quite reconcile the appearance of Broderick-Hartley with the image of Hitler's secretary stamped on my mind during our journey downriver fifty years earlier.

It was not until the spring of 1996 that Susan Kemp at last felt able to revel the truth to me. Even after retiring from the M Section, she had some access to its records, and so was able to help. Belatedly I learnt that in 1989, when I started work on this book, the Section had deliberately led me to believe that Bormann died in Hampshire in April 1956, in the hope that I would publish the date and so get it generally accepted. What they had not bargained for, however, was that Hanne Nelson would come forward with her story in the hope of getting it published. At first they told me they supported her version of events, and confirmed to me that she was who she claimed to be, at and after our meeting in the Sussex restaurant. Only when they realised I was adamant that Hartley was not Bormann did they at last decide to come clean.

The truth was that between 1945 and 1956 Bormann was based (as I have shown) in England. During those years, however, he made several trips to Brazil, Argentina, other countries in South America, and elsewhere, always under the control and surveillance of the M Section and the CIA (successors of the OSS). The leader of the CIA's control and protection team in South America was none other than Barbara Brabenov, who reported that when Bormann first set eyes on her again both of them were overcome by emotion, and tough CIA operatives watched in amazement as their star agent embraced the world's most wanted war criminal. According to Susan, the results of their partnership were 'superlative': wanted Nazis were run to earth, hoards of cash, jewellery and gold were recovered, and other important things accomplished, among them the containment of attempts to rebuild the Third Reich in exile through financial and economic domination of the free world.

Nevertheless, the government was still nervous about having

the convicted war criminal in England, and early in April 1956, just before the official visit of the Soviet leaders Bulganin and Khrushchev, Susan was sent for by the Prime Minister, Anthony Eden, who launched into a diatribe about the problems caused by all the suspicion that we were harbouring Bormann. Before she could say anything, Eden lost control – as I also had seen him do – and began to bang on the desk as he screamed obscenities: 'We're cosseting him like a f***ing VIP!' he yelled. 'I want him out of the country before these bloody Russians get here. Why don't you just cut the bloody man's head off and throw him in the sea?'

As usual, with the tantrum over, Eden abruptly reverted to his normal, suave self, giving Susan a big smile and saying with the utmost courtesy, 'Be so good, my dear Miss Kemp, as to escort him out of the country by April 25th'.

Susan did almost exactly that. In Hampshire, as I have recorded, it was announced that Herr Schuler had died, and a coffin bearing his name was buried in the village graveyard near the riding school. On 29 April 1956 Bormann was flown under escort to Argentina, and there once again joined forces with Brabenov. By then, however, his health was failing: he was still only fifty-five, but he wanted somewhere to settle down in obscurity. He found his haven in Paraguay, where he lived quietly until, after a long illness, he died in February 1959. He was buried in the local cemetery, but some time later, in a deal concluded by the CIA, the Paraguayan government and German intelligence, his remains were exhumed and taken back to Berlin. They were reburied in the sand beneath the Ulap Fairground, where they were conveniently found in 1972. I say 'some time later' because Susan could not give me details of this operation, which she heard of only at second hand. All the same, her account of Bormann's last years is strikingly similar to that of Hugh Thomas, who reached much the same conclusion by means of acute detective work.

Early in 1996 I travelled to Bavaria and met Gerhardt Bormann, one of Martin's sons, in the company of the family lawyer, Dr Florian Besold, and a first-class interpreter, Dr G.K. Kindermann. The meeting took place in the Bormanns' house on the outskirts of Freising, near Munich. Also present were Gerhardt's wife and son, and the atmosphere was thoroughly cordial. Conditioned as they were by years of belief that Martin Bormann had died in 1945, the family received the story of Operation James Bond with a good deal of scepticism. Nevertheless, I think they were shaken when I showed them copies of the letter from Ian Fleming and the memorandum from Mountbatten, confirming that the rescue of Piglet had taken place. There was also one point, trivial yet telling, at which the truth suddenly struck home. Through the interpreter I asked Gerhardt (who speaks practically no English) whether, as a boy, he had owned a pony. The answer was, 'No, that was my brother Martin.'

'And when the family had to move,' I went on, 'he was upset because he couldn't keep the pony any longer.'

Until then Gerhardt had remained impassive, reminding me strongly of his father, with his broad features and wary eyes. But now he suddenly came alive. With a startled look he said to the interpreter, 'How on earth could he have known that?'

The answer was simple. Martin Bormann senior had told this sad little story to the girls at the riding school in Hampshire.

Our interview in Freising ended amicably, if indecisively. I made a point of emphasising that my book would not harp on Bormann's war record: on the contrary, I described how in 1945, when I knew nothing of his recent past, I had formed an emotional bond with him during our journey down the waterways, and everyone in the party had become fond of him.

The family said they would like time to think about what I had told them, but Gerhardt reiterated his conviction that the bones and skull dug up in Berlin, and now preserved in a vault in Wiesbaden, are those of his father. As I was leaving, Dr Besold remarked that the way to settle the issue once and for all would be to arrange a DNA test, comparing a sample from the bones with hair or blood from a surviving member of the family. I myself very much hope that such a test will be carried out; if it is, I am confident that it will confirm the authenticity of the remains, and that it will show that the bones were brought back from Paraguay.

In 1945, as I have said, the ethics of Operation James Bond did not concern us. As naval officers, we merely carried out orders in the final stages of a global war. Since then, however, I have frequently worried about the moral questions which our actions raised. Clearly the nation's leaders carried colossal responsibilities in a time of national emergency, and their decisions must have been influenced by the extraordinary pressures under which they were working.

But were Churchill (and later Attlee) right to shield a Nazi war criminal for largely financial reasons? Why did they not hand him over to the Nuremberg Tribunal once the first major tranche of the stolen assets – some 95 per cent – had been recovered? It is true that to have done so would have meant breaking the guarantee of safe conduct which Fleming and I had given in the bunker; but should normal standards of behaviour have been applied to a known criminal?

I feel bound to point out that in the end it was not Churchill who sanctioned Bormann's eleven-year stay in Britain. The new Labour administration came to power in July 1945, before the interrogation of Bormann had finished, and before the Nuremberg Tribunal issued it notices calling for his arrest. The decision to allow him to remain in hiding must therefore have been taken by Attlee, with the backing of President Truman. (As Churchill's deputy during the war years, Attlee had of course been privy to the secrets of Op JB.)

Only later did I become aware that the man we saved from the gallows was a monster. During our journey downriver, as I have tried to show, he behaved in an entirely reasonable manner: he was co-operative, friendly and constructive, and gave no sign of harbouring violent tendencies or evil ideas.

To understand the last and most extraordinary twist of this story, one must know something of the mentality of Desmond Morton. I have already explained that he was secretive to the point of paranoia; what I have perhaps not emphasised enough is that he loved coups – intelligence coups, political coups, military coups, even theatrical coups. Best of all, in his view, were those coups which only he, or only he and one or two trusted associates, knew about. The abduction of Bormann and the recovery of Nazi assets undoubtedly formed the greatest coup of his career. It was as if the operations involved were the acts of a Wagnerian opera, for which he himself had written the libretto and the music, even if (as he grudgingly conceded) luck and the Royal Navy had played a part in the success of the drama.

Yet in his view Act III of the opera was not yet complete. It needed a *dénouement*, a final *coup de théâtre* with which to bring down the curtain on the grand entertainment he had devised. Not only that: he somehow managed to persuade himself that the extraordinary course of action he proposed to take was the correct one, and operationally sound. For my account of what followed, I rely heavily on Susan Kemp, who was at the centre of this Wagnerian climax.

In September 1946 she was stationed at Düsseldorf, in the Rhineland, directing Operation Andrew Preston. At the same time Barbara Brabenov was also in Germany, running Operation Midas Touch. One day they both received orders to present themselves outside the Palace of Justice in Nuremberg at 11 a.m. on Tuesday, 1 October. Although both knew that the trial of the Nazi war criminals had been in progress for months, neither realised that 1 October was a date of any special significance. In fact, it was the day on which the final judgments were given and the sentences read out.

Having arrived in separate jeeps, the two women met by appointment at one of the secure checkpoints guarded by American military police.

Dead on time, along came Morton in bowler hat, black overcoat and dark pin-stripe suit, carrying a rolled umbrella. With him were two Royal Marine Commando captains, escorting a squat powerfully built man dressed in an ill-fitting British battledress, and wearing the insignia of a major in the Intelligence Corps. He also sported a pair of large spectacles. For a moment Brabenov did not recognise him, so much had he changed since she had last seen him. Then suddenly she realised it was Bormann. When she and Susan both exclaimed, 'Fred! Hello!' and smiled at him, Morton was furious: it was not in such an undignified fashion that he wished his final act to unfold.

The party of six was escorted into the building by an American colonel and a major of Special Military Police. They went past the main doors of the court room in which the International Military Tribunal was sitting, along some corridors and up a flight of stairs to a fairly small room apparently reserved for official visitors or observers who did not wish to be seen by people in the courtroom below. Simultaneous translation was available, and the proceedings were relayed through headphones plugged in to every seat.

As they were being shown to their places, Morton suddenly said, 'You're here as silent witnesses.' Susan and Barbara sat down in one row of chairs with Bormann between them. Morton and the two Royal Marine officers were in the row behind. All around were other VIPs. In the wall ahead was a glass panel through which they could see down into the courtroom. There below them, in full view, sat the former Nazi leaders.

The Allied judges had been taking it in turns to read out the Tribunal's verdicts, and at that moment the Soviet judge, General I.T. Nikitchenko, was reading the verdict on Hans Fritzsche, who was found not guilty. Presently Nikitchenko came to the last of the defendants, Martin Bormann. Compared with some of the earlier judgments, this was relatively short. There was insufficient evidence, the Tribunal had decided, to convict Bormann on Count One of the indictment, Crimes against Peace: 'The evidence does not show that [in the late 1930s] Bormann knew of Hitler's plans to prepare, initiate or wage aggressive wars.' But on Counts Three and Four, War Crimes and Crimes against Humanity, things were very different.

The judgment emphasised that Bormann had 'controlled the ruthless exploitation of the subjected populace' in conquered territories; that he was 'extremely active in the persecution of the Jews'; that he had been prominent in the slave labour programme, had prohibited decent burials for Russian prisoners of war, and had been responsible for the lynching of Allied airmen. The Tribunal agreed that Bormann's counsel, Dr Friedrich Bergold, had 'laboured under difficulties', but pointed out that he had been unable to refute the evidence they had gathered:

In the face of these documents, which bear Bormann's signature, it is difficult to see how he could do so even were the defendant present. Counsel has argued that Bormann is dead, and that the Tribunal should not avail itself of Article 12 of the Charter, which gives it the right to take proceedings *in absentia*. But the evidence of death is not conclusive, and the Tribunal, as previously stated, is determined to try him *in absentia*.

In conclusion, Nikitchenko announced that the Tribunal had found Bormann not guilty on Count One, but guilty on Counts Three and Four.*

As these thunderous ironies rolled over him, Bormann stared down transfixed at his former colleagues. When she put a hand on his arm, Susan found that he was shuddering.

At 1.45 p.m. the president of the Tribunal, Lord Justice Lawrence, announced that the court would adjourn, and sit again at ten minutes to three. During the recess Morton and his party walked outside the Palace of Justice. Somebody had provided them with sandwiches and coffee, but Bormann ate nothing. By ten to three they were back in their places in the VIP gallery to hear the sentences passed.

Now, instead of all siting in court together, the defendants were brought in one at a time to hear their fate. The first was Goering. The president read out his sentence in a voice that was quiet but solemn and authoritative:

Defendant Hermann Wilhelm Goering, on the Counts of the Indictment on which you have been convicted, the International Military Tribunal sentences you to death by hanging.

Next came Hess, who received life imprisonment; then Ribbentrop (death by hanging), Keitel, Kaltenbrunner and the rest. For the final sentence, no prisoner came in:

The Tribunal sentences the defendant Martin Bormann, on the Counts of the Indictment on which he has been convicted, to death by hanging.

As those fateful words rang out, Bormann himself sat still as a statue, icy calm. Lord Justice Lawrence rose to make a short announcement, to the effect that the Soviet member of the Tribunal

* Quotations from Volume 1 of the official record, *The Trial of the Major War Criminals before the International Military Tribunal*, 1947.

desired to record his dissent from some of the decisions, and that his opinion would be put in writing and published later.

Then suddenly everyone in the VIP gallery was on the move. Morton's party was shepherded down the stairs, but at the bottom they were blocked and almost knocked down by a stampede of journalists racing for the telephones. Such was the excitement that for a moment Susan feared somebody had rumbled their companion. In the event he left quietly with his escorts, to be returned to the safety and jurisdiction of the United Kingdom.

So Morton engineered his *dénouement*, creating a supreme historical precedent. He had already ordered Susan to make no report on what had happened that day – but he knew that by ordering her to attend he had ensured that she would record the event secretly. So she did. That evening, back in Düsseldorf, she made some private notes, which Brabenov later confirmed were accurate. Thirty years on, when she went to copy Morton's papers privily after he had threatened to destroy them, she came across a single sheet of paper headed: 'NUREMBERG – 1. 10. 46.'

It read:

JUSTICE MUST NOT ONLY BE DONE
BUT MUST 'BE SEEN' TO BE DONE
D.J.F.M.

Appendix

The K–XVII Incident

The decision to destroy the Dutch submarine K–XVII was taken
for the following reasons.

On 28 November 1941, when Commander Besançon sighted
the Japanese fleet apparently heading for Pearl Harbour, he
promptly signalled in code to the Commander-in-Chief, Royal
Navy Far Eastern Command, under whose authority the Dutch
were operating. His message was intercepted by the M Section
code and cypher office in Singapore. Within hours, copies of
the signal arrived in Washington for the eyes of General
Donovan only, and in London, for Major Desmond Morton.
Both men informed their masters, Roosevelt and Churchill. All
four already knew of the planned attack on Pearl Harbour, and
all had prayed that it would come about.

At that time, eighty per cent of the American people were
vehemently isolationist, and against war with either Japan or
Germany. If Roosevelt declared war on Japan without any attack
on American assets, the odds were that he would have been
impeached. Conversely – as Donovan and Morton had secretly
agreed – if America stayed out of the war, the Japanese would
be left virtually unopposed to ravage India, Australia, New
Zealand and many other countries in the Pacific and Indian
oceans. To liberate such countries later might well have proved
impossible. Besides, Britain and her allies desperately needed
American help against Germany – and if the Japanese attacked

Pearl Harbour, it was certain that America would come into the war.

Yet if the British and American supremos knew of the impending attack, why had the American forces in Pearl Harbour not been put on full alert? And why were the U.S. warships not ordered to sea, where they would have been much safer, and able to fight back? Professional opinion of the day believed that the base could be successfully defended. So why was nothing done?

The answer is simple. In Hawaii there were thousands of Japanese expatriates. Most were fiercely loyal to their adopted country, but a sizeable minority were not, and some of these had been spying for their homeland. Also, the Japanese Consulate–General was hyperactive. Had the base been put on full alert, Japanese High Command would have learnt about it in a few hours. The attack would have been cancelled by order of Emperor Hirohito, who had insisted that the assault be a complete surprise. Roosevelt would have lost his pretext for bringing America into the war, with disastrous results for the Allies.

What had all this to do with K–XVII? The connection is clear. If ever it became public that Roosevelt and Churchill had known of the plan to attack Pearl Harbour, and had done nothing to forestall it, not only their careers, but quite probably the whole alliance, would have foundered. The Japanese would have been free to conquer and pillage.

The ship's company of K–XVII knew they had sighted the Japanese fleet and reported it to the highest authority. No matter how well-intentioned, such witnesses could prove dangerous. The Allied secret intelligence chiefs therefore decided that no risk could be taken, and the Dutch submariners were silenced.

Index

Christopher Creighton's name is abbreviated to CC.

Aldred, A.B., 129–30, 138

Ampleforth College, CC at, 12, 15, 16; school records rearranged, 15; discipline, 81; CC's music examination, 93

Attlee, Clement (*later* 1st Earl Attlee), 218, 240

Austria, Germans in Vienna, 43; Wren operator in Vienna, 43–4; Germany and, 45; Falkiner in, 45–9, 51–3; CC and Fleming *en route* for Berlin, 119

Axmann, Artur, 226

Bergold, Friedrich, 242

Berlin, CC meets Canaris, 25–6; focus of Allied encirclement, 76; CC makes intensive study of, 107–8; defences on Müggelsee, 117; Operation JBV, 118; devastation, 120; waterways, 120–1; Foreign Office, 121, 122; destitution, 121–2; JBV reinforcements at Müggelsee, 140; abduction plan, 146; clearing of waterways, 147; River Spree, 147, 148, 157; chaos prevailing in, 147–8; CC

and JBC land, 153–4; Freedom Fighters, 155; kayaks hidden, 155; underground escape routes discovered, 155; JBC down Spree by kayak, 156–7; stench of death pervades, 158; Brabenov sees off vigilantes, 158–9; CC and companions in Foreign Ministry bunker, 161–8; Russian forces in, 164, 166, 169, 172, 179, 180; in its death throes, 171–2; skeletons allegedly of Bormann and Stumpfegger, 226

Bernadotte, Folke, Count, 72, 163

Besançon, Lieutenant-Commander, 81, 112

Besold, Dr Florian, 238–9

Birdham, Birdham transcript, 23n; M Section operational service arm at, 41; part of Combined Operations, 58; house and grounds, 58–9; CC welcomed, 65; Fleming at, 72, 75; German Freedom Fighters, 75–6, 89, 91–2; news of Falkiner's death, 77; off duty periods, 92; music, 93, 95–6; failed personnel, 97; CC and Fleming return to, 105;

kayaks delivered, 109; Morton, 115; Blunt and Hollis, 133–5; Brabenov, 141; Morton and Donovan, 145; Bormann, 216, 220; McIndoe works on Bormann, 217; Marlene Grant's visits to Bormann, 220, 221

Bletchley Park, 47, 49, 78, 155, 182

Bloem, Israel, leader of German Freedom Fighters, 75–6; appearance, 76, 89; Brownshirts mutilate, 89–90; personality, 90; Fleming and, 90; CC and, 90, 202; selects Freedom Fighters for Birdham, 91; violinist, 96, 145; and Shulberg, 114; orders to his agents in Berlin, 114–15; detailed in command group, 149; and Freedom Fighters in Berlin, 155; reports on Soviet forces in Berlin, 164; in kayak escape party, 179; translates *werder*, 183; at Schwanenwerder, 184; dependability, 185; Russian speaker, 187; wants to wait for JB7, 187; dressed as Soviet lieutenant-colonel, 191; disposes of Russian rapists, 200; in lead towards Havelberg, 201–2; blown to pieces, 202; dipped ensigns for, 210; named among the dead, 214

Blunt, Anthony, to M Section for training, 133; appearance, 133; behaviour, 134; CC and, 134–5; Morton reprimands, 135; CC and George VI discuss, 136, 137; in breach of orders, 138; disturbing information about, 186; and Brabenov, 203

Bormann, Gerhardt, 238–9

Bormann, Martin, witnesses CC's meeting with Hitler, 22, 23; Birdham transcript, 23n, 73n; loathes Ribbentrop, 23; describes Hitler in a tantrum, 33; position of power, 72; and Hitler, 72, 73, 104; code-name, 74; Ribbentrop and, 102, 104, 123; CC and Fleming discuss strategy over, 105; and Ribbentrop's proposals, 116; personal retreat of, 122; appearance, 124–5; meetings with CC and Fleming, 124–6, 163–4; medical and dental records, 157; in underground bunker in Foreign Ministry, 163–8 *passim*; Fleming's orders to CC concerning, 166; exposes CC as double agent, 167; Fleming and, 167–8; reports Hitler's death, 169; and Günther, 173, 177; body-search, 174; Hitler's will, 174; forged identity card, 174–5; leads breakout, 175; and exploding tank, 176; Kayak escape party, 178, 179, 182; physical condition, 179–80, 195; CC's orders on, 185, 187, 188; kneels to pray, 189; restrictions on, 194; disguise, 194, 195; personality, 195, 218; stories of Wittelsbach dynasty, 196; his safety of paramount importance, 202; handed over to Commando escort, 205; CC and, 205, 218; provides necessary signatures, 215–16; debriefing, 216; charged with War Crimes etc., 217; appearance, demeanour and voice altered, 217; piano-playing, 218, 235; and recovery of Nazi loot, 218; on verge of breakdown, 219; Kemp finds safe environment for, 219–20; Marlene Grant and, 220–21; received into Roman Catholic Church, 221; agents search for, 221; indestructible rumour of his escape from Europe, 222; riding, 222, 235; as Herr Schuler, 222–3; Trevor-Roper's conclusion about, 226; post-war international hunt for, 226; search officially terminated, 227; his grave, 233,

236; later life, 233–6; Nuremberg Tribunal's verdict, 242–3; condemned to death, 243

Boult, Sir Adrian, 13

Brabenov, Barbara W., liaison officer with M Section, 130, 142; arrives at Birdham, 141; Donovan and, 142, 145, 148; appearance, 142; personality, 142, 185; training, 142–3; Cowboys and Indians, 143; Russian speaker, 144, 187, 192–3; volunteers for Op.JB, 144; dines with secret circle, 145; 'Yankee Doodle Dandy', 148; code-name, 149; and Fleming, 149, 165; to Berlin, 153; identity of pick-up targets, 156; down Spree by kayak, 156; carries Bormann's medical and dental records, 157; sees off SS vigilante group, 158–9; and the dying baby, 159; and chamber pots, 161–2; and CC, 162, 170, 172–3, 211, 223–4; and Bormann, 163–4, 165, 166, 205; disables SS men, 167; clothing for breakout, 173; Hitler's will, 174; and exploding tank, 176; signals JBPU, 177; perceives kayaks, 177; and Schwanenwerder, 184; receives Donovan's signal on Blunt, 186; wants to wait for JB7, 187; in the lead to Potsdam Bridge, 191; confronts Soviet captain, 192–3; and Russians, 194; kills Russian captain, 199–200; Kemp and, 201; hoists 'Old Glory', 204; on reconnaissance for boats, 207; boards flotilla leader, 208; deals with Russian major on river Havel, 209–10; and Russian general, 211, 213; 'Battle Hymn', 214; Operation Midas Touch, 218–19

Braun, Eva, 225, 227

Braun, Wernher von, 216

Braunschweig (Brunswick), 152

Canaris, Wilhelm, 19–21, 25, 166, 167

Cherbourg, CC witnesses Operation Jubilee, 20–1; CC meets Rommel in, 25–7; CC in SS prison, 28–30

Churchill, Mary (later Lady Soames), 12, 51

Churchill, (Sir) Winston, and Morton, 10, 132–3; CC and, 11–12, 16, 81, 83–5; deception operations, 16n; planning for D-Day operations, 18; Valentine Fleming and, 37; and Ian Fleming, 39, 42, 51; code-name, 50, 231; against employing women on operations, 51; letter to Swiss Finance Minister, 69, 70; spiral staircase at Ministry of Works, 80; and Brabenov's award, 193n; and Operation James Bond, 224; letter to CC, 227–8; and Bormann, 240

Cohen, Jacob, 203

Conyers, Mary, 210

Courtneidge, (Dame) Cicely, 13

Creighton, Christopher, rendezvous in Dublin with Unified German Secret Service, 1–7; and Ribbentrop, 10, 101–5, 122–4, 162–3; Churchill and, 11, 16, 81, 83–5; Mountbatten and, 13, 15–16, 80; noms de guerre, 13, 56, 231; appointed to M Section, 14; instruction in RAF as undercover agent, 14–15; and Canaris, 19–20; betrays Operation Jubilee, 20–1; meets Ribbentrop and Hitler, 21–3; with COPP, 23, 24; informs Nazis about Operation Overlord, 24; Exercise Tiger, 24; meeting with Rommel, 25–8; interrogation by Gestapo, 28–30; rescue, 30–1; and Falkiner, 32–3, 94, 116; Fleming reads file on, 42–3; search for shipwrecked American servicemen, 55; Fleming and, 56–8, 118; promotion, 57–8; Secret

Musical Telegraphy Transmissions, 94–5, 100, 105; in Lisbon, 97; in Switzerland, 98; adopts Waffen-SS identity, 99, 119; wires piano as transmitter, 100; Operation Subend, 112–13; to Berlin, 119–21; John Davis, double agent, 127; dentist and plastic surgeon for Bormann's double, 129–30; interview with Eisenhower, 131–2; discusses Blunt with George VI, 135–7

Birdham:

    Kemp, 60, 63–5; Commando training, 67–8; physical training, 89; return to, 105, 129; Bloem, 90; music, 95–6; Fierstein, 118; intensive study of geography of Berlin, 107–8; Blunt, 133–5; and assassination of Günther, 140; Brabenov, 141; Cowboys and Indians, 143; secret circle of M Section dine, 145–6; rehearsal of abduction plan, 146; Donovan and, 148; 'Yankee Doodle Dandy', 148; parachute training, 149; Bormann's adaptation for life in England, 216

Operation JB:

    clothing and equipment, 151, 173; position of authority, 153; parachutes into Berlin, 153–4; countersigns Bloem's report, 155; down Spree by kayak, 156; calls Morgan on transceiver, 160; in underground Foreign Ministry bunker, 161–2, 163–8; Bormann exposes him as double agent, 166–7; and Schulberg, 172–3; about to kill Günther, 176; and exploding tank, 176; escape party in kayaks, 178–83; and raft of corpses, 181; sanitary arrangements, 183; escape party's respite at Schwanenwerder, 183–5;

overall command, 185; misses Fleming's experience and wisdom, 185, 187–8; Potsdam Bridge presents problem, 186–7, 188; prays aloud, 189; changes order of approach to Potsdam Bridge, 191; receives signal of German surrender, 196–7; and dead Russian captain, 200; Bloem, 201–2; plans to reach Elbe overland, 203; leads party ashore, 204; hands Bormann over, 205; prayer for deliverance of JB7, 206; cutting-out action for JB7, 207–14; a party to distract attention of Russians, 212

post-war:

    training at RADA, 223; in show business, 225; Ismay and, 227; Churchill's letter, 228; Fleming's letter and gift of money, 229; Mountbatten's resumé of CC's involvement in Op.JB, 231; last encounter with Morton, 232; learns of Bormann's later life, 233; and Hanne Nelson, 236; concern over moral questions raised by Op.JB, 236–7

personal matters:

    appearance, 1; boyhood, 10, 11–12, 13, 14; black angel experiences, 16–17, 18, 65, 153, 170; feelings of guilt, 79–80, 81; and Falkiner's death, 77–9, 81, 82–7, 95, 149; music, 93–4, 95–6, 148, 218; lineage, 111; and Fleming, 110–13, 116; anxiety about assassination of Günther, 161, 170, 173; comforts Brabenov, 201; Bloem's death, 203

personal relationships:

    Bormann: quest for, 72–4; meetings with Fleming and, 124–6, 163–4; not trusted,

171; in bunker, 174; in kayak escape from Berlin, 179–80, 195; CC's orders on, 185, 187, 188; last encounter, 218

Morton:
builds up CC's dual personality, 1; godfather and guardian, 1; intends CC for intelligence agent, 14; sends him into Royal Navy, 18; double-crosses him, 24; visits him in Royal Naval hospital, 31–2; meeting in Cabinet War Room, 80, 82–5; greets CC on bank of Elbe, 204, 205; and plan to cut out JB7, 208; last meeting, 232

Cunningham, Sir Andrew, (later Viscount Cunningham), 58n, 103n

Darlan, François, 38
Dartmouth, Royal Naval College, 12, 13, 81
Davis, Jack Ainsworth-, Cambridge friends, Olympic Champion, 9; and Ribbentrop, 9–10, 230; scholar and musician, 13; personality, 14, 230; and Mountbatten, 15–16, 230, 231; works with McIndoe, 101; oarsman, 107; ignorant of CC's wartime service, 230
Davis, John Ainsworth (CC), Germans' belief about character of, 1; told not to use his own name, 13; M Section fabricates background and character, 15; contributions to image as traitor, 18; discharged from Navy, 127
Davis, Marguerite 'Daisy' Ainsworth-, 11, 13, 69
Donegal, 14, 215
Dönitz, Karl, 163n
Donovan, W.J., Morton and, 133, 145, 146; and Brabenov, 142, 145; his position mirrors Morton's, 144; history, 145; and Roosevelt, 145; personality, 145; at Birdham, 145–6; and abduction plan, 146; information on Blunt, 186; and transfer of Nazi assets, 215, 216
Dublin, 2–3, 4, 5–7, 19

Eisenhower, Dwight D., Exercise Tiger, 24, 25; recovery of Nazi assets, 39; interviews CC and Fleming, 131–2; and Brabenov, 144; signal to Brabenov, 149
Elbe river, 108, 187, 203, 204, 209

Falkiner, Patricia, and CC, 32–3, 77–8, 94; appearance, 32, 46; swims across Salzach, 45–6; history, 46–7, 84–5; reaches safe house, 48; transmits signal to Liechtenstein, 48–9; tortured, 51–2; suicide, 53; news of her death, 77; Op.JB, 78; Gerhardt's statement, 115–16; code-name, 149; remembered, 214
Fervent, HMS, 55–8
Fierstein, Hannah, 114, 117–18, 214
Fleming, Ann, 229
Fleming, Eve, 51
Fleming, Ian Lancaster, home on 'secret recall' from Far East, 35; deputy director M Section, 36; Morton and, 36, 38–44 passim, 50–51, 110; family background, 36–7; appearance, 37; history, 37, 38; personality, 37, 75, 92, 97, 111, 113, 229; Churchill and, 39, 42, 51; orders to recover Nazi assets, 39; reads CC's file, 42–3; attitude to women, 44, 109; code-names, 50, 74; and CC, 56–8, 74, 110–13, 152, 178, 216, 228–9; discusses Nazi assets with Swiss Finance Minister, 69–70; is shown German treasure in vault of National Bank of Basle, 71; quest for Bormann, 72; at Birdham, 72, 75, 92; security, 74; Kemp

and, 75, 109; Kemp telephones, 79; and row between CC and Morton, 83, 86–7; returns to Far East, 89; and Bloem 0, 96; in Lisbon, 97; in Switzerland, 98; adopts Waffen-SS identity, 99, 119; at Weinheim, 99–105; makes radio contact with M Section control, 100, 105; and 30th Assault Unit, 103, 110; and Ribbentrop, 103–4, 123–4, 162–3; physical training, 109; use of firearms, 109–10; lineage, 110–11; and Fierstein, 118; to Berlin, 120, 153; and Bormann, 124–6, 164, 167–8, 174; interviews with Eisenhower, 131–2; dislikes Blunt, 133; gives orders about Bormann's abduction, 139–40; Cowboys and Indians, 143; and Donovan, 145; tells Donovan of conditions in Berlin, 147, 148; parachuting, 149; signal to Eisenhower, 149; parachutes into action, 153; countersigns Bloem's report, 155; identity of pick-up targets, 156; down Spree by kayak, 156; in Foreign Ministry underground bunker, 163–8; and Brabenov, 165; his order to CC, 166; unconcerned about discovery by Russians, 171; clothing for breakout, 173; and exploding tank, 176; recalled to London, 178; recovery of German navy archives, 215; and transfer of Nazi assets, 215; and CC's acting training, 223, 224; cover-up of Op.JB to safeguard, 224–5; *Casino Royale*, 228; and guarantee of safe conduct for Bormann, 240

Fleming, Peter, 35, 37
Fleming, Valentine, 37
Fletcher, Peter, 156
Fouchet, Claudine, 71

Garfield, Brian, 86n

Gay, Noel, 13
George VI, King, as Duke of York, 9; and M Section, 10; covertly approves procedure, 58n; and CC, 135–7; and recovery of Nazi loot, 218; and Bormann, 231
Gerhardt, Hans, 45n, 46, 51–3, 115
German Freedom Fighters, arrive at Birdham, 75–6; personnel, 90–92; Kemp and, 92; help with study of Berlin, 107; Fleming and, 113; Operation JBV, 117–18; in Berlin, 155; prepare Schwanenwerder for JB, 185; dispose of Russian rapists, 200; surrogate daughters for Bormann from, 219
Gibbons, Carroll, 93
Gloucester, Prince Henry, Duke of, 9, 231
Godfrey, John, 35, 37, 38
Grant, Marlene Schuler, 219, 220–21, 222
Grant, Peter, 219, 220
Grosser Müggelsee, size, 107; closely surveyed, 117; blocked, 117; JBV parachutes into, 118; reinforcements despatched to, 140; Op.JB plans, 146; mines and explosives removed from, 147; JB forces round, 153; JBC parachute landings, 154; kayaks hidden, 155; Schulberg's group to leave, 172
Gülpersee, 196–7
Günther, Otto, Kemp and, 138, 139; Fleming's orders about future of, 139–40; parachute instruction, 149; head bandage, 152, 156, 175; and Brabenov, 161–2; CC dreads assassinating, 161, 170, 173; Bormann and, 163–4, 177; body-search, 173; given Bormann's diary, 174; breakout, 175; killed, 176

Hall, Sir Reginald 'Blinker', 12
Havel river (*see also* Potsdam Bridge), 107; course, 108; mines and

explosives removed from, 147;
Spree joins, 180; Op.JB excape
party down, 180–83; lake, 181;
Schwannenwerder peninsula,
183–4; JBC, 192; lying-up spot
on island in, 193; flotilla paddles
down, 197; Soviets camped on
bank of, 197; blown-up bridges
and sunken vessels, 201; flows
into Elbe, 204; Soviet battalion
reported, 207; CC and LCPs
proceed up, 209

Havelberg, 201–2, 203, 210

Hess, Rudolf, 72

Hitler, Adolf, and CC, 21, 22; wants
to see CC again, 33; Bormann
and, 72, 73, 216–17; code-name,
74; death, 169; his will, 174, 226;
Trevor-Roper's conclusion about
death of, 226; Hugh Thomas
and identity of Hitler's alleged
corpse, 226–7

Hollis, Roger, 133–4, 135, 137

Hulbert, Claude, 13

Hulbert, Jack, 13

Hurst, Caroline, in Lisbon, 97;
history, 116; arranges transport,
119; German and Russian
speaker, 149

Ignatius, Mother, 46, 68

Ireland (*see also* Dublin), CC's Nazi
contacts in, 24; cash deposited
for CC in, 25; U-boat refuelling
bases, 215

Isle of Man, 97, 135

Ismay, Hastings (*later* 1st Baron
Ismay), 81, 227

JBC, abduction plan, 146; orders to
parachute into Berlin, 149; flying
to Berlin, 153; communication
with JB pick-up, 177; to aid of JB7,
208–14

JB7, JBV renamed, 140; already on
Berlin waterways, 153; stolen

motorboats, 154; in control of
houses and facilities, 155; CC calls
on transceiver, 160; Hurst signals
good news, 184; JBC uncertain
what to do about, 187; reaches
Wannsee, 194; CC's orders to,
203; prayer for safe deliverance
of, 206; Soviet battalion encamped
near, 207, 210; CC and JBC to
aid of, 207–14; hiding south of
Verble, 209; Kemp signals, 212;
withdraws, 213

JBV, drop into Müggelsee, 116–18;
Fierstein, 117–18; Shulberg, 118,
140; success, 121; reinforcements,
129; strength, 140

Jerome, Jenny (Lady Randolph
Churchill), 51

Jones, David, 156, 178, 179, 181

Kemp, Susan, training and
accomplishments, 59–60; and
CC, 60, 63–5, 78–9, 87, 96, 182,
232–3; action stations, 60–63;
death-clasp, 68; meeting with
Fleming and CC, 72; and Fleming,
75, 76, 109, 140, 178; and German
Freedom Fighters, 76, 92; and
Falkiner, 77; CC's number one, 87;
and Gerhardt's statement, 115–16;
and search for Bormann's double,
129, 130–31, 138; and Blunt,
137–8, 186; and Günther, 139; and
Brabenov, 142, 186, 201; Cowboys
and Indians, 143; in command
group, 149; to Berlin, 153;
identity of pick-up targets, 156; in
command of operation in Berlin,
169; in command of pick-up group,
172; leads kayak escape party,
178, 179, 182, 183; in shock,
180; at Schwanenwerder, 184;
second-in-command of Op.JB, 184;
wants to wait for JB7, 187; leads
flotilla, 193; battle ensigns, 204;

calls JB group to attention, 205; on reconnaissance for boats, 207; in WRNS uniform, 208–9; rescue of JB7, 212, 213; Operation Andrew, 216; finds safe environment for Bormann, 219–20, 222; Operation Piglet, 220; Mountbatten and, 231; Mountbatten's letter in her keeping, 231–2; code-name, 231

Kindermann, Dr G. K., 239

Korda, Zoltan, 49

Kuhlhausen, 198–200

Lambert, Father Jerome, 17

Lang, Jochen von, 226

Lawson, Jane, 100

Laycock, (Sir) Robert, 58

Lewis, Jenny, 138

Liffey, river, 1, 3

Lisbon, 21, 97

London, Room 39, Admiralty, 35, 36, 225; Room 60, Ministry of Works, 36, 38; CC at Ministry of Works, 79, 80; Cabinet War Room, 82; Bormann housed in Highgate, 219, 220

Lycett, Andrew, 230

M Section, Morton founds and runs, 10, 41; *noms de guerre*, 13; CC and, 14, 57; falsifies record of John Davis, 15; Fleming, 36; launcing major undercover operation, 38; and Nazi assets, 39–40; background, 41; reports only to Prime Minister, 42; Birdham operational headquarters, 41, 58; operational Wren in Vienna, 43–4; Falkiner, 47, 49, 78; wireless telegraphy control station, 49; selection for, 68–9; hunts down Standartenführer, 116n; Operation JBV, 116–18; and search for Bormann's double, 129; Brabenov, 132; records doctored in name of Martin Bormann, 139; uniforms

manufactured, 140; implications for Op.JB, 143–4; similarities between OSS and, 144–5; Donovan and Brabenov dine with secret circle, 145–6; JB7 in Berlin, 154, 155; reports Fleming out of Germany, 184; JBC makes radio contact, 203; Bormann, 217, 219, 236; Hitler's will, 226; builds up CC's fictitious character, 230; Kemp, 231; has copies of Morton's records, 233

McIndoe, Archibald, 101, 130, 138, 217

McIndoe, Venora, 130

Marshall, Joan, 178

Martindale, C.C., 115

Mathews, Dame Vera Laughton, 47, 69

Miklas, Wilhelm, 45

Montagu, Ewen, 16n

Montgomery, Bernard (*later* 1st Viscount Montgomery), 81

Moore, Roger, 223

Morgan, John, Kemp and, 61; CC and, 63, 160; switches live bullets with dummies, 64; and German Freedom Fighters, 91; down Spree by kayak, 156–7; and raft of corpses, 181; at Schwanenwerder, 184; Bormann and, 205

Morton, Desmond, 86n; M Section, 1, 41, 68, 69; history, 10; appearance, 10–11, 204; personality, 11, 41, 42, 83, 144, 148; and CC's family, 11; and CC's mother, 11, 13; considers CC a likely intelligence agent, 12; and CC, 14, 18, 21, 24, 31–2, 80, 82–5, 205, 208, 232; planning for D-Day invasion, 18; orders CC to make contact with Canaris, 19; double-crosses CC about Allied landings, 24; Operation Tiger Hunt, 25; and CC's L-pill, 29; and Fleming, 36, 38–44 *passim*, 50–51, 110; security, 42, 74, 84; code-name, 50, 231; and Churchill, 50, 132–3; and quest for Bormann, 72, 74; and German Freedom Fighters, 76; and Falkiner, 78, 84–5; and Secret Musical Telegraphy Transmissions, 94; ghost stories, 115, 145–6; and John Davis's discharge, 127; search for Bormann's double, 129; leaks information to Americans, 133; and Donovan, 133, 145; sends Blunt and Hollis to Birdham, 133; and Blunt, 135; and Donovan, 144, 145; signals German surrender, 196–7; greets JBC, 204; and Bormann, 205, 217, 219, 220, 221; suggests a prayer, 205; wants things done through proper channels, 208; emotional signal to CC and JBC, 214; and transfer of Nazi assets, 215, 216; and benefit to West of Nazi expertise, 216; and recovery of remaining Nazi loot, 218; arranges for CC to have acting training, 223; and Trevor-Roper, 226; death, 232

Mosley, Sir Oswald, 15, 91
Mountbatten, Lord Louis (*later* Earl Mountbatten), and CC's father, 9, 15–16, 230, 231; and CC, 12, 13, 80, 231, 232; and CC, 12, 13, 80, 231; and CC's mother, 13; jazz drummer, 13; Operation Mincemeat, 16n; has CC drafted into COPP, 23; Birdham, 58; signal to CC, 135; death, 232

Nelson, Johanne, 234, 235, 236
Nelson, Vanessa, 234
Nielson, Tachin, 210
Nobs, Ernest, 69–70
Nuremberg, trials, 163; International Military Tribunal, 217, 241–3

Obolensky, Prince Alexander, 10

Olivier, (Sir) Laurence (*later* Baron Olivier), 223
Op.JB, name, 74; and German Freedom Fighters, 75; Fleming, 89; Brabenov, 132, 144; Blunt and Hollis, 133; George VI and, 137; implications for, 143–4; members expendable, 178; down Spree towards Weidendamm Bridge, 179

Potsdam Bridge, Russians in control of, 185, 186, 188, 191, 194; CC decides to steer for, 188; flotilla follows Brabenov through, 193
Pound, Sir Dudley, 12, 58
Prewitt, Joan, 61, 62

Rawlins, John, 156, 178, 192, 211, 212
Ribbentrop, Joachim von, and CC's father, 9–10; and CC, 10, 21, 73, 101–4; Foreign Minister, 12; confirms knowledge of CC, 19; gives false impression of his accomplishments to Hitler, 23; Bormann and, 23, 123; code-name, 74; and Fleming, 103–4; CC and Fleming discuss strategy over, 105; CC and Fleming meet him in Berlin, 122–4, 162–3; later history, 163n; Mountbatten and, 231
Richardson, (Sir) Ralph, 224
Rommel, Erwin, 25–8
Roosevelt, Franklin D., 145
Rundstedt, Gerd von, 20

Saunders, Caroline, action stations, 61, 62; appearance, 113; and Fleming, 178; and approaching LCPs, reports Fleming's getaway, 182; signals news of JB7, 184, 210; repeats signal to Shulberg, 212; Operation Midas Touch, 219
Schellenberg, Walter, 30
Scott, (Sir) Peter, 1
Seyss-Inquardt, Arthur, 45

Schulberg, Christa, appearance
and personality, 200; incident
of unexploded grenade, 114;
Operation JBV, 118, 121, 126–7,
140; her force renamed JB7, 140;
welcomes CC, 154; to follow pick-
up flotilla, 172; JB7 withdraws,
213; speaks names of the dead,
214; Saunders and, 219
Simpson, William H., 205
Southampton, HMS *Tormentor*, 25
Spree, river, course of, 107–8, 157;
through Rahnsdorf, 117; mines
and booby-traps, 127; Op.JB
plans, 146; mines and explosives
removed from, 147; incendiary
devices, 147; at low level, 148,
157; JBC by kayak down, 156–7;
sunken barges, 172, 177; Op.JB
escape party down, 178–80; into
Havel, 180
Stalin, Joseph, 225
Stephenson, Sir William, 224
Stumpfegger, Ludwig, 175, 176, 226
Switzerland, 40, 69–70, 98

Thomas, Hugh, 226–7, 238
Thorndike, Dame Sybil, 223
Trevor-Roper, Hugh (*later* Baron
Dacre), 225–6

Truman, Harry S., 240

Vernon, HMS, mine-disposal experts,
129, 147, 179; casualities, 214

Wannsee, 107, 185, 194
Webb, Bill, 178
Wiesenthal, Simon, 226
Wild, Peter, 208, 211, 212
Wilhelmina, Queen of the
Netherlands, 113
Windsor, Duke of, 136
Wirrell, Penny, action stations, 60,
61, 62; signals officer, 77; and
Blunt, 134; Brabenov signals, 177;
kayak escape party, 178; Admiralty
signal, 196
Wright, Jenny, CC and, 30; doctor,
110; appearance and personality,
113; kayak escape party, 178;
brandy, 196; and dead Russian
captain, 200

York, Duke of (*later* King George VI,
q.v.), 9

Zhukov, Georgy Konstantinovich,
143